PRACTICE FOR

ADVANCED MATHEMATICS

STATISTICS

ALAN SMITH

Hodder & Stoughton
A MEMBER OF THE HODDER HEADLINE GROUP

INTRODUCTION

Practice for Advanced Mathematics: Statistics provides an extensive bank of practice questions for the aspiring A or AS level mathematics student.

It is assumed that the book will be used to support taught lessons, or as a revision guide, and thus the development or proof of results from first principles has been kept to a minimum. Each topic is introduced with a brief overview of key points, followed by one or more worked examples.

The main exercises contain questions of two kinds. **A** questions are short questions intended to practise one simple skill, such as calculating a Spearman coefficient. **B** questions are slightly longer; they usually involve two or more skills, and are beginning to approach the standard of many A level questions, though they are still reasonably short.

At the end of each chapter is a set of ten **C** questions: these are set at A level standard, and can be a little longer than the **B** questions.

In order to solve many of the questions you will need a good set of statistical tables and/or a graphics calculator. The worked answers have been constructed using the *MEI Student Handbook* and built-in functions on a Casio fx9850 calculator; you may obtain slightly different numerical answers using other tables or a different graphics calculator.

I would like to thank the pupils and staff at the Royal Mathematical School, Christ's Hospital, who have trialled many of the questions in this book. Special thanks are due to my wife, Rosemarie, who has typed and proof-read the text, and provided unstinting support and encouragement throughout.

Orders: please contact Bookpoint Ltd, 39 Milton Park, Abingdon, Oxon OX14 4TD. Telephone: (44) 01235 400414, Fax: (44) 01235 400454. Lines are open from 9.00–6.00, Monday to Saturday, with a 24 hour message answering service. Email address: orders@bookpoint.co.uk

British Library Cataloguing in Publication Data
A catalogue record for this title is available from The British Library

ISBN 0 340 70165 X

First published 1998

Impression number	10	9	8	7	6	5	4	3	2	1
Year		2004	2003	2002	2001	2000	1999	1998		

Copyright © 1998 Alan Smith

Cover photo from Tony Stone Images

Typeset by Wearset, Boldon, Tyne and Wear.
Printed in Great Britain for Hodder & Stoughton Educational, a division of Hodder Headline Plc, 338 Euston Road, London NW1 3BH by Scotprint Ltd, Musselburgh, Scotland.

CONTENTS

Chapter 1

DATA HANDLING AND BASIC PROBABILITY

1.1 Discrete and continuous variables, central tendency and dispersion

Key points

Statistical variables are usually either discrete or continuous.

Discrete variables take definite, distinct values, and are often recorded by counting:
- the number of people on a bus   (5, 6, 7, etc.)
- the age (in completed years) of a child   (10, 11, 12, etc.)
- the marks scored in a 25-question multiple-choice test (19, 20, 21, etc.).

Continuous variables may take intermediate values as well; they are often recorded by measuring, to a limited level of accuracy:
- the speed of a bus   (23.228749 . . . mph)
- the height (in metres) of a child (1.29 . . . metres)
- the weight of a cauliflower.

There are many important distinctions between how to handle these different types of data. For example, a set of discrete data might have a **mode**, while a set of continuous data would have a **modal class** instead. Before solving any problem in statistics you must decide whether the variable in question is discrete or continuous.

Four measures of central tendency and three measures of dispersion occur in most statistical applications, and these measures are explained in this section. You should already be familiar with them from GCSE or similar work.

Suppose we have a set of observations taking a variety of values—e.g. the number of people sitting in cars during rush-hour traffic. We might want to describe a 'typical' or 'average' value—we would do this by using a measure of **central tendency**. There are many ways of describing this 'average' value, including:
- **mean**, the ordinary arithmetic average
- **median**, half the values are above it, half below
- **mode**, the most common value
- **midrange value**, the mean of the highest and lowest values.

We may also wish to describe the amount of variation within the data set—this is done using a measure of **dispersion**. Again, there are several ways to do this, including:
- **range**, the difference between the highest and lowest values

- **interquartile range**, often found using a cumulative frequency curve, although for a small discrete set of data it may be found numerically
- **standard deviation**, the square root of the variance.

Remember that

> **variance = the mean of the squares minus the square of the mean**

Example I

In the morning traffic, I observed the number of people sitting in 12 different cars. The figures were:

| 2 | 1 | 1 | 3 | 2 | 5 | 4 | 1 | 2 | 4 | 1 | 1 |

Calculate the mean and the mode of these data. Also calculate the standard deviation. Illustrate the data with a diagram.

Solution

For the mean, begin by summing the values: $\Sigma x = 2 + 1 + \ldots + 1 = 27$.
$\therefore$ The mean $= 27 \div 12 = 2{\cdot}25$ people.

To find the mode, draw up a frequency table:

Number of people, x	1	2	3	4	5
Frequency, f	5	3	1	2	1

This tells you that the value 4 occurred in the data set on 2 occasions.

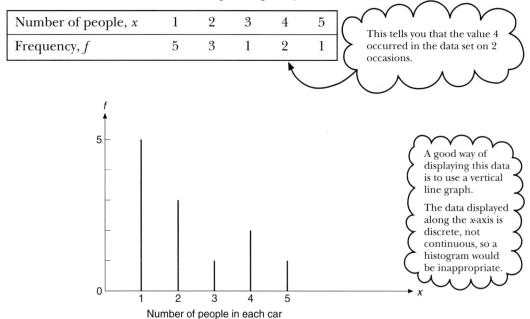

Number of people in each car

A good way of displaying this data is to use a vertical line graph.

The data displayed along the x-axis is discrete, not continuous, so a histogram would be inappropriate.

From the table the highest frequency is 5, and so the mode = 1 person.

To find the standard deviation, we compute $\Sigma x^2 = 2^2 + 1^2 + \ldots + 1^2 = 83$

So the variance is

$$s^2 = \frac{\sum x^2}{n} - \bar{x}^2$$

$$= \frac{83}{12} - 2 \cdot 25^2$$

$$= 1 \cdot 854$$

and, square rooting, the standard deviation is $1 \cdot 362$.

Example 2

The ages of 17 members of a stamp club are as follows:

12	25	45	17	28	33	35	39	71	32	16	15	26	44	47
30	42													

(i)   Construct a stem-and-leaf diagram to show these data.

(ii)   Find the median and the midrange value.

(iii) Explain why it would not be sensible to try to find the mode.

Solution

(i)

> The first data point is 12. It has a stem of 10 and a leaf of 2.

```
10 | 2 7 6 5              10 | 2 5 6 7
20 | 5 8 6               20 | 5 6 8
30 | 3 5 9 2 0           30 | 0 (2) 3 5 9
40 | 5 4 7 2             40 | 2 4 5 7
50 |                    50 |
60 |                    60 |
70 | 1                  70 | 1
```

> This is a one-pass stem-and-leaf diagram—the data have been sorted into rows as we have worked through the data, but the rows themselves are still jumbled.

> Now by sorting out the order within each row we obtain the two-pass diagram. The median is found by looking for the middle number in the two-pass diagram.

(ii)   The median value is 32. The midrange value is $(12 + 71) \div 2 = 41 \cdot 5$

(iii) There is no mode—all the values occur only once.

Example 3

The scores obtained by seven French students in a grammar test are:

$$72 \quad 65 \quad 78 \quad 60 \quad 62 \quad 32 \quad 58$$

(i) Calculate the mean and the standard deviation of these seven scores.

(ii) Explain carefully whether the scores contain any outliers. (An **outlier** is a value which lies more than two standard deviations away from the mean.)

Solution

(i) $\Sigma x = 72 + 65 + \ldots + 58 = 427$

The mean is $\bar{x} = \dfrac{427}{7} = 61$

$\Sigma x^2 = 72^2 + 65^2 + \ldots + 58^2 = 27\,325$

The variance is $s^2 = \text{Var}(X) = \dfrac{27\,325}{7} - 61^2 = 182 \cdot 57$

The standard deviation is $s = \sqrt{\text{Var}(X)} = \sqrt{182 \cdot 57} = 13 \cdot 51$

(ii) $\bar{x} \pm 2s$ is $61 \pm 27 \cdot 02$, i.e. from $33 \cdot 98$ up to $88 \cdot 02$, so the score of 32 is an outlier.

Example 4

A cricketer decides to analyse the scores obtained during his last 20 innings. They are summarised in this table:

Score	0–9	10–19	20–29	30–39	40–49	50–59	60+
Frequency	4	2	6	5	1	2	0

(i) Write down the modal group.

(ii) Calculate estimates of the mean and the standard deviation.

Solution

(i) From the table, the modal group is 20 to 29.

(ii) To find the mean, each group is replaced with its midpoint:

Midpoint, x	Frequency, f	xf	x^2f
4.5	4	18	81
14·5	2	29	420·5
24·5	6	147	3601·5
34·5	5	172·5	5951·25
44·5	1	44·5	1980·25
54·5	2	109	5940·5
		520	**17 975**

Mean: $\bar{x} = \dfrac{\sum x \cdot f}{n} = \dfrac{520}{20} = 26$

Variance: $s^2 = \dfrac{\sum x^2 \cdot f}{n} - \bar{x}^2 = \dfrac{17\,975}{20} - 26^2 = 222 \cdot 75$

Values for the mean and standard deviation are estimates because the midpoint values have been used—the original data have been lost.

So the standard deviation is $\sqrt{222 \cdot 75} = 14 \cdot 92$

As the median splits a data set into two halves, so the upper quartile and lower quartile split it into four quarters. There is a simple way of doing this for a small discrete set, as shown in Example 5, but quartiles are more usually encountered in connection with a cumulative frequency diagram as in Example 6.

Example 5

Here are the masses of 15 fish of a certain species, measured to the nearest 5 grams:

| 120 | 55 | 65 | 100 | 65 | 60 | 70 | 85 | 75 | 60 | 105 | 100 | 115 | 140 | 95 |

Calculate:

(i)   the median

(ii)   the midrange value

(iii)   the upper and lower quartiles

(iv)   the interquartile range.

Solution

First we need to order the data, with the smallest first:

| 55 | 60 | 60 | 65 | 65 | 70 | 75 | 85 | 95 | 100 | 100 | 105 | 115 | 120 | 140 |

(i)   Median = 8th value (7 below, 7 above) = 85

(ii)   Midrange = mean of 55 and 140 = 195 ÷ 2 = 97.5

(iii)   Upper quartile = 12th value (median of last 7 values) = 105

Lower quartile = 4th value (median of first 7 values) = 65

(iv)   Interquartile range = 105 − 65 = 40

Example 6

Seventy-five competitors take part in a cross-country race. The times taken to complete the race are given in the table below:

Time, X minutes	Number, f, of competitors
$X \leq 15$	0
$15 < X \leq 20$	5
$20 < X \leq 25$	23
$25 < X \leq 30$	20
$30 < X \leq 35$	17
$35 < X \leq 40$	10
$40 < X$	0

(i)   Draw up a table of cumulative frequencies.

(ii)   Construct a cumulative frequency curve.

(iii)   Use your graph to find the median and the interquartile range.

Solution

(i)

Upper bound of interval	Frequency, f	Cumulative frequency
15	0	0
20	5	5
25	23	28
30	20	48
35	17	65
40	10	75

The cumulative frequency is a running total, e.g. $0 + 5 + 23 = 28$

(ii)

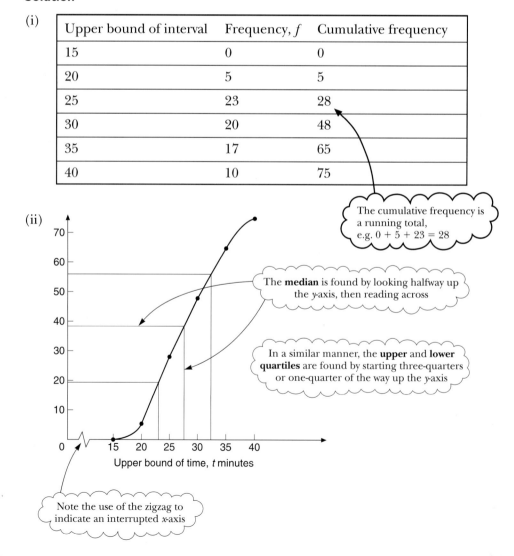

Upper bound of time, t minutes

The **median** is found by looking halfway up the y-axis, then reading across

In a similar manner, the **upper** and **lower** quartiles are found by starting three-quarters or one-quarter of the way up the y-axis

Note the use of the zigzag to indicate an interrupted x-axis

(iii) From the graph,

median = 28 minutes

interquartile range = $32 - 23 = 9$ minutes.

Exercise 1.1

In questions **A1** to **A6** you are given a small set of discrete data. In each case find the mean, median, mode and midrange value. Find also the range and the standard deviation.

A1 2, 3, 5, 6, 6, 7, 10, 10, 10, 14

A2 2, 4, 5, 6, 7, 7, 9, 10, 11

A3 103, 115, 118, 118, 125

A4 42, 23, 15, 36, 56, 47, 60, 70, 44, 61

A5 0, 0, 1, 3, 6, 7, 7, 10, 12

A6 31, 28, 31, 30, 31, 30, 31, 31, 30, 31, 30, 31

In questions **A7** to **A10** you are given a table of data. State whether you think the variable is discrete or continuous, and find the mean, standard deviation and mode (or modal class).

A7

Number of goals	0	1	2	3	4	5 or more
Frequency	12	14	8	3	1	0

A8

Time taken (seconds)	0–10	10–20	20–30	30–40
Frequency	6	11	14	3

A9

Number of spelling mistakes per page	0	1	2	3	4	5 or more
Frequency	4	11	2	5	1	0

A10

Mass of coin (grams)	under 30	30–32	32–34	34–35	35–40	over 40
Frequency	0	3	6	9	2	0

B1 Thirty children in a primary school were asked the age of the youngest member of their family (including themselves) at the last birthday. The results were:

8	7	4	7	3	7	8	1	5	2
0	3	2	1	3	2	8	7	8	1
8	4	3	8	8	1	2	5	6	6

(i) Find the mean age, and find also the standard deviation of these ages.

(ii) State the value of the mode.

(iii) Explain carefully whether or not you think the value of 0 has to be an error.

B2 A librarian wants to order copies of 17 new paperback books. The prices quoted for the books, in pounds, are as follows:

10·49	8·20	11·99	8·49	6·50	6·75
5·99	9·50	13·99	10·99	8·99	9·75
7·25	7·99	8·99	5·50	8·50	

(i) Construct a stem-and-leaf diagram to display these data. Use pounds for the stem and pence for the leaves.

(ii) State the value of the median of this set of data.

(iii) State the modal value.

B3 A market researcher notes the annual salary of 50 people who have replied to a questionnaire:

continued

Exercise 1.1 *continued*

Salary, X, pounds	Frequency
$0 < X \leq 12\,000$	1
$12\,000 < X \leq 16\,000$	8
$16\,000 < X \leq 20\,000$	11
$20\,000 < X \leq 25\,000$	16
$25\,000 < X \leq 40\,000$	14

(i) Using midpoints of each interval, calculate an estimate of the mean salary and the corresponding standard deviation.

(ii) Using upper limits of each interval, construct a table of cumulative frequencies. Use this table to draw up a cumulative frequency curve, and from the graph obtain values for the median and the interquartile range.

B4 Forty motorists are asked how many parking fines they have received during the last 12 months. Their replies are:

0	0	1	2	0	2	1	0	0	1
3	2	2	0	0	0	1	2	0	1
6	1	0	1	1	0	3	2	1	2
0	1	4	1	0	1	8	0	1	0

(i) Draw up a frequency table to show these data.

(ii) State the mode.

(iii) Calculate the value of the mean and the standard deviation.

(iv) Find the midrange value, and explain why it is not a very useful measure in this particular case.

B5 An electronic detector is set up to count the number of people disembarking from tube trains at a London Underground station. The numbers of people disembarking from a sample of 60 trains are summarised in this table:

Number of people per train	Frequency
0 to 10	2
11 to 20	8
21 to 30	12
31 to 40	15
41 to 50	12
51 to 60	8
61 to 70	3
over 70	0

(i) Carefully calculate the midpoint of each class. Hence calculate estimates of the mean and standard deviation of these data. Explain briefly why your values can only be estimates.

(ii) Draw up a table of cumulative frequencies, and use it to construct a cumulative frequency graph.

(iii) Use your graph to obtain values for: (a) the median, and (b) the upper and lower quartiles.

B6 Bags of cement are supposed to weigh 25 kilograms. Forty bags are chosen at random, and their weights are recorded as in the table:

Weight, grams	Frequency
24 700–24 800	1
24 800–24 900	0
24 900–25 000	4
25 000–25 100	18
25 100–25 200	11
25 200–25 300	5
25 300–25 400	1

(i) Calculate estimates of the mean and standard deviation of the weight of a bag of cement.

(ii) Each bag carries a label which claims 'Average weight 25 kg'. Comment briefly on whether you think this claim is justified.

1.2 Data presentation

Key points

In this section you are reminded of various diagrams used for display of data. Some of these were introduced in Section 1.1; you should be familiar with most of the others from GCSE or similar work.

This list summarises some of the most popular devices for data display:

- **Stem-and-Leaf Diagram**

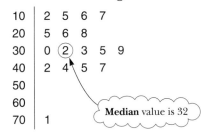

Used for discrete data. It produces a display similar to a bar graph or vertical line graph on its side, with the added advantage that the original data are not lost when grouped. The median may be found by looking for the middle number—but make sure that you are using a two-pass diagram when doing this.

- **Vertical Line Graph**

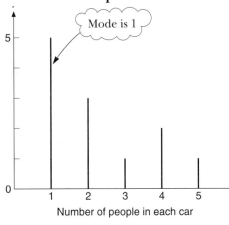

Number of people in each car

Used for discrete data. It produces a display similar to a vertical bar graph, but with thin vertical lines. Do not join the points together—this would imply that the *x*-axis is continuous. The mode will be the value with the highest frequency.

- **Bar Chart**

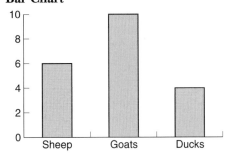

Used for categorical data, e.g. colours, animals, etc. It is simply a plot of frequency against category. The vertical bars should not touch each other. Bar charts are of limited use in A-level work, though they are used extensively in news articles, presentations, etc.

● **Histogram**

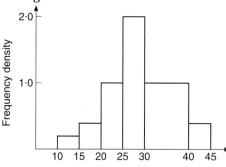

Used for continuous data, with frequencies corresponding to the area within each column. As the columns may not all be of equal width it is a good idea to plot frequency density along the y-axis—this is frequency divided by the width of the column. Do not leave gaps between the columns. Histograms are often wrongly confused with bar charts.

● **Frequency Polygon**

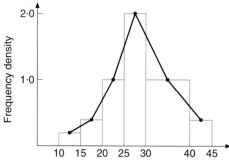

Used for continuous data. The frequency polygon is a close relative of the histogram—it may be obtained from a histogram by joining up the midpoints of the tops of the columns.

● **Time Series Chart**

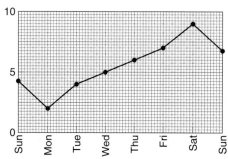

Used to show how a quantity varies with time, i.e. the x-axis is continuous. A classic time series chart shows values at daily (or weekly or monthly) intervals—be careful when judging intermediate values.

- **Pie Chart**

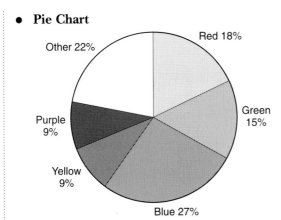

Like the bar chart, this is used for categorical data. The categories are shown as sectors of a circle, so it is often convenient to re-scale the given frequencies until they total 360. Beware of pseudo-3D pie charts, which can exaggerate the sectors nearest you. Like the bar chart, pie charts are of limited use in A-level work.

- **Cumulative Frequency**

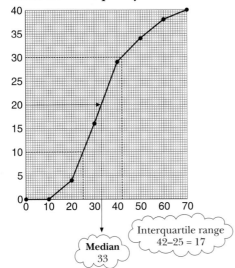

Used for discrete data (cumulative frequency polygon) or for continuous data (cumulative frequency curve, or ogive). The median, quartiles and interquartile range may all be found conveniently from a cumulative frequency graph. When drawing up a table of cumulative frequencies from grouped data be sure to use the *upper limit* of each class, not the midpoint.

- **Box and Whisker Diagram**

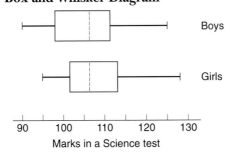

Used for discrete or continuous data. This is a plot of the upper and lower quartiles (the box) with the extreme maximum and minimum values (the whiskers). The median is shown as a dotted line within the box. This diagram is especially useful when comparing two or more data sets (e.g. heights of boys and girls).

When a set of data (or a complete distribution) is displayed on a graph it may exhibit **skew**. This means that there is a tail making the distribution far from symmetric.

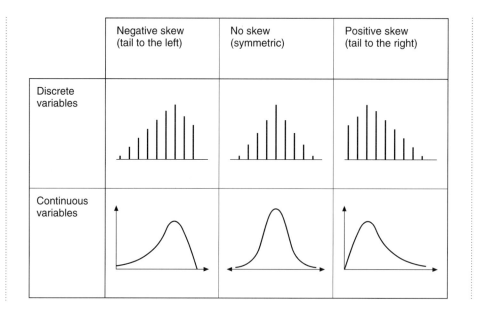

	Negative skew (tail to the left)	No skew (symmetric)	Positive skew (tail to the right)
Discrete variables			
Continuous variables			

Exercise 1.2

In questions **A1** to **A6** you are given a set of data and a corresponding diagram. In each case the diagram contains a serious error. Study the data carefully to see how the diagram has been made, and describe the error.

A1

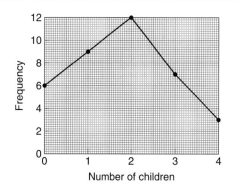

Number of children in family	Frequency
0	6
1	9
2	12
3	7
4	3
5 or more	0

A2

Marks in a French test	Boys	Girls
Minimum	35	40
Lower quartile	40	45
Median	42	46
Upper quartile	50	50
Maximum	65	65

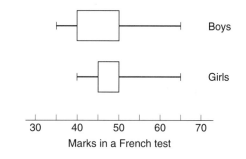

Exercise 1.2   *continued*

A3

Method of travel to work	Frequency
Walk	15
Car	25
Bus	7
Cycle	4
Other	3

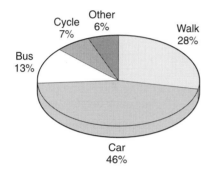

Methods of travel

A4

Distance jumped, X, feet	Frequency
$0 \leq X \leq 1$	0
$1 \leq X \leq 3$	2
$3 \leq X \leq 5$	5
$5 \leq X \leq 7$	6
$7 \leq X \leq 9$	3
$9 \leq X$	0

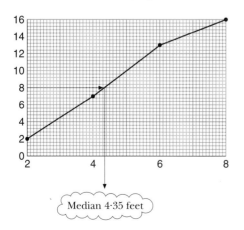

Distance jumped

Median 4·35 feet

A5 Number of runs scored by a batsman

44	25	13	48	29	36	85	12	10	5
28	17	12	47	36	21	11	33	12	0

00	5 0
10	3 2 0 7 2 1 2
20	5 9 8 1
30	6 6 3
40	4 8 7
80	5

B1 Diane decides to investigate the ages at which men and women get married. She asks some of her married friends how old they were when they got married and summarises the results in this table:

Age of marriage	Frequency (Men)	Frequency (Women)
under 20	0	0
20 and under 25	0	5
25 and under 30	7	10
30 and under 35	9	14
35 and under 40	13	8
40 and under 50	10	5
50 and under 60	3	1
60 and under 80	1	0
over 80	0	0

(i)   Redraw the table to show frequency density for men and women.

(ii) Draw two histograms, one for men and one for women, to show the age at marriage.

(iii) Comment briefly on any similarities or differences between the two distributions which you can see from your diagrams.

continued

B2 The table shows the number of rain-free Saturdays and Sundays at a certain seaside resort in July over a period of 50 years:

3	2	3	2	1	5	2	4	6	10
4	3	6	5	3	4	4	0	3	2
2	2	4	6	5	5	4	5	8	5
1	1	0	3	3	6	7	1	1	2
4	4	9	8	4	3	5	3	6	3

(i) Rewrite the data in the form of a table of frequencies.

(ii) State the median and the mode.

(iii) Illustrate the data with a diagram. Describe the kind of skewness, if there is any.

B3 A fell-running club organises a competition in which competitors are timed over a foot race on local hills. There are two categories of competitor: All-comers (for all age groups) and Veterans (over 40s). The times, in minutes, taken by the two categories are summarised in the table:

	All-comers	Veterans
Minimum	25	26
Lower quartile	36	40
Median	41	48
Upper quartile	45	53
Maximum	59	58

(i) Illustrate both sets of data with a pair of box-and-whisker diagrams.

(ii) Comment briefly on any similarities or differences between the two categories of runner, with regard to:

(a) central tendency;

(b) dispersion;

(c) skewness.

B4 Pat is a taxi driver. He decides to record the number of passengers he picks up for each of 25 airport bookings in his eight-seater minibus:

Number of passengers	Frequency
1	1
2	0
3	2
4	5
5	7
6	8
7	2
8	0

(i) Calculate the mean and standard deviation of these data.

(ii) Illustrate the data with a suitable diagram.

(iii) The table suggests that groups of 7 or 8 passengers are unlikely to book Pat's eight-seater minibus. Suggest one reason for this.

B5 Olivia and Shane have submitted a statistical report as part of their Year 7 mathematics project. The report includes this table and the following diagram:

Type of CD	Olivia's collection	Shane's collection
Classical	18	9
Rock/Pop	5	37
Jazz	3	12
World Music	6	2
Other	4	12

(i) Explain carefully why the diagrams provide a misleading comparison between the two CD collections.

(ii) Redraw the pie charts so that the comparison is fairer.

Exercise 1.2 *continued*

Olivia's collection

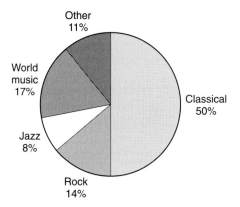

Shane's collection

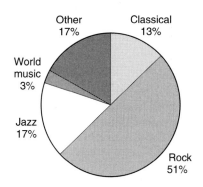

1.3 Tree diagrams and sample spaces

Key points

You should already be familiar with tree diagrams and sample space diagrams from your GCSE, or similar work. In this section, we use them to solve simple problems in conditional probability.

Tree diagrams are usually used when several trials are conducted, each of which has only two or three possible outcomes. Probabilities are multiplied along the branches to give final values which must all sum to 1.

Conditional probability arises whenever we need to find the probability of A occurring given that B has occurred. In the case of tree diagram or sample space problems, the best approach is often to restrict the set of outcomes (see Examples 2 and 3). Conditional probability problems may also be tackled by using Bayes' Theorem:

$$\text{Probability of A given B} = \frac{\text{Probability of A and B}}{\text{Probability of B}}$$

which is often written symbolically:

$$P(A \mid B) = \frac{P(A \cap B)}{P(B)}$$

Example 1

A spinner is labelled in such a way that it only scores 0 or 1. The probability of scoring a 0 is 0·3, and the probability of scoring a 1 is 0·7. The spinner is spun three times. Find

(i)   the probability of getting three zeros;

(ii) the probability that the total of all three throws is 1.

Solution

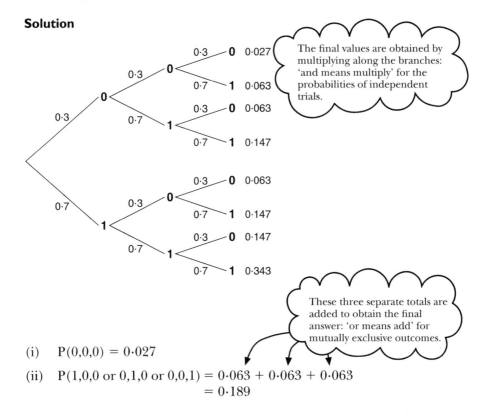

The final values are obtained by multiplying along the branches: 'and means multiply' for the probabilities of independent trials.

These three separate totals are added to obtain the final answer: 'or means add' for mutually exclusive outcomes.

(i)   P(0,0,0) = 0·027

(ii) P(1,0,0 or 0,1,0 or 0,0,1) = 0·063 + 0·063 + 0·063
                                 = 0·189

Example 2

In a certain Cumbrian village the weather may be modelled by describing each day as either fair or foul. If the weather is fair one day then the probability that it is fair the next day is 0·2; if the weather is foul one day then the probability that it is foul the next day is 0·7.

Today is Wednesday and the weather is fair.

(i)   Draw a tree diagram to show the possible states for the weather on Thursday, Friday and Saturday.

(ii) Find the probability that the weather on Saturday is fair.

(iii) Given that the weather on Saturday does, in fact, turn out to be foul, find the probability that the weather on Thursday turns out to be foul.

Solution

(i)

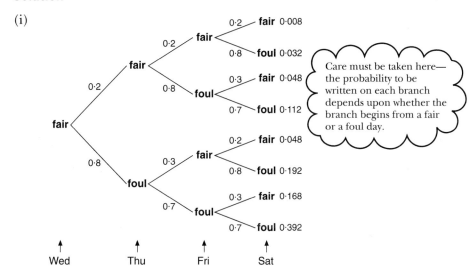

Care must be taken here—the probability to be written on each branch depends upon whether the branch begins from a fair or a foul day.

(ii) $P(\text{Sat fair}) = 0 \cdot 008 + 0 \cdot 048 + 0 \cdot 048 + 0 \cdot 168$
$\qquad\qquad\;\; = 0 \cdot 272$

(iii)   If we are now given that Saturday is foul

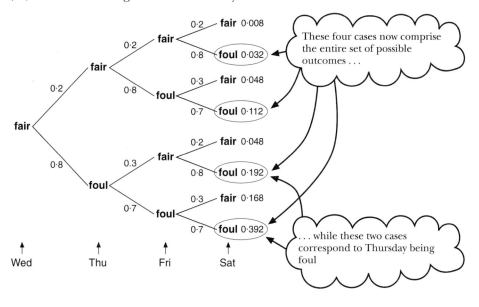

These four cases now comprise the entire set of possible outcomes . . .

. . . while these two cases correspond to Thursday being foul

$$P(\text{Thursday foul given Saturday foul}) = \frac{0 \cdot 192 + 0 \cdot 392}{0 \cdot 032 + 0 \cdot 112 + 0 \cdot 192 + 0 \cdot 392}$$

$$= 0 \cdot 802$$

Example 3

Two fair dice are thrown together, and the total score is recorded.

(i)   Draw a sample space diagram to show the 36 possible combinations of scores.

(ii) Use your diagram to find the probability that the total score is

    (a) eight; (b) prime.

(iii) Given that one of the dice shows a five, calculate the probability that the total is eight.

Solution

(i)

	1	2	3	4	5	6
1	2	3	4	5	6	7
2	3	4	5	6	7	8
3	4	5	6	7	8	9
4	5	6	7	8	9	10
5	6	7	8	9	10	11
6	7	8	9	10	11	12

(ii) (a) A score of 8 may be achieved in 5 different ways.

$$\therefore P(8) = \frac{5}{36}$$

    (b) The primes are 2, 3, 5, 7, 11, which are achieved in 1, 2, 4, 6 and 2 ways, respectively, i.e. a total of 15 ways.

$$\therefore P(\text{prime}) = \frac{15}{36} = \frac{5}{12}$$

(iii) Given that one of the dice shows a five, the set of 36 outcomes is now reduced to these 11:

	1	2	3	4	5	6
1	2	3	4	5	6	7
2	3	4	5	6	7	8
3	4	5	6	7	(8)	9
4	5	6	7	8	9	10
5	6	7	(8)	9	10	11
6	7	8	9	10	11	12

$$\therefore P(8) = \frac{2}{11}$$

Exercise 1.3

In questions **A1** to **A4**, decide whether to use a tree diagram or a sample space diagram. Draw the appropriate diagram, and use it to calculate the required probabilities.

A1 On my journey to work I have to pass through three sets of traffic lights. The probability that I have to stop at the first set of lights is 0·6; at the second 0·5 and at the third 0·2. You can assume that these probabilities are independent.

   (i) Find the probability that I have to stop at all three sets of lights.

   (ii) Find the probability that I have to stop at exactly one set of lights.

A2 When baby Bethany cries for a nappy change she is changed either by her mother, father or sister, with probability 0·5, 0·3 and 0·2, respectively. One afternoon Bethany cries for three nappy changes.

   (i) Find the probability that she is changed all three times by her mother.

   (ii) Find the probability that she is changed exactly once by her sister.

   (iii) Find the probability that she is changed each of the three times by different people.

A3 From a set of five cards numbered 1, 2, 3, 4, 5, one card is chosen at random and then replaced; a second card is then also chosen at random. Find the probability that:

   (i) the total score is 6;

   (ii) the two scores differ by 2;

   (iii) the total is 7 or 8.

A4 I throw an ordinary six-sided die, labelled 1, 2, 3, 4, 5, 6 and I also draw a card from three bearing the numbers 2, 3 and 4. The numbers on the die and the card are then multiplied together to give a total score.

   (i) Find the probability that the score is 8.

   (ii) Find the probability that the score is even.

   (iii) Find the probability that the score is greater than 9.

Revision questions

C1 A certain electrical accessory is available at 12 different shops in this country. The price, in pounds, charged by each shop is shown in the table:

95.00	95.99	110.00
105.99	103.50	102.99
155.00	112.00	107.50
99.99	105.00	108.25

   (i) Calculate the mean and standard deviation of these data.

An outlier is defined as a value which lies more than two standard deviations away from the mean.

   (ii) Explain carefully whether there are any outliers in this particular data set.

As a result of changes in the cost of production all 12 shops decide to increase their prices by £2.00.

   (iii) Explain the effect that this will have on (a) the mean, and (b) the standard deviation. *continued*

C2 Two dice are thrown together and the total score is recorded:

Total score	Frequency
2	1
3	3
4	4
5	3
6	7
7	9
8	8
9	5
10	4
11	4
12	2

(i) Write down the modal score, the median and the midrange value.

(ii) State the value of the range, and explain briefly why it does not convey much information about the compactness of the data.

(iii) Calculate the mean and the standard deviation, giving your answers correct to 2 decimal places.

(iv) Illustrate the distribution with a vertical line graph. Comment on whether you think the data looks positively skewed, negatively skewed, or approximately symmetrical.

C3 The diagram shows a cumulative frequency curve for the heights of geraniums in a garden centre.

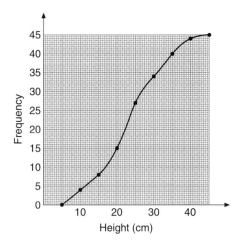

Use the diagram to obtain values for:

(i) the median

(ii) the interquartile range.

Later in the summer all of the plants have grown by 5 cm. Describe the effect that this will have on the shape of the cumulative frequency curve.

C4 The table shows the price, in pounds, of 20 of the most popular dishes at a local Tandoori restaurant:

3.80	3.50	1.20	2.25	3.90	3.80	3.60	0.99	3.80	3.80
4.05	1.99	0.30	3.80	3.50	3.80	0.60	3.50	5.20	3.70

(i) Illustrate the data in a stem-and-leaf diagram, using pounds for the stem and pence for the leaves. Comment briefly on any values which lie well away from the main part of the data.

(ii) Calculate the mean and standard deviation of the data. Say whether you think the value of £0.30 is an outlier.

(iii) Explain briefly why the value of £0.30 need not necessarily be a mistake, even though it lies well away from the main part of the data.

C5 A small village supermarket hires out videotapes. The running times of the tapes are given in the following table:

Running time (minutes)	Number of tapes
under 10	0
10–20	1
20–40	5
40–60	9
60–70	8
70–80	11
80–90	10
90–100	16
100–105	9
105–110	11
110–115	13
115–120	12
120–130	13
130–140	6
over 140	0

(i) Copy and complete this table of frequency densities:

Running time (minutes)	Frequency	Frequency density
under 10	0	0
10–20	1	0·1
20–40	5	0·25

(ii) Illustrate the data with a histogram.

(iii) Calculate the mean running time. Mark this value clearly on your histogram.

(iv) State the type of skewness exhibited by the data.

C6 An old medical book says that the average person needs eight hours sleep per night. Dr Fisher decides to investigate this statement by looking at the number of hours sleep that his hospital patients have. The results for a sample of 30 patients are summarised in the table:

Number of hours sleep	Frequency
less than 4	0
4–5	3
5–6	8
6–6·5	7
6·5–7	5
7–7·5	4
7·5–8	2
8–9	1
over 9	0

(i) Illustrate the data with a histogram.

(ii) Calculate estimates of the mean and the standard deviation. Explain briefly why these can only be estimates.

(iii) Describe briefly the type of skewness exhibited by the data.

(iv) To what extent do you think this sample can be considered to be representative of the population as a whole?

C7 (i) A bag contains five counters, numbered 1, 2, 3, 4 and 5. A counter is selected at random, replaced, and then a second counter is selected at random. Find the probability that

    (a) the total is at least 5;

    (b) the total is 8;

    (c) the total is 8, given that one of the counters is 5.

(ii) Now suppose that the process is repeated, but the first counter is *not* replaced before the second is drawn. Repeat the three calculations.

Revision questions *continued*

C8 A sports enthusiast decides to model the results of a Test match between the English and Australian cricket sides as follows:

- The weather throughout the match may be described either as rainy, overcast or sunny with probabilities 0·2, 0·5 and 0·3, respectively.
- The match may result in a win for England, a win for Australia, or a draw.
- If the weather is rainy then the probability that England wins is 0·5 and the probability that Australia wins is 0·3.
- If the weather is overcast then the probability that England wins is 0·6 and the probability that Australia wins is 0·3.
- If the weather is sunny then the probability that England wins is 0·2 and the probability that Australia wins is 0·7.

(i) Illustrate the model with a tree diagram.

(ii) Find the probability that England wins.

(iii) Given that Australia wins, find the probability that the weather was sunny.

C9 A motoring organisation sets up a voluntary safety checkpoint at a motorway service station. Motorists can submit their vehicles for three safety checks, on brakes, lights and steering.

The probability that a vehicle fails the brakes test is 0·3; the corresponding figures for lights and steering are 0·4 and 0·1, respectively.

(i) Find the probability that a randomly-chosen vehicle fails at least one of the three checks.

(ii) Given that a vehicle does fail at least one of the three checks, find the probability that it fails the brakes check.

(iii) During the day a total of 350 vehicles are checked. Calculate the expected number of vehicles which will pass all three checks.

C10 A two-digit number is formed as follows:
- the tens digit is chosen at random from the digits 1, 2, 3 and 4;
- the units digit is chosen at random from the digits 1, 3, 5, 7, 9.

Draw up a sample space diagram to show the possible two-digit numbers which could be formed. Hence find the probability that

(i) the two digits are equal;

(ii) the product of the two digits is more than 12;

(iii) the two-digit number is prime;

(iv) the two-digit number is prime given that the tens digit is even;

(v) the tens digit is even given that the two-digit number is prime.

Chapter 2

DISCRETE AND CONTINUOUS VARIABLES

Key points

As we mentioned in the last chapter, statistical variables are either **discrete** or **continuous**. Discrete variables take **distinct values** which may be specified exactly:
- the number of people in a car   (1, 2, 3, . . .)
- the time showing on a digital watch   (12:44, 12:45, . . .).

Continuous variables take **intermediate values** as well; they may only be specified to a certain number of decimal places:
- the amount of fuel in a fuel tank   (16·32514 . . . litres)
- the time at which a solar eclipse began   (12:44 and 13·62433 . . . seconds).

Calculations based on discrete variables usually involve **summation** (i.e. multiplying and adding), while those based on continuous variables depend upon **integration**, so it is important to be able to distinguish between them. The methods described in this section apply to discrete random variables only.

Discrete random variables are often given in the form of a **list** or a **table** of values, with matching probabilities. This is known as a **probability distribution**.

The mean, $E(X)$, of a discrete random variable X is obtained by multiplying each value of X by the corresponding probability, and adding all the results:

$$E(X) = \Sigma x \cdot p_x$$

Note that a capital letter X is used for the name of the random variable, but each of the actual values it may take is denoted by a small letter x with corresponding probability p_x. Each p_x must lie between 0 and 1, and they must all add up to 1.

The mean $E(X)$ is also called the **expected value** or **expectation** of X. It need not be a whole number, even if all of the x's are.

The **variance** $\mathrm{Var}(X)$ is defined as

$$\mathrm{Var}(X) = \Sigma x^2 \cdot p_x - [E(X)]^2$$

and is often remembered in words by the rule

> **variance = the mean of the squares minus the square of the mean**

The **standard deviation** is simply the square root of the variance.

The definitions of mean, variance and standard deviation used here are similar to those in Section 1.2, but observe how the notation is amended:

Set of data points (Chapter 1)	Entire distribution (Chapter 2)
mean $= \bar{x}$	mean $= \mathrm{E}(X) = \mu$
variance $= s^2$	variance $= \mathrm{Var}(X) = \sigma^2$

Example 1

A fair six-sided die is renumbered so that its faces read 1, 1, 1, 2, 2, 3. The random variable X denotes the score showing when the dice is thrown once.

(i)   Draw up a table to show the probability of distribution of X.

(ii) Calculate $\mathrm{E}(X)$.

(iii) In a game a pair of such dice are thrown together a large number of times. Show that a total score of 5 could be expected approximately 11% of the time.

Solution

(i)

Score, X	1	2	3
Probability, p_x	$\frac{1}{2}$	$\frac{1}{3}$	$\frac{1}{6}$

(ii) $\mathrm{E}(X) = 1 \times \frac{1}{2} + 2 \times \frac{1}{3} + 3 \times \frac{1}{6}$

$= \frac{1}{2} + \frac{2}{3} + \frac{1}{2}$

$= 1\frac{2}{3}$

(iii) $\mathrm{P}(2 \text{ then } 3) = \frac{1}{3} \times \frac{1}{6} = \frac{1}{18}$

$\mathrm{P}(3 \text{ then } 2) = \frac{1}{6} \times \frac{1}{3} = \frac{1}{18}$

$\therefore \mathrm{P}(\text{total } 5) = \frac{1}{18} + \frac{1}{18} = \frac{1}{9} = 0{\cdot}111 \ (3 \text{ d.p.}) \approx 11\%.$

Example 2

Ebenezer saves 1p, 2p and 5p coins in a bottle. The distribution of the types of coin is modelled as in this table:

Value of coin, X pence	1	2	5
Probability	0·2	0·3	0·5

(i)   Calculate E(X).

(ii) Show that Var(X) is a little over 3.

(iii) Ebenezer wants to save up £5.00. Use your answer to part (i) to show
      that he will expect to save just over 150 coins.

Solution

(i)   E(X) $= 1 \times 0\cdot2 + 2 \times 0\cdot3 + 5 \times 0\cdot5$

              $= 0\cdot2 + 0\cdot6 + 2\cdot5$

              $= 3\cdot3$

(ii) Var(X)$= 1^2 \times 0\cdot2 + 2^2 \times 0\cdot3 + 5^2 \times 0\cdot5 - 3\cdot3^2$

              $= 0\cdot2 + 1\cdot2 + 12\cdot5 - 10\cdot89$

              $= 13\cdot9 - 10\cdot89$

              $= 3\cdot01$

      which is a little over 3 as required.

(iii) E(X) $= 3\cdot3$

      $\therefore$ Expected number of coins for £5.00 is $500 \div 3\cdot3 = 151\cdot51$

      which is just over 150 coins as required.

Exercise 2.1

In questions **A1** and **A2** explain why the tables
could not represent probability distributions:

A1

X	0	1	2
p	0·4	0·3	0·5

A2

X	10	11	12	13
p	0·4	0·3	0·4	−0·1

In questions **A3** to **A8** calculate (i) E(X);
(ii) Var(X) and (iii) $\sigma = \sqrt{\text{Var}(X)}$.

A3

X	1	2	5
p	$\frac{1}{2}$	$\frac{1}{4}$	$\frac{1}{4}$

A4

X	1	2	3	10
p	0·4	0·3	0·2	0·1

A5

X	0	5	10	50
p	0·1	0·3	0·5	0·1

A6

X	−1	0	1
p	$\frac{1}{7}$	$\frac{5}{7}$	$\frac{1}{7}$

A7

X	−5	5	10
p	0·25	0·15	0·6

A8

X	−4	−3	−2	−1	0
p	0·1	0·2	0·3	0·2	0·2

A9 Look at this probability distribution:

X	1	2	3	10
p	k	$2k$	$3k$	$10k$

(i)   Using the result that all the
      probabilities must add up to 1, find
      the value of k.

(ii) Hence find E(X) and Var(X).

continued

Exercise 2.1 *continued*

A10 The tabulated probability distribution has an ink blot concealing one of the values:

X	-1	1	3	5
p	0·05	✸	0·25	0·35

(i) Find the missing value concealed by the ink blot.

(ii) Hence find $E(X)$ and $Var(X)$.

B1 Louise claims that her homework marks last term may be modelled by the following probability distribution:

Mark, X	16	17	18	19	20
Probability	0·05	0·05	0·1	0·2	0·6

(i) Calculate $E(X)$.

(ii) Calculate $Var(X)$.

In order to earn a commendation Louise needs to score more than 365 marks from the 20 homeworks set this term.

(iii) Explain, with reasoning, whether Louise is likely to earn a commendation this term. State clearly any assumptions you are making.

B2 When Andy plays darts he always aims at the treble 20. He usually hits single 20 instead, and sometimes drifts left or right, hitting 1 or 5 (or their trebles).

Andy's score with a single throw may be modelled by the following distribution:

Score, X	20	60	1	3	5	15
Probability	0·6	0·2	0·08	0·02	0·08	0·02

(i) Calculate $E(X)$.

(ii) Show that $Var(X)$ is a little under 350, and find the value of the standard deviation correct to 1 decimal place.

(iii) Andy wishes to score 180 with his next three throws. Show that the likelihood of this happening is approximately 1%.

B3 Linford is preparing for an Olympic 100 m final. He might win a Gold (3 points), Silver (2 points) or Bronze (1 point), or

perhaps no medal at all. He models his chances of success as follows:

Number of points, X	3	2	1	0
Probability	0·05	0·15	0·2	0·6

(i) Calculate $E(X)$.

(ii) Find the standard deviation of X.

Sally is preparing for the 400 m final. She uses an identical distribution to model her chances of success.

(iii) Find the probability that the two athletes score exactly 2 points between them.

B4 The table shows the approximate values of National Lottery prizes, along with their approximate probabilities:

Prize, X, £	Probability
0	p
10	0.017 5
65	0.000 968
1 500	0.000 018 0
100 000	0.000 000 429
2 000 000	0.000 000 071 5

source: adapted from Camelot flyer, 1994

(i) Find the value of p, correct to 4 decimal places.

(ii) Find the expected prize $E(X)$, stating your final answer in pence correct to the nearest penny.

(iii) Tickets cost £1.00 each. Matthew buys three each week for 50 weeks of the year. Find his expected loss over the course of one year. (Expected loss = costs minus winnings.)

B5 A random variable X takes values of 0, 1, 2 and 3 with probabilities k, $k/2$, $k/3$ and $k/6$, respectively.

(i) State two conditions which k, $k/2$, $k/3$ and $k/6$ must fulfil in order to form a valid probability distribution.

(ii) Show that $k = \frac{1}{2}$.

Exercise 2.1 *continued*

(iii) Show that $E(X) \approx 0.833$.

(iv) Find $Var(X)$ and hence obtain the standard deviation of X correct to 3 d.p.

B6 A random variable X is defined by the probability distribution below:

X	1	2	3	5	10
Probability	a	b	0.35	0.25	0.1

(i) State a result about the sum of the probabilities for a probability distribution. Hence write down an equation containing a and b.

(ii) It is known that $E(X) = 3.7$. Use this information to obtain a second equation containing a and b.

(iii) Solve the simultaneous equations obtained in (i) and (ii).

(iv) Find the value of $Var(X)$.

B7 Clive runs a small mail-order shoe business. The (British) sizes of the shoes he sells are modelled by the following probability distribution:

Shoe size, X	4	5	6	7	8	9	10
Probability	0.1	0.1	0.2	0.2	0.3	0.05	0.05

(i) Calculate $E(X)$ and $Var(X)$.

(ii) Write down the standard deviation of X.

An outlier is a value which lies more than 2 standard deviations away from the mean.

(iii) Calculate the probability that the next pair of shoes Clive sells is an outlier.

(iv) Suggest one aspect of real behaviour which is not described by this model.

B8 The table below is a complete probability distribution for the values X with corresponding probabilities Y:

X	a	$3a$	$5a$	$7a$
Y	$10b$	$5b$	$3b$	$2b$

(i) Write down an equation for the sum

of the probabilities, and solve this to show that $b = 0.05$.

It is known that $E(X) = 10.8$.

(ii) Write down an equation for $E(X)$ and solve it to find the value of a.

(iii) Calculate $Var(X)$.

B9 Virginia has been studying the number of occupants in cars during morning rush-hour traffic outside her school. She proposes the following model:

Number of occupants, X	1	2	3	4	more than 4
Probability	0.4	0.2	0.15	0.15	0.1

(i) Explain why it is not possible to calculate $E(X)$ directly from this model.

(ii) Suggest an amendment to Virginia's model which will enable $E(X)$ to be calculated.

(iii) Calculate $E(X)$ and $Var(X)$ for this amended model.

(iv) Explain one aspect of real behaviour which is described by Virginia's original model but not by your amended model.

B10 Jill runs a small bed and breakfast business, catering for up to four guests. She looks at last year's records, and suggests that the number of guests staying on any randomly chosen night might be modelled by this distribution:

Number of guests, X	0	1	2	3	4
Probability	0.2	0.1	0.2	0.3	0.2

(i) Calculate $E(X)$, the mean number of guests per night.

(ii) Calculate $Var(X)$.

Jill computes the probability that she will be fully booked next Christmas Day and Boxing Day as follows:

probability = $0.2 \times 0.2 = 0.04$

(iii) Give two different reasons why this calculation might not be appropriate.

Key points

Calculations based on **discrete variables** involve **summation**; those for **continuous variables** depend upon **integration**. The methods described in this section apply to **continuous random variables** only.

Discrete random variables are usually given as an algebraic formula, $f(x)$, defined over a specific domain of values $a \leq x \leq b$. The formula $\mathbf{f(x)}$ is called the **probability density function** or **pdf**.

The probability that the random variable X lies between two particular values s and t is given by the integral

$$P(s \leq X \leq t) = \int_{s}^{t} f(x) \, dx$$

The mean $E(X)$ of a continuous random variable X is obtained by multiplying each value of X by the corresponding probability, and integrating:

$$E(X) = \int_{a}^{b} x \cdot f(x) \, dx$$

Notice that a capital letter X is used for the name of the random variable, but the values within the domain are denoted by a smaller letter x with corresponding probability density $f(x)$.

The variance $\text{Var}(X)$ is similarly defined as

$$\text{Var}(X) = \int_{a}^{b} x^2 \cdot f(x) - [E(X)]^2$$

and may be remembered by the usual rule:

variance = the mean of the squares minus the square of the mean

In order for a function to form a valid pdf two conditions must apply:
- $f(x)$ is never negative
- $\int_{a}^{b} f(x) \, dx = 1$.

Example 1

The random variable X has the probability density function

$$f(x) = \begin{cases} \frac{1}{18}(x^2 + 3) & 0 \leq x \leq 3 \\ 0 & \text{otherwise} \end{cases}$$

(i) Show that $E(X) = 1\frac{7}{8}$.

(ii) Find the probability that X lies between 1 and 2.

Solution

(i) $E(X) = \displaystyle\int_0^3 x \cdot \tfrac{1}{18}(x^2 + 3)\,dx$

$= \tfrac{1}{18} \displaystyle\int_0^3 x \cdot (x^2 + 3)\,dx$

$= \tfrac{1}{18} \displaystyle\int_0^3 x^3 + 3x\,dx$

$= \tfrac{1}{18}\left[\dfrac{x^4}{4} + \dfrac{3x^2}{2}\right]_0^3$

$= \tfrac{1}{18}\left[\dfrac{81}{4} + \dfrac{27}{2}\right] - 0$

$= 1\frac{7}{8}.$

(ii) $p(1 \le X \le 2) = \displaystyle\int_1^2 \tfrac{1}{18}(x^2 + 3)\,dx$

$= \tfrac{1}{18} \displaystyle\int_1^2 (x^2 + 3)\,dx$

$= \tfrac{1}{18}\left[\dfrac{x^3}{3} + 3x\right]_1^2$

$= \tfrac{1}{18}\left[\dfrac{8}{3} + 6\right] - \tfrac{1}{18}\left[\dfrac{1}{3} + 3\right]$

$= \tfrac{8}{27}.$

Example 2

The random variable X is defined by the probability density function

$$f(x) = \begin{cases} k(x + 4) & 2 \le x \le 6 \\ 0 & \text{otherwise} \end{cases}$$

(i) Use integration to obtain the value of the constant k.

(ii) Show that $E(X) = 4\frac{1}{6}$.

(iii) Obtain the value of $Var(X)$, correct to 3 decimal places.

Solution

(i) $\displaystyle\int_2^6 k(x+4)\,dx = k\int_2^6 x+4\,dx$

$$= k\left[\frac{x^2}{2}+4x\right]_2^6$$

$$= k\left[\frac{36}{2}+24\right] - k\left[\frac{4}{2}+8\right]$$

$$= 32k$$

$$= 1 \text{ for a pdf}$$

$\therefore$ The constant $k = \frac{1}{32}$.

(ii) $\displaystyle\mathrm{E}(X) = \int x\cdot \mathrm{f}(x)\,dx$

$$= \int_2^6 x\cdot k(x+4)\,dx$$

> Note that the k is taken out as a factor at the start here . . .

$$= k\int_2^6 x^2+4x\,dx$$

$$= k\left[\frac{x^3}{3}+2x^2\right]_2^6$$

$$= k\left[\frac{216}{3}+72\right] - k\left[\frac{8}{3}+8\right]$$

$$= \frac{400k}{3}$$

> . . . but the value $k = \frac{1}{32}$ is not substituted in until the end.

$$= 4\tfrac{1}{6}.$$

(iii) $\displaystyle\mathrm{Var}(X) = \int x^2\cdot \mathrm{f}(x)\,dx - [\mathrm{E}(X)]^2$

$$= \int_2^6 x^2\cdot k(x+4)\,dx - [4\tfrac{1}{6}]^2$$

$$= k\int_2^6 x^3+4x^2\,dx - [4\tfrac{1}{6}]^2$$

> A common mistake is to become so absorbed in the integral that you forget to include the $-[\mathrm{E}(X)]^2$

$$= k\left[\frac{x^4}{4}+\frac{4x^3}{3}\right]_2^6 - [4\tfrac{1}{6}]^2$$

$$= k\left[\frac{1296}{4}+\frac{864}{3}\right] - k\left[\frac{16}{4}+\frac{32}{3}\right] - [4\tfrac{1}{6}]^2$$

$$= \frac{1792k}{3} - [4\tfrac{1}{6}]^2$$

$$= 1{\cdot}306.$$

Exercise 2.2

In questions **A1** and **A2** explain why the given expressions could not represent probability density functions:

A1
$$f(x) = \begin{cases} 2 - x & 0 \le x \le 2 \\ 0 & \text{otherwise} \end{cases}$$

A2
$$f(x) = \begin{cases} x - \frac{1}{2} & 0 \le x \le 2 \\ 0 & \text{otherwise} \end{cases}$$

In questions **A3** and **A4** calculate (i) $E(X)$; (ii) $P(2 \le X \le 3)$

A3
$$f(x) = \begin{cases} \frac{1}{6}(2x - 1) & 1 \le x \le 3 \\ 0 & \text{otherwise} \end{cases}$$

A4
$$f(x) = \begin{cases} \frac{2}{9}(3x - x^2) & 0 \le x \le 3 \\ 0 & \text{otherwise} \end{cases}$$

In questions **A5** and **A6** you are to use the result that the total area under a pdf is 1 in order to find the value of the constant k.

A5
$$f(x) = \begin{cases} k(3x^2 + 2x + 1) & 1 \le x \le 2 \\ 0 & \text{otherwise} \end{cases}$$

A6
$$f(x) = \begin{cases} 4k(x - x^3) & 0 \le x \le 1 \\ 0 & \text{otherwise} \end{cases}$$

In questions **A7** to **A10** calculate (i) $E(X)$; (ii) $Var(X)$, and (iii) sketch the given pdf.

A7
$$f(x) = \begin{cases} \frac{1}{6}(4 - x) & 0 \le x \le 2 \\ 0 & \text{otherwise} \end{cases}$$

A8
$$f(x) = \begin{cases} 6(x - x^2) & 0 \le x \le 1 \\ 0 & \text{otherwise} \end{cases}$$

A9
$$f(x) = \begin{cases} \frac{4}{27}(x^3 + 2x) & 1 \le x \le 2 \\ 0 & \text{otherwise} \end{cases}$$

A10
$$f(x) = \begin{cases} \frac{12}{11}(x^3 + 2x^2) & 0 \le x \le 1 \\ 0 & \text{otherwise} \end{cases}$$

B1 The continuous random variable X has the pdf $f(x) = \frac{3}{4}(x^2 + 2x)$ for $0 \le x \le 1$ and zero otherwise. Calculate:

(i) $P(0 \le X \le \frac{1}{2})$; (ii) $E(X)$;
(iii) $Var(X)$

B2 The continuous random variable X has the pdf $f(x) = k(10 - 3x)$ for $1 \le x \le 3$ and zero otherwise.

(i) Use integration to show that $k = \frac{1}{8}$.

(ii) Calculate $E(X)$ and $Var(X)$.

B3 The continuous random variable X has the pdf $f(x) = k(4x - 3)$ for $1 \le x \le 4$ and zero otherwise.

(i) Use integration to find the value of the constant k.

(ii) Show that $P(2 \le x \le 3)$ is $\frac{1}{3}$.

(iii) Calculate $E(X)$ and $Var(X)$.

B4 The continuous random variable X has the pdf $f(x) = \frac{12}{13}(x^3 - 2x^2 + 3x)$ for $0 \le x \le 1$ and zero otherwise.

(i) Calculate $E(X)$ and $Var(X)$.

(ii) Sketch the pdf.

B5 The time T, in hours, taken for a certain manufacturing process is modelled by a continuous random variable with pdf $f(t) = \frac{3}{4}(t - 1)(3 - t)$ for $1 \le t \le 3$ and zero otherwise. Calculate the probability that a single random observation of T is less than 2 hours.

B6 The weight W kilograms of an adult male fish of a certain species is modelled by a continuous random variable with pdf $f(w) = k(2w^3 - w)$ for $1 \le w \le 2$ and zero otherwise.

(i) Use calculus to find the value of the constant k.

(ii) Calculate $E(W)$ and $Var(W)$.

2.3 Cumulative distribution functions

Sometimes we want to know the area under a probability density function, from the left-hand side, up to some value x. The procedure is to integrate the pdf; this gives rise to the **cumulative distribution function** or cdf.

Consider the random variable X with pdf

$$f(x) = \begin{cases} \frac{1}{4}(2x + 1) & 1 \le x \le 2 \\ 0 & \text{otherwise} \end{cases}$$

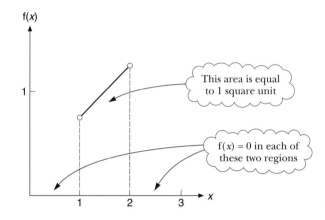

The cumulative distribution function $F(x)$ counts the total area under the graph (from the left) up to the ordinate x:

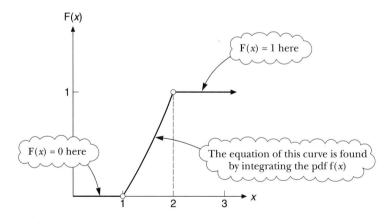

Since the cdf $F(x)$ is found by integrating the pdf $f(x)$, there will be a constant of integration—which is not always equal to zero. Take care with this constant!

Some questions require the median or the mode to be found. The median m is the value such that 50% of the distribution lies below it and 50% above and is found by solving the equation $F(m) = 0.5$. The mode, x, is the value of x for which the pdf $f(x)$ has a maximum, and is often found by solving the equation $f'(x) = 0$. If $f'(x) = 0$ has no solutions then the mode occurs at one end of the domain.

Example 1

The random variable X has probability density function

$$f(x) = \begin{cases} \frac{1}{4}(2x + 1) & 1 \leq x \leq 2 \\ 0 & \text{otherwise} \end{cases}$$

(i)   Find the cumulative distribution function $F(x)$.

(ii)   Find the probability that X lies between $1 \cdot 5$ and $1 \cdot 6$.

(iii)   Find the value of t such that $P(1 \leq X \leq t) = 0 \cdot 4$.

Solution

(i)   To find the cdf we integrate the pdf:

$$F(x) = \int f(x)\,dx$$

$$= \int \tfrac{1}{4}(2x + 1)\,dx$$

$$= \tfrac{1}{4}[x^2 + x] + c.$$

At the beginning of the domain the cdf is zero.

$\therefore F(x) = 0$ when $x = 1$.

$0 = \tfrac{1}{4}[1^2 + 1] + c$

$ = \tfrac{1}{2} + c$

$\therefore c = -\tfrac{1}{2}$

Thus the required cumulative distribution function is

$$F(x) = \begin{cases} 0 & x < 1 \\ \frac{1}{4}(x^2 + x) - \frac{1}{2} & 1 \leq x \leq 2 \\ 1 & x > 2 \end{cases}$$

(ii)   To find the probability that X lies between $1 \cdot 5$ and $1 \cdot 6$ use the cdf:

$$P(1 \cdot 5 \leq X \leq 1 \cdot 6) = F(1 \cdot 6) - F(1 \cdot 5)$$

$$= \tfrac{1}{4}(1 \cdot 6^2 + 1 \cdot 6) - \tfrac{1}{2} - [\tfrac{1}{4}(1 \cdot 5^2 + 1 \cdot 5) - \tfrac{1}{2}]$$

$$= 0 \cdot 1025$$

(iii)   If $P(1 \leq X \leq t) = 0 \cdot 4$ then $F(t) = 0 \cdot 4$.

$$\therefore \tfrac{1}{4}(t^2 + t) - \tfrac{1}{2} = 0 \cdot 4$$

Multiplying by 4 and simplifying,

$t^2 + t - 3{\cdot}6 = 0$

Solving this by the quadratic equation formula gives $t = 1{\cdot}462$ or $t = -2{\cdot}462$.

As the domain is $1 \leq X \leq 2$ we can reject the value $t = -2{\cdot}462$.

$\therefore t = 1{\cdot}462$

Example 2

The random variable X has probability density function

$$f(x) = \begin{cases} \frac{1}{54}(4x^3 - 3x^2) & 1 \leq x \leq 3 \\ 0 & \text{otherwise} \end{cases}$$

(i)   Find the cumulative distribution function $F(x)$. Sketch its graph.

(ii) Find the value of the mode.

(iii) Show that the value of the median is just below $2{\cdot}58$.

Solution

(i)   Integrating the pdf we have

$$F(x) = \int f(x)\,dx$$

$$= \int \frac{1}{54}(4x^3 - 3x^2)\,dx$$

$$= \frac{1}{54}[x^4 - x^3] + c.$$

At the beginning of the domain the cdf is zero.

$\therefore F(x) = 0$ when $x = 1$.

$0 = \frac{1}{54}[1^4 - 1^3] + c$

$= 0 + c$

$\therefore c = 0$

Thus the required cumulative distribution function is

$$F(x) = \begin{cases} 0 & x < 1 \\ \frac{1}{54}(x^4 - x^3) & 1 \leq x \leq 3 \\ 1 & x > 3 \end{cases}$$

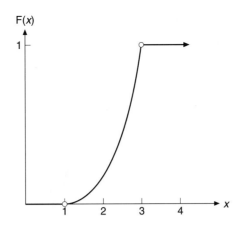

(ii) For the mode we need to solve the equation $f'(x) = 0$

$f'(x) = \frac{1}{54}(12x^2 - 6x)$

$= 0$ for max/min

$\therefore 12x^2 = 6x$ so $2x = 1$ and hence $x = \frac{1}{2}$.

This value does not lie within the domain $1 \leq x \leq 3$ so the mode must occur at one of the end points. From the sketch we can see that this will be the upper end, so the mode is 3.

(iii) For the median set $F(m) = \frac{1}{2}$.

$\frac{1}{54}(m^4 - m^3) = \frac{1}{2}$

$m^4 - m^3 = 27$

$m^4 - m^3 - 27 = 0$

Solving this by trial and improvement we have

$2 \cdot 57^4 - 2 \cdot 57^3 - 27 = -0 \cdot 3499$

$2 \cdot 58^4 - 2 \cdot 58^3 - 27 = 0 \cdot 1341$

so there is a solution between $2 \cdot 57$ and $2 \cdot 58$.

$\therefore$ The median is just below $2 \cdot 58$.

Exercise 2.3

In questions **A1** to **A6** use integration to find the cumulative distribution function corresponding to the given probability density function f(x).

A1
$$f(x) = \begin{cases} \frac{1}{8}(3x + 1) & 0 \le x \le 2 \\ 0 & \text{otherwise} \end{cases}$$

A2
$$f(x) = \begin{cases} 6(3 - x)(x - 4) & 3 \le x \le 4 \\ 0 & \text{otherwise} \end{cases}$$

A3
$$f(x) = \begin{cases} \frac{1}{6}(5 - x) & 1 \le x \le 3 \\ 0 & \text{otherwise} \end{cases}$$

A4
$$f(x) = \begin{cases} \frac{3}{44}(x^2 + x + 1) & 1 \le x \le 3 \\ 0 & \text{otherwise} \end{cases}$$

A5
$$f(x) = \begin{cases} \frac{1}{16}(10 - x^3) & 0 \le x \le 2 \\ 0 & \text{otherwise} \end{cases}$$

A6
$$f(x) = \begin{cases} \frac{32}{27}(3x^2 - 2x^3) & 0 \le x \le 1\frac{1}{2} \\ 0 & \text{otherwise} \end{cases}$$

A7 Find the mode of the distribution given in question **A2**.

A8 Find the median of the distribution given in question **A1**.

A9 Find the mode of the distribution given in question **A3**.

A10 Find the median of the distribution given in question **A3**.

B1 (i) Find the value of k in order that the function $f(x) = k(4 - \frac{1}{2}x)$ is a valid probability density function over the domain $2 \le x \le 4$.

   (ii) Find the corresponding cumulative distribution function F(x).

B2 (i) Sketch the graph of $y = x^3 - x$.

   (ii) Show that the portion of the function $f(x) = k(x^3 - x)$ between $x = 1$ and $x = 2$ forms a valid probability density function provided $k = \frac{4}{9}$.

   (iii) Find the modal value of this distribution.

B3 (i) Write down two conditions which must apply in order for a function f(x) to form a valid probability density function over the domain $a \le x \le b$.

   (ii) Sketch the graph of $f(x) = \frac{6}{7}(2x^2 + x)$ over the domain $0 \le x \le 1$. Show that this function meets both conditions in (i) above.

   (iii) Find the corresponding cumulative distribution function F(x).

   (iv) Find the mode of the random variable with this function f(x) as its pdf.

B4 The random variable X has the following pdf:
$$f(x) = \begin{cases} \frac{3}{35}(2x^2 - 1) & 2 \le x \le 3 \\ 0 & \text{otherwise} \end{cases}$$

   (i) Find an expression for the cumulative distribution function F(x).

   (ii) Show that the median lies between 2·6 and 2·7, and find its value correct to 2 decimal places.

   (iii) Find the value of the mode.

B5 The random variable X has the following pdf:
$$f(x) = \begin{cases} \frac{3}{25}(x^2 + 4x) & 1 \le x \le 2 \\ 0 & \text{otherwise} \end{cases}$$

   (i) Find an expression for the cumulative distribution function F(x).

   (ii) Show that F(1·6) is approximately equal to 0·5. Explain why the median is a little over or a little under 0·5.

   (iii) Find the value of the mode.

B6 The random variable X has the following pdf:
$$f(x) = \begin{cases} k(x^3 - 2x) & 2 \le x \le 4 \\ 0 & \text{otherwise} \end{cases}$$

   (i) Use integration to show that the value of k is $\frac{1}{48}$.

Exercise 2.3 *continued*

(ii) Find an expression for the cumulative distribution function $F(x)$.

(iii) Find the value of the mode.

(iv) Calculate the expectation $E(X)$.

2.4 Expectation algebra

Key points

Sometimes we want to know the expectation or variance of a **linear function** of a random variable X, or a **linear combination** of several **independent** observations of X. The results in this section apply equally to both continuous and discrete random variables.

For linear functions of a random variable X the following results apply:

$$E(aX + b) = aE(X) + b$$
$$Var(aX + b) = a^2 Var(X)$$

Note that the variance is not affected by the +b.

For the sum of two independent variables X and Y:

$$E(X + Y) = E(X) + E(Y)$$
$$Var(X + Y) = Var(X) + Var(Y)$$

Even if the variables are subtracted, you still add the variances:

$$E(X - Y) = E(X) - E(Y)$$
$$Var(X - Y) = Var(X) + Var(Y)$$

Example 1

The random variable X has mean 20 and standard deviation 6. Find the mean and standard deviation of the random variable $Y = 2X + 3$.

Solution

$E(X) = 20$

$\therefore E(Y) = E(2X + 3)$

$\qquad = 2E(X) + 3$

$\qquad = 2 \times 20 + 3$

$\qquad = 43$

$Var(X) = 36$

$$\therefore \text{Var}(Y) = \text{Var}(2X + 3)$$
$$= 2^2 \text{Var}(X)$$
$$= 4 \times 36$$
$$= 144$$

$\therefore$ Standard deviation $= 12$

Example 2

The random variable X has mean 20 and standard deviation 6, while the random variable Y has mean 10 and standard deviation 8. Find the mean and standard deviation of (i) $X + Y$; (ii) $3X - 2Y$.

Solution

(i) $E(X + Y)$ $= E(X) + E(Y)$
$$= 20 + 10$$
$$= 30$$
$$\text{Var}(X + Y) = \text{Var}(X) + \text{Var}(Y)$$
$$= 6^2 + 8^2$$
$$= 100$$

$\therefore$ Standard deviation $= 10$.

(ii) $E(3X) = 3 \times 20 = 60$

$E(2Y) = 2 \times 10 = 20$

$\therefore E(3X - 2Y) = 60 - 20 = 40$

$\text{Var}(3X) = 9 \times \text{Var}(X) = 9 \times 6^2 = 324$

$\text{Var}(2Y) = 4 \times \text{Var}(Y) = 4 \times 8^2 = 256$

$\therefore \text{Var}(3X - 2Y) = 324 + 256 = 580$

Standard deviation $= \sqrt{580} = 24 \cdot 1$.

Exercise 2.4

A1 $E(X) = 25$ and $Var(X) = 12$. Find $E(3X + 1)$ and $Var(3X + 1)$.

A2 $E(X) = 60$ and $Var(X) = 16$. Find $E(2X - 10)$ and $Var(2X - 10)$.

A3 $E(X) = 55$ and $Var(X) = 10$. Find $E(2X - 20)$ and $Var(2X - 20)$.

A4 $E(X) = 32$ and $Var(X) = 5$. Find $E(X - 32)$ and $Var(X - 32)$.

A5 The random variable X has mean 15 and standard deviation 2. Find the mean and standard deviation of the random variable $3X - 10$.

B1 $E(X) = 15$ and $Var(X) = 9$. $E(Y) = 25$ and $Var(Y) = 16$. Find $E(X + Y)$ and $Var(X + Y)$.

B2 $E(X) = 50$ and $Var(X) = 10$. $E(Y) = 40$ and $Var(Y) = 20$. Find $E(X - Y)$ and $Var(X - Y)$.

B3 $E(X) = 45$ and $Var(X) = 9$. $E(Y) = 35$ and $Var(Y) = 11$. Find $E(2X + 3Y)$ and $Var(2X + 3Y)$.

B4 $E(X) = 100$ and $Var(X) = 25$. $E(Y) = 150$ and $Var(Y) = 16$. Find $E(3X - 2Y)$ and $Var(3X - 2Y)$.

B5 The body length of a certain species of insect is a random variable with mean 80 mm and standard deviation 15 mm, while the head length is an independent random variable with mean 30 mm and standard deviation 8 mm. Find the mean and standard deviation of the random variable obtained by adding the head length and body length together.

Revision questions

C1 The random variable X has the following probability distribution:

X	10	11	12	13	14	15
Probability	k	0·1	0·25	0·4	0·1	$2k$

(i) Calculate the value of the constant k.

(ii) Find the mean $E(X)$ and the variance $Var(X)$.

Two independent observations X_1 and X_2 are taken. Find

(iii) $P(X_1 + X_2 = 20)$,

(iv) $P(X_1 + X_2 \leq 29)$.

C2 A normal-looking die has been fixed so that the scores obtained are as in this probability table:

Score, X	1	2	3	4	5	6
Probability	k	k	k	$2k$	$2k$	$3k$

(i) Calculate the value of the constant k.

(ii) Find the mean $E(X)$ and the variance $Var(X)$.

(iii) The die is thrown twice. Calculate the probability that the same score is obtained on both throws.

C3 A lottery company sets up a game in which tickets cost £1. The prizes and their corresponding probabilities are:

Prize, X, £	0	1	10	100
Probability	0·9	0·05	0·045	0·005

(i) Find the mean and variance of X. Hence explain why the game may be said to be fair.

After running for six months the lottery revises its rules. The cost of each ticket is increased to £5, and the values of the prizes, £Y, become four times those given in the table above.

(ii)   Write down the mean and variance of Y. Explain why the game may no longer be described as fair.

C4   The number of children recorded as absent from Class 3D on a Monday morning during the Summer Term may be modelled by the following probability distribution:

Number of absent children, X	0	1	2	3
Probability	0·6	0·25	0·1	0·05

(i)   Calculate the expectation $E(X)$ and the variance $Var(X)$.

(ii)   Write down the expectation and the variance of Y, the total number of recorded absences on the 14 Mondays during the Summer Term.

(iii)   Use the model to calculate the probability that exactly one absence is recorded in total for the first 2 Mondays of the Summer Term.

C5   Since reaching the age of 30 I have noticed that the number of cards I receive each birthday may be modelled by the following distribution:

Number of birthday cards, X	4	5	6	7	8
Probability	0·1	0·4	0·3	0·15	0·05

(i)   Calculate the expectation $E(X)$ and the variance $Var(X)$.

My wife is likely to receive twice as many cards each year as I do.

(ii)   Draw up a table for the distribution of Y, the number of birthday cards my wife receives each birthday.

(iii)   Write down the mean and variance of Y.

(iv)   Describe one unrealistic aspect of this second model.

C6   The continuous random variable X has this probability density function:

$$f(x) = \begin{cases} k(x^3 + x) & 1 \le x \le 3 \\ 0 & \text{otherwise} \end{cases}$$

(i)   Use integration to show that $k = \frac{1}{24}$.

(ii)   Find the cumulative distribution function $F(x)$.

(iii)   Calculate $E(X)$ and $Var(X)$.

(iv)   Find the modal value of the distribution.

C7   My postman always comes past my door between 8.05 and 8.10 a.m. I model his arrival time as T minutes past 8.00, where the random variable T has the following probability density function:

$$f(t) = \begin{cases} k(5 - t)(t - 10) & 5 \le t \le 10 \\ 0 & \text{otherwise} \end{cases}$$

(i)   Find the value of k, giving your answer as an exact fraction in its lowest terms.

(ii)   Find the probability that, on a randomly chosen morning, the postman arrives between 8.05 and 8.07 a.m.

(iii)   Find the modal arrival time.

C8   The continuous random variable X has the cumulative distribution function given by:

$$F(x) = \begin{cases} 0 & x < 0 \\ k(a + 10x - x^2) & 0 \le x \le 1 \\ 1 & x > 1 \end{cases}$$

(i)   Write down the value of $F(0)$. Hence find the value of the constant a.

(ii)   Write down the value of $F(1)$. Hence find the value of the constant k.

(iii)   Find the two solutions to the equation $F(x) = \frac{1}{2}$. Hence find the value of the median, m.

(iv)   Find the mode of this distribution.

C9   Quiklite instant barbecue briquettes are sold in bags with a nominal weight of 2 kg.

In fact the weight, W, of each bag is a random variable with the following probability density function:

$$f(w) = \begin{cases} \frac{3}{4}(9 - w)^2(11 - w) & 9 \le w \le 11 \\ 0 & \text{otherwise} \end{cases}$$

(i) Sketch the graph of $f(w)$ and show that it meets the two conditions to form a valid pdf.

(ii) Find the modal value of W.

(iii) Find an expression for the cumulative distribution function $F(w)$. Use your expression to show that the median value of W is approximately 10·23.

(iv) Find the mean and variance of W.

Mr Callaghan buys ten bags of Quiklite briquettes.

(v) Write down the mean and variance of the total weight of the ten bags.

C10 The continuous random variable X has this probability density function:

$$f(x) = \begin{cases} 0\cdot4(x - 2) & 2 \le x \le 3 \\ 0\cdot1(7 - x) & 3 \le x \le 7 \\ 0 & \text{otherwise} \end{cases}$$

(i) Sketch the graph of this distribution.

(ii) Find the cumulative distribution function $F(x)$.

(iii) Calculate $E(X)$ and $Var(X)$.

(iv) Write down the value of the mode.

(v) Explain how you can tell that the median, m, lies in the interval $3 \le m \le 7$. Find the median correct to 2 decimal places.

Chapter 3

DISCRETE DISTRIBUTIONS

Key points

The **Binomial distribution** is an example of a **discrete distribution**. Binomial problems can be solved directly (either by computation or tables), or, under certain circumstances, by using an approximating Poisson or Normal distribution.

This section deals with direct solutions to Binomial problems.

Typical situations in which the Binomial distribution should be used include:
- the number of 6s when four dice are thrown
- the number of church weddings in a sample of 20 weddings
- the number of prizes won by a woman with 10 raffle tickets.

A **Binomial model** relies on these modelling assumptions:
- there is a fixed number of trials, n
- each trial results in a success or a failure (e.g., heads or tails, win or lose)
- the trials are independent
- at each trial there is a fixed probability, p, of success.

A Binomial distribution is characterised by two parameters, namely the number of trials, n, and the probability of an individual success, p. We write $X \sim B(10, 0 \cdot 3)$, for example, to mean that 'the random variable X has a Binomial distribution with $n = 10$ trials, each of which has a fixed probability $p = 0 \cdot 3$ of success'.

Probabilities are computed using the formula

$$P(X = r) = {}^nC_r \times p^r \times (1 - p)^{n-r} \text{ where } r = 0, 1, 2, 3 \text{ up to } n.$$

The mean and the variance of X are found in the following way:

$$\text{if } X \sim B(n, p) \text{ then } E(X) = np$$
$$\text{Var}(X) = np(1 - p) = npq$$
$$\text{where } q = (1 - p)$$

Some A-level syllabuses let you use cumulative Binomial tables. These allow useful shortcuts, but remember that not every Binomial distribution can be listed: you need to know how to calculate the probabilities directly.

Example 1

The random variable X is known to be distributed $B(8, 0 \cdot 2)$. Calculate

(i) $P(X = 6)$; (ii) $P(X \leq 2)$; (iii) $P(X > 6)$.

Find also $E(X)$ and $Var(X)$.

Solution

(i) $P(X = 6) = {}^8C_6 \times 0 \cdot 2^6 \times 0 \cdot 8^2$

Remember to set out the working in full. Take care to use ${}^8C_6$ correctly.

$\qquad\qquad\quad = 28 \times 0 \cdot 2^6 \times 0 \cdot 8^2$

$\qquad\qquad\quad = 0 \cdot 001147$

(ii) $P(X \leq 2) = P(X = 0) + P(X = 1) + P(X = 2)$

$\qquad\qquad\quad = {}^8C_0 \times 0 \cdot 2^0 \times 0 \cdot 8^8 + {}^8C_1 \times 0 \cdot 2^1 \times 0 \cdot 8^7 + {}^8C_2 \times 0 \cdot 2^2 \times 0 \cdot 8^6$

$\qquad\qquad\quad = 1 \times 0 \cdot 2^0 \times 0 \cdot 8^8 + 8 \times 0 \cdot 2^1 \times 0 \cdot 8^7 + 28 \times 0 \cdot 2^2 \times 0 \cdot 8^6$

$\qquad\qquad\quad = 0 \cdot 16777 + 0 \cdot 33554 + 0 \cdot 29360$

$\qquad\qquad\quad = 0 \cdot 797$

(iii) $P(X > 6) = P(X = 7) + P(X = 8)$

$\qquad\qquad\quad = {}^8C_7 \times 0 \cdot 2^7 \times 0 \cdot 8^1 + {}^8C_8 \times 0 \cdot 2^8 \times 0 \cdot 8^0$

$\qquad\qquad\quad = 8 \times 0 \cdot 2^7 \times 0 \cdot 8^1 + 1 \times 0 \cdot 2^8 \times 0 \cdot 8^0$

$\qquad\qquad\quad = 0 \cdot 00008192 + 0 \cdot 00000256$

$\qquad\qquad\quad = 0 \cdot 0000845$

Also $E(X) = np = 8 \times 0 \cdot 2 = 1 \cdot 6$

$Var(X) \quad = np(1 - p) = 8 \times 0 \cdot 2 \times 0 \cdot 8 = 1 \cdot 28$

Example 2

An author claims that 30% of the letters in a large novel are vowels. Ten letters are to be chosen at random, and checked to see how many of them are vowels.

(i) Explain why a Binomial distribution $B(n, p)$ might be an appropriate model, stating suitable values of n and p.

(ii) Calculate the probability that exactly 6 of the letters are vowels.

(iii) Use cumulative Binomial tables to find the probability that at least 7 of the 10 letters are vowels.

Solution

(i) Each letter has a fixed probability $0 \cdot 3$ of being a vowel, and there is a fixed number of 10 trials. Assuming the letters are chosen independently of one another a Binomial model $B(n, p)$ is appropriate, with $n = 10$ and $p = 0 \cdot 3$.

43

(ii)   Using $X \sim B(10,0.3)$ $P(X = 6) = {}^{10}C_6 \times 0.3^6 \times 0.7^4$

$$= 210 \times 0.3^6 \times 0.7^4$$

$$= 0.0368$$

(iii) $P(X \geq 7)$ $= 1 - P(X \leq 6)$

$$= 1 - 0.9894$$

$$= 0.0106$$

This is obtained from cumulative Binomial tables.

Exercise 3.1

A1 If $X \sim B(8,0.2)$ find (i) $P(X = 3)$;
(ii) $P(X = 2)$; (iii) $P(X \leq 3)$.

A2 If $X \sim B(12,\frac{1}{6})$ find (i) $E(X)$; (ii) $Var(X)$;
(iii) $P(X = 4)$; (iv) $P(X \leq 4)$.

A3 If $X \sim B(6,\frac{1}{2})$ find (i) $P(X = 3)$;
(ii) $P(X = 4)$; (iii) $P(X \leq 3)$.

A4 If $X \sim B(9,0.4)$ find (i) $E(X)$; (ii) $Var(X)$;
(iii) $P(X = 4)$; (iv) $P(X \leq 4)$.

A5 If $X \sim B(6,0.25)$ find (i) $P(X = 3)$;
(ii) $P(X = 1)$; (iii) $P(X < 2)$.

A6 If $X \sim B(18,\frac{1}{3})$ find (i) $E(X)$; (ii) $Var(X)$;
(iii) $P(X = 4)$; (iv) $P(X > 4)$.

A7 If $X \sim B(8,\frac{3}{4})$ find (i) $P(X = 6)$;
(ii) $P(X = 4)$; (iii) $P(X \geq 3)$.

A8 If $X \sim B(20,0.1)$ find (i) $E(X)$;
(ii) $Var(X)$; (iii) $P(X = 2)$; (iv) $P(X \leq 2)$.

A9 $X \sim B(n, p)$ and it is known that $n = 10$ and $E(X) = 6$.

(i)   Use the result $E(X) = np$ to calculate the value of p.

(ii)   Hence find $P(X = 4)$.

A10 $X \sim B(n, p)$ and it is known that $p = 0.4$ and $Var(X) = 1.2$.

(i)   Use the result $Var(X) = np(1 - p)$ to calculate the value of n.

(ii)   Hence find $P(X = 4)$.

B1 Megan takes her camera on a walking holiday. There are 36 photographs on each film, and she expects 10% of her photographs to be failures.

Use the Binomial model $B(36,0.1)$ to find:

(i)   the probability that her first film contains exactly 3 failures;

(ii)   the probability that her second film contains exactly 2 failures;

(iii) the expected number of failures in a total of five films.

In fact Megan ended up with only 6 failures in a total of five films.

(iv) Suggest one reason why this figure is very different from the answer to part (iii).

B2 William is working as a traffic warden. He believes that a randomly chosen car in his area will be parked illegally with probability 0.15. William walks along a single street containing 20 parked cars. Use a Binomial model $B(20,0.15)$ to find:

(i)   the probability that exactly 4 cars are parked illegally;

(ii)   the probability that exactly 3 cars are parked illegally;

(iii) the probability that no more than 4 cars are parked illegally.

Suggest one reason why a Binomial model might not be valid.

B3 Duncan is planning to take part in a series of 10 international motor races. He estimates the probability of failing to finish in any given race as 0.1, his performance in each race being independent of the others.

(i)   Explain why the number of races, X, in which he fails to finish may be modelled by a Binomial distribution B(n, p) and state suitable values for n and p.

(ii) Use your model to compute
(a) P($X = 1$); (b) P($X = 2$).

(iii) Use cumulative Binomial tables to find the probability that Duncan fails to complete at least 3 races.

B4 Charlene works as a policewoman on traffic duty. She reckons that a randomly chosen tyre on a randomly chosen car will be defective with probability 0·15.

Charlene wants to set up a Binomial model B(n, p) to describe the probability that exactly r defective tyres are observed in a random sample of 4 tyres.

(i) State clearly the model Charlene should set up, and use it to find the probability that $r = 4$. Comment on whether this is a likely or unlikely outcome.

(ii) All four tyres on the next car that Charlene stops are defective. Explain carefully whether you think this is surprising, in view of your answer to part (i).

B5 David reads this headline in a newspaper:

> **SHOCK SURVEY!**
> **65% OF A-LEVEL MATHS**
> **CANDIDATES ARE MALE,**
> **35% ARE FEMALE**

Taking these figures to be exact:

(i) Describe a suitable Binomial model to describe the likelihood of obtaining exactly r males in a random group of 10 candidates.

(ii) Use your model to calculate the probability that $r = 4$.

(iii) Use cumulative tables to find the probability that $r \geq 9$.

David observes that all 10 of the candidates in his maths set at school are male.

(iv) Explain carefully whether this observation contradicts the newspaper headline.

B6 A raffle competition has 20 prizes, and 250 tickets are sold.

(i) Show that the probability that a random ticket wins a prize is 0·08.

Natalie buys 10 tickets. She believes that the number of prizes she will win can be approximately modelled by the Binomial distribution B(10,0·08). Using this model, calculate the probability that she wins

(ii) no prizes;

(iii) exactly one prize;

(iv) exactly two prizes.

B7 A shipping company claims that its passenger services sail on time with probability 0·95.

Using a Binomial model B(18,0·95) to find the probability that in a random selection of 18 passenger services

(i) exactly 16 sail on time;

(ii) at least 16 sail on time.

During the month of August, the company has scheduled 580 services.

(iii) Assuming a suitable Binomial model, find the mean and standard deviation of the number of services which sail on time in August.

(iv) State one possible objection to the use of a Binomial model in describing the sailings during the month of August.

B8 A fairground stall advertises the following game rules:

> **Throw 3 darts for 50p:**
> **Win £20 if all 3 hit the bull!**

Eric is a talented darts player. Each time he throws a dart he reckons to hit the bull with (independent) probability of 0·2.

Eric decides to play the game. Calculate the probability that he scores

(i) exactly 2 bulls;

(ii) exactly 3 bulls. *continued*

Explain carefully whether Eric should expect to win money or lose money, if he were to play this game a great many times.

B9 Janine is a novice canoeist. For any given one-hour lesson she reckons there is a 20% chance that she will capsize.

(i) Calculate the probability that in six randomly chosen lessons she will capsize in exactly two of them.

Janine takes a course of 30 lessons, after which she will qualify as a canoe instructor. Steven says 'Using a Binomial model B(30,0·2) the expected number of lessons in which Janine capsizes will be $30 \times 0·2 = 6$.'

(ii) Explain carefully whether you think it is reasonable for Steven to use this model.

B10 Sarfraz is preparing for a musical concert. He has to perform five pieces of music, and he reckons that the probability of playing any one given piece correctly is 0·8.

Using a suitable Binomial model calculate the probability that he plays

(i) all five pieces correctly;

(ii) at least four correctly;

(iii) all of them incorrectly.

3.2 Hypothesis tests using the Binomial distribution

Key points

The aim is to test whether a Binomial model is consistent with some observed results. The value of n is known, but p is not. The null hypothesis H_0 suggests a working value for p, while the alternative hypothesis H_1 contains an inequality.

The complete test procedure follows this pattern:

- **Step 1**   State the model to be tested

  e.g. 'Let $X \sim B(20, p)$', p is only symbolic at this stage.

- **Step 2**   State null and alternative hypotheses

  Use H_0 and H_1 notation. H_0 is always 'p = a value'.

- **Step 3**   Check the significance level to be used

  Usually given in the question. If you need to set your own level then tell the examiner you are doing so. 5% is a standard choice.

- **Step 4**   Establish the type of tail

  One tail upper, one tail lower or two-tail.

- **Step 5**   Restate the model using the value of p supplied by H_0

  e.g. 'Under H_0 $X \sim B(20, \frac{1}{6})$'

- **Step 6**   Identify the critical region(s), usually by using cumulative Binomial tables

  State the critical region(s); either list the values or use an inequality.

- **Step 7**   Compare the test value X_{test} with the critical region(s)

  > If X_{test} is not within the critical region then accept H_0, otherwise reject H_0 in favour of H_1.

- **Step 8**   Draw a diagram or write an inequality to show the comparison

  > Warning! Binomial models are discrete so avoid using continuous curves in your diagram.

- **Step 9**   State the conclusion formally

  > State 'Accept H_0' or 'Reject H_0 in favour of H_1'.

- **Step 10**   Restate it in plain English

  > e.g. 'There is evidence (at 5% level) that the politician is overstating his support.'

Finally, be prepared to comment on the reliability of your conclusion. If the sample has not been collected in a genuinely random way, then the conclusion may be unsound (as in Example 2 below).

Example I

Panos is playing a game with a normal-looking six-sided die. He suspects that the score does not result in an even number as often as it should for a fair die, so he throws the die 20 times, obtaining an even number on 8 occasions.

(i)   State a statistical model to be tested, including null and alternative hypotheses.

(ii)   Carry out your test at the 5% significance level, stating your conclusion clearly.

Solution

Let X be the number of even scores obtained in 20 throws.

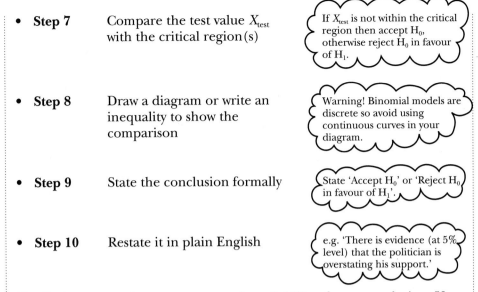

> At this stage the probability is denoted by a letter p.

$X \sim B(20, p)$ **(Step 1)**

$H_0: p = \frac{1}{2}$ **(Step 2)**

> The null hypothesis H_0 supplies the missing value of p.

$H_1: p < \frac{1}{2}$

47

5% significance level, one-tail (lower tail) test. **(Steps 3 & 4)**

Under H_0, $X \sim B(20, \frac{1}{2})$ **(Step 5)**

Using cumulative tables of $B(20, \frac{1}{2})$,

$P(X \le 5) = 0.0207$

$P(X \le 6) = 0.0577$

> The critical region is a lower tail so start at 0 and count upwards until the cumulative probability is just below 5%.

$\therefore$ Critical region = {0, 1, 2, 3, 4, 5} **(Step 6)**

$X_{\text{test}} = 8$ does not lie in the critical region **(Step 7)**

(Step 8)

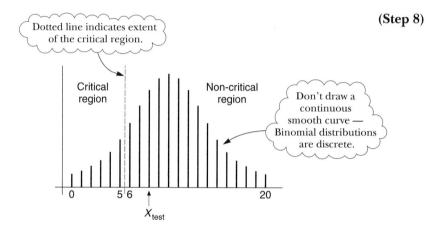

> Dotted line indicates extent of the critical region.

Critical region

Non-critical region

> Don't draw a continuous smooth curve — Binomial distributions are discrete.

X_{test}

Accept H_0 **(Step 9)**

There is no evidence (at 5% level) that the number of even scores is unusually low. **(Step 10)**

Example 2

A magazine claims that 40% of all adults in this country wear glasses. Anna doubts the validity of this figure, as the magazine is not renowned for the accuracy of its claims. Anna decides to set up a Binomial model and test it at the 5% level. She takes a sample of 18 adults, and notices that exactly 13 of them wear glasses.

(i)   Explain clearly the assumptions needed for the Binomial model to be valid, and comment on the nature of the sample being used.

(ii) State suitable null and alternative hypotheses for Anna's test.

(iii) Carry out the test at the 5% significance level, stating your conclusion clearly.

In fact the 18 adults were all members of Anna's netball club.

(iv) Explain carefully whether your conclusion is still valid.

Solution

The Binomial model requires a fixed number of trials, each with a fixed probability of success. The trials should be independent. The sample should be random.

Let X be the number of adults wearing glasses in a random sample of 18.

$X \sim B(18, p)$

$H_0: p = 0.4$

$H_1: p \neq 0.4$

*This time a two-tail test, as the alternative to H_0 is that p is **different** from 0.4—it could be greater or less.*

5% significance level, two-tail test.

5% is shared between the two tails, 2.5% in each.

Under H_0, $X \sim B(18, 0.4)$

Using cumulative tables of $B(18, 0.4)$,

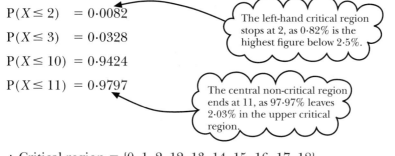

$P(X \leq 2) = 0.0082$

$P(X \leq 3) = 0.0328$

$P(X \leq 10) = 0.9424$

$P(X \leq 11) = 0.9797$

The left-hand critical region stops at 2, as 0.82% is the highest figure below 2.5%.

The central non-critical region ends at 11, as 97.97% leaves 2.03% in the upper critical region.

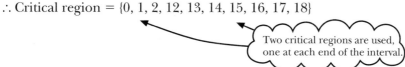

∴ Critical region = {0, 1, 2, 12, 13, 14, 15, 16, 17, 18}

Two critical regions are used, one at each end of the interval.

$X_{test} = 13$ lies in the critical region.

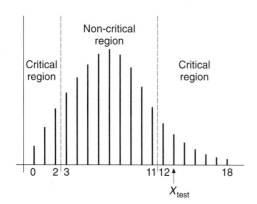

Non-critical region

Critical region

Critical region

X_{test}

The 5% two-tail test is, in effect, two separate one-tail tests, each at the 2.5% level.

Reject H_0 in favour of H_1. There is evidence (at 5% level) that the magazine's figure is not accurate.

(iv) The 18 people were all members of Anna's netball club and so they do not comprise a random sample, therefore the conclusion may not be valid. (The condition of independence is violated.)

Exercise 3.2

In questions **A1** to **A6** list the values which would make up the critical region for the test at the indicated significance level.

A1 Under H_0 $X \sim B(10, 0 \cdot 5)$. One tail (lower tail). 5% significance level.

A2 Under H_0 $X \sim B(9, 0 \cdot 6)$. One tail (upper tail). 5% significance level.

A3 Under H_0 $X \sim B(14, 0 \cdot 4)$. Two tail. 5% significance level.

A4 Under H_0 $X \sim B(15, \frac{2}{3})$. One tail (lower tail). 10% significance level.

A5 Under H_0 $X \sim B(20, 0 \cdot 25)$. One tail (upper tail). 1% significance level.

A6 Under H_0 $X \sim B(16, 0 \cdot 8)$. Two tail. 10% significance level.

In questions **A7** to **A10** you are given a Binomial model, null (H_0) and alternative (H_1) hypotheses, a significance level and a test value (X_{test}). List the values comprising the critical region, and state whether H_0 should be accepted or rejected.

A7 $X \sim B(12, p)$

$H_0: p = 0 \cdot 4$

$H_1: p < 0 \cdot 4$

5% significance level

$X_{test} = 2$

A8 $X \sim B(15, p)$

$H_0: p = 0 \cdot 25$

$H_1: p > 0 \cdot 25$

10% significance level

$X_{test} = 7$

A9 $X \sim B(14, p)$

$H_0: p = 0 \cdot 65$

$H_1: p \neq 0 \cdot 65$

5% significance level

$X_{test} = 5$

A10 $X \sim B(17, p)$

$H_0: p = 0 \cdot 75$

$H_1: p \neq 0 \cdot 75$

2% significance level

$X_{test} = 16$

B1 A presidential candidate claims that 30% of the public would vote for him in the next election. One of his aides thinks the true figure is not that high, so he asks a random sample of 20 voters: only 4 of them say they would vote for the candidate.

(i) State suitable null and alternative hypotheses.

(ii) Carry out your test at the 5% significance level, stating your conclusion clearly.

B2 Tom likes to play bagatelle—a game in which small balls are fired around a board. Some balls drop into holes and score points, but most do not. Tom knows that, on average, 40% of the balls score points.

One Christmas Tom obtains a new bagatelle board. He suspects that the new board enables a higher proportion of balls to score. To test this hypothesis he fires 10 balls, and notices that 6 balls score points.

(i) State a statistical model to be tested, including null and alternative hypotheses.

Exercise 3.2 *continued*

(ii) Carry out your test at the 5% significance level, stating your conclusion clearly.

(iii) In fact the 10 balls were fired one after the other, so they do not form a 'random sample'. To what extent do you think this may invalidate your test?

B3 A machine is designed to fill matchboxes with an average of 50 matches. Over a long period of time it is established that 25% of the boxes filled by the machine contain less than this average number.

The machine is serviced, and a quality control engineer then examines the next 12 boxes to be filled to see whether this percentage has changed. He finds that 7 of the 12 boxes contain less than 50 matches.

(i) State suitable null and alternative hypotheses. Explain carefully why your alternative hypothesis takes the form it does.

(ii) Carry out the test at the 10% significance level, stating your conclusion clearly.

B4 Marianne is an ice skater, and she has been chosen to dance a solo on the opening night of a new ice rink. The dance contains some difficult moves, and during training she estimates that the probability of not falling during the dance is only 0·8.

Marianne decides to take a special course of training exercises to try to increase this probability. After completion of the special course she performs the solo 20 times, and falls once.

(i) State suitable null and alternative hypotheses in order to test whether the probability of not falling has increased.

(ii) Carry out the test at the 10% significance level, stating the conclusion clearly.

B5 Oliver is the manager of his local soccer club's first team. One summer he analyses the team's record over the last five years,

and finds that matches ended in goalless draws with probability 0·35.

At the start of the new season his team adopts a more aggressive style, with the intention of reducing the likelihood of goalless draws. Later in the season the supporters' club magazine carries this headline:

> Team's new style is a success: only 3 of the first 12 games were goalless draws!

You have been asked to carry out a formal hypothesis test on these data.

(i) State suitable null and alternative hypotheses. Explain carefully why your alternative hypothesis takes the form it does.

(ii) Carry out your test at the 5% significance level, stating your conclusion clearly.

(iii) Explain carefully whether all of the requirements for a Binomial model have been met. To what extent is your conclusion valid?

B6 Rosemarie likes to grow geraniums from seed. She knows that, using her usual methods, the probability of any individual seed germinating successfully is 0·65.

This spring Rosemarie decides to use a new type of compost. She notices that of 14 seeds planted in this new compost exactly 11 germinate successfully.

(i) Carry out a hypothesis test at the 5% level to see whether there is any evidence that the new compost has made any difference to the probability of a successful germination. State your hypotheses and conclusion clearly.

(ii) In fact all 14 seeds were planted in the same seed tray. To what extent does this extra information invalidate the conclusion to your test?

B7 At the start of a cricket match the umpire

continued

Exercise 3.2   *continued*

tosses a coin; the team which wins the toss may choose whether to bat or field first. The umpire suspects that the coin he traditionally uses may not be fair, so he records the results of the next 16 tosses with this coin, observing that 'Heads' occurs in exactly 5 cases.

You are required to carry out a formal hypothesis test on these data.

(i)   State suitable null and alternative hypotheses. Explain carefully why your alternative hypothesis takes the form it does.

(ii)   Carry out your test at the 10% significance level, stating the conclusion clearly.

(iii)   Another umpire says, 'The sample is not random because he took the results of 16 consecutive tosses.' Does this objection invalidate the conclusion?

B8   Ginnie is making model cars with plaster of Paris. Many of the models break because they crack when she removes them from the mould; she estimates the probability of any one car breaking to be 0·2.

Ginnie changes to a new brand of plaster, in the hope of reducing the probability of a car breaking. Of the first 12 models made with the new plaster only 1 breaks.

(i)   State suitable null and alternative hypotheses.

(ii)   Carry out the test at the 10% significance level.

(iii)   Explain carefully why these data could not have been tested at the 5% level.

(iv)   Comment on the method of sampling.

B9   An astrologer claims that 30% of the population read their horoscope regularly. A student thinks this figure is too high, so

he asks a random sample of 12 people, 'Do you read your horoscope regularly?' Two say 'Yes' and the other ten say 'No'.

(i)   State suitable null and alternative hypotheses to be tested.

(ii)   Carry out the hypothesis test at the 5% significance level.

(iii)   Explain briefly whether you think the student's question is a sensible one.

B10   Susan is playing a general knowledge quiz game on a computer. Each question is followed by three suggested responses – A, B, C – of which only one is correct. There are nine categories of question:

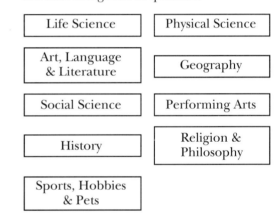

Susan claims to have a good general knowledge, but her father suspects that she is guessing randomly. To test his hypothesis he watches her answer 15 questions, and notices that she answers 7 of them correctly.

(i)   State suitable null and alternative hypotheses for the test.

(ii)   Carry out the hypothesis test at the 5% significance level.

The 15 questions were, in fact, all from the Sports, Hobbies & Pets category.

(iii)   To what extent does this additional information affect your conclusion?

3.3 The Poisson distribution

Key points

The **Poisson distribution** is an example of a **discrete** distribution. It may arise in one of two forms:
- as a distribution in its own right
- as an approximation to the Binomial distribution for large n and small p.

This section deals with the Poisson distribution in its own right.

Typical situations in which the Poisson distribution is used include:
- the number of faults in a reel of cable
- the number of cases of malaria seen by a doctor in three months
- the number of fish caught by an angler in a day.

Modelling assumptions are that the occurrences are
- random
- independent
- uniform—in the sense that the mean number of occurrences is proportional to the time (or distance) interval.

A Poisson distribution is characterised by one parameter denoted by λ (lambda). We write $X \sim \text{Po}(2 \cdot 3)$, for example, to mean that 'the random variable X is Poisson distributed with $\lambda = 2 \cdot 3$'. (Notice that λ does not need to be a whole number, but X must take whole number values.)

Probabilities are computed using the formula

$$P(X = r) = \frac{e^{-\lambda}\lambda^r}{r!} \text{ where } r = 0, 1, 2, 3, \dots$$

The parameter λ is equal to both the mean and the variance of X, i.e.

$$\text{if } X \sim \text{Po}(\lambda) \text{ then } E(X) = \text{Var}(X) = \lambda$$

Some A-level syllabuses let you use cumulative Poisson tables. These allow useful shortcuts, but remember that not every Poisson distribution can be listed: you must know how to calculate the probabilities directly.

If two independent Poisson variables are added the result is another Poisson variable:

$$\text{if } X \sim \text{Po}(\lambda) \text{ and } Y \sim \text{Po}(\mu), \text{ and } T = X + Y \text{ then } T \sim \text{Po}(\lambda + \mu)$$

This **reproductive property** of the Poisson distribution is exploited in Example 2 below.

Example 1

Doctor Jones is about to spend three months working in an overseas clinic. He has been told to expect to see, on average, three cases of malaria every year. [Malaria is a disease which may be caused by a bite from an infected mosquito.]

(i) Find the expected number of cases of malaria in a three-month period. [Consider a year to be made up of 12 equal months.]

(ii) Show that the probability that Dr Jones sees exactly one case of malaria in the three-month period is approximately 0·354.

(iii) Calculate the probability that Dr Jones sees no more than three cases in a period of three months.

(iv) In fact Dr Jones saw six cases of malaria during the three-month period. Suggest one reason why a Poisson distribution might not be appropriate in modelling the number of cases of malaria seen by Dr Jones.

Solution

(i) Let X be the number of cases of malaria seen in 3 months.

Then $E(X) = 3 \times \frac{3}{12} = 0.75$ cases per three months.

(ii) Let $X \sim Po(0.75)$

$$P(X = 1) = \frac{e^{-0.75} \times 0.75^1}{1!}$$

$$= 0.354275$$

$$= 0.354$$

(iii) $P(X \le 3) = P(X = 0) + P(X = 1) + P(X = 2) + P(X = 3)$

$$= \frac{e^{-0.75} \times 0.75^0}{0!} + \frac{e^{-0.75} \times 0.75^1}{1!} +$$

$$\frac{e^{-0.75} \times 0.75^2}{2!} \quad \frac{e^{-0.75} \times 0.75^3}{3!}$$

$$= 0.472 + 0.354 + 0.133 + 0.033$$

$$= 0.993$$

(iv) It may well be that diseases such as malaria tend to occur in outbreaks (where infected mosquitoes live) and so occurrences will not be independent.

Example 2

Izaak goes fishing on Wednesday and Friday. The number of fish he catches each day can be modelled by independent Poisson distributions with parameters 3·5 and 2·4, respectively.

(i) Write down the distribution of T, the total number of fish caught during both days.

(ii) Find the probability that he catches no more than two fish in total.

Solution

(i) Let $W \sim Po(3·5)$ and $F \sim Po(2·4)$. $T = W + F$. Then $T \sim Po(5·9)$

(ii) $P(T \leq 2) = P(T = 0) + P(T = 1) + P(T = 2)$

$$= \frac{e^{-5·9} \times 5·9^0}{0!} + \frac{e^{-5·9} \times 5·9^1}{1!} + \frac{e^{-5·9} \times 5·9^2}{2!}$$

$$= 0·0027 + 0·0162 + 0·0477$$

$$= 0·0666$$

Exercise 3.3

A1 Let $X \sim Po(2)$. Calculate:

(i) $P(X = 0)$; (ii) $P(X = 1)$;
(iii) $P(X = 2)$; (iv) $P(X = 3)$.

A2 Let $X \sim Po(4)$. Calculate:

(i) $P(X = 1)$; (ii) $P(X = 3)$;
(iii) $P(X = 4)$; (iv) $P(X = 5)$.

A3 Let $X \sim Po(5)$. Calculate:

(i) $P(X = 1)$; (ii) $P(X = 3)$;
(iii) $P(X = 5)$; (iv) $P(X = 6)$.

A4 Let $X \sim Po(1·5)$. Calculate:

(i) $P(X = 0)$; (ii) $P(X = 1)$;
(iii) $P(X = 2)$; (iv) $P(X \leq 2)$.

A5 Let $X \sim Po(4·2)$. Calculate:

(i) $P(X = 1)$; (ii) $P(X = 3)$;
(iii) $P(X < 2)$; (iv) $P(X \geq 2)$.

A6 Let $X \sim Po(1·8)$. Calculate:

(i) $P(X = 0)$; (ii) $P(X = 1)$;
(iii) $P(X = 2)$; (iv) $P(X \geq 1)$.

A7 Let $T \sim Po(2·5)$. Calculate: (i) $P(T = 0)$;
(ii) $P(T = 1)$; (iii) $P(T = 2)$.

Use cumulative Poisson tables to find:
(iv) $P(T \leq 6)$; (v) $P(T \geq 4)$.

A8 Let $T \sim Po(3·4)$. Calculate: (i) $P(T = 0)$;
(ii) $P(T = 1)$; (iii) $P(T = 2)$.

Use cumulative Poisson tables to find:
(iv) $P(T \leq 6)$; (v) $P(T \geq 4)$.

A9 Let $X \sim Po(4·2)$ and $Y \sim Po(2·4)$. Calculate:

(i) $P(X = 3)$; (ii) $P(Y = 2)$;
(iii) $P(Y \leq 2)$; (iv) $P(X > 3)$.

A10 Anu and Maire have been studying graphs of Poisson distributions.

(i) Anu says 'All Poisson distributions are positively skewed.' Is he right?

(ii) Maire says 'When you plot a Poisson distribution $X \sim Po(\lambda)$, and λ happens to be a whole number, then the modal value of X will be λ.' Is she right?

B1 An amateur astronomer enjoys photographing the night sky. Each month he processes his films, and keeps only the very best photographs. The number he keeps per month may be modelled by a Poisson distribution with parameter $3·5$.

(i) Calculate the probability that he keeps exactly 4 photographs in January.

(ii) Write down the distribution for T, the total number he keeps in January, February and March.

(iii) Calculate the probability that he keeps at least four photographs in total during the period from January to March.

B2 A bank keeps records of the number of bad cheques presented each week during a 50-week accounting period, as in the table:

continued **55**

Exercise 3.3   *continued*

Number of bad cheques	0	1	2	3	4	5
Number of weeks	12	17	12	5	2	2

(i)   Show that the mean of these data is approximately 1·5.

(ii)   Use Po(1·5) as a model to calculate the probability of exactly one bad cheque being presented in a given week.

(iii)   Calculate the experimental probability of exactly one bad cheque being presented in a given week, using the data in the table.

(iv)   Comment briefly on the agreement between your answers to parts (ii) and (iii).

B3   A boy is watching vehicles travelling along a motorway. All the vehicles he sees are either cars or lorries; the numbers of each may be modelled by two independent Poisson distributions. The mean number of cars per minute is 5·1, and the mean number of lorries per minute is 6·3.

(i)   Find the probability that he sees exactly 3 cars in a given period of one minute.

(ii)   Find the probability that he sees exactly 2 lorries in a given period of one minute.

Let T denote the total number of vehicles he observes in any one-minute period.

(iii)   Write down the distribution of T, and hence find the probability that he observes a total of exactly 10 vehicles in a given one-minute period.

(iv)   Find the probability that he observes less than 2 vehicles in a given period of ten seconds.

B4   Sarah has a collection of old LP records. Some of these are scratched, with an average of 3 scratches per record. Using a Poisson distribution as a model, calculate the probability that:

(i)   a randomly chosen record contains no scratches;

(ii)   a randomly chosen record contains at least three scratches;

(iii)   two randomly chosen records contain exactly two scratches each;

(iv)   two randomly chosen records contain a total of four scratches.

B5   The number of goals scored by Alford United in a soccer match is Poisson distributed with mean 1·6, while the number scored by Bexford Rovers is Poisson distributed with mean 1·1. When Alford play against Bexford find the probability that:

(i)   Alford win 1–0

(ii)   the score is 2–1 (to either team)

(iii)   four goals are scored in total.

B6   A doctor sees on average three cases of a broken arm during a month of 30 days.

(i)   How many broken arms would she expect to see in one day, on average?

(ii)   Use a suitable Poisson distribution to find the probability that she sees exactly four cases of broken arms in one day.

(iii)   After a railway accident the doctor does, in fact, see exactly four cases of broken arms in one day. Explain why a Poisson model would not be appropriate in this particular context.

B7   The number of cats rescued by an Animal Shelter each day may be modelled by a Poisson distribution with parameter 2·5, while the number of dogs rescued per day may be modelled by an independent Poisson distribution with parameter 3·2. Calculate the probability that on a randomly chosen day the Shelter rescues:

(i)   exactly two cats;

(ii)   exactly three dogs;

(iii)   exactly five cats and dogs in total.

Exercise 3.3 *continued*

B8 Carole enjoys skiing. She reckons that she falls on average once every five days.

   (i)   Calculate the expected number of falls: (a) in one day; (b) in six days.

She is going on a six-day skiing holiday next winter, over the Christmas period. Calculate the probability that she has:

   (ii)   exactly two falls on Christmas Day;

   (iii)   exactly three falls on Boxing Day;

   (iv)   no falls at all throughout the six days.

B9 The first round of the Euro 96 soccer finals began with 24 'league' matches. The numbers of goals scored by each team in each match are summarised in this table:

Number of goals	0	1	2	3	4
Frequency	16	18	6	7	1

   (i)   Explain why the total number of data points n in the table is 48, not 24.

   (ii)   Show that the mean number of goals per team per match is about $1 \cdot 15$.

   (iii)   Taking $\lambda = 1 \cdot 15$ as an exact value, use the model $Po(1 \cdot 15)$ to calculate the probabilities of scoring 0, 1, 2, 3 and 4 goals.

   (iv)   Multiply your answers to (iii) by the number of data points, n, to produce a list of frequencies based on the Poisson model.

   (v)   Comment on the agreement between the actual results and those predicted by the Poisson model.

B10 Some comets are discovered visually by comet-hunters who sweep the sky with large binoculars or a telescope. It is expected that on average one discovery might be made for each 400 hours of time spent sweeping.

   (i)   Assuming that a comet-hunter spends two hours sweeping the sky on each clear night, and that there are ten clear nights in each month, calculate the number of hours spent sweeping in twelve months. Hence show that the expected number of discoveries per year is $0 \cdot 6$.

   (ii)   Explain why the number of discoveries per year might be modelled by a Poisson distribution.

   (iii)   Use (i) and (ii) to find the probability that a comet-hunter discovers:

      (a)   no comet in a period of one year;

      (b)   exactly one comet in a period of one year;

      (c)   exactly three comets in a period of two years.

Historical note: The most successful visual comet-hunter of all time, Jean Louis Pons, made 37 discoveries between 1801 and 1831.

3.4 Poisson approximation to a Binomial distribution

Key points

The Poisson distribution is often used as an approximation to the Binomial distribution for large n and small p, as the Poisson probabilities are easier to calculate.

The Poisson approximation to a Binomial distribution may be made provided n is large. In addition p must be quite small, otherwise the two distributions would not exhibit similar amounts of positive skew. The usual guidelines are:

- n should be quite large

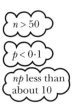

$n > 50$

- p should be quite small

$p < 0.1$

- np should not be too big.

np less than about 10

> Then use $Po(\lambda)$ as an approximation to $B(n, p)$ with $\lambda = np$.

These conditions should be checked before making any approximation.

Example 1

Séan enjoys solving hard crossword puzzles. His favourite is *The Listener* crossword, which is published each Saturday. From past experience he knows that the probability of failing to solve any given puzzle is 0·05. During the first six months of the year Séan attempts 26 puzzles.

(i)   State a suitable distribution for the number of puzzles which he fails to solve during the first six months of the year. Explain carefully why this distribution cannot be approximated by a Poisson distribution.

(ii)   Calculate the probability that Séan fails to solve exactly two of the 26 puzzles.

Séan's ambition is to solve all 52 puzzles set during the whole year.

(iii)   State a suitable distribution for the number of puzzles which he fails to solve during the whole year. State also a suitable approximating Poisson distribution.

(iv)   Calculate the probability that Séan solves all 52 puzzles.

Solution

(i)   Let X be the number of puzzles which Séan fails to solve out of 26. Then X is distributed Binomially, $X \sim B(26, 0.05)$. For this model, $n = 26$, $p = 0.05$ and $np = 26 \times 0.05 = 1.3$. A Poisson approximation may not be used because n is too small.

> Binomial is the only approach here, because n is small.

(ii) $P(X = 2) = {}^{26}C_2 \times 0.05^2 \times 0.95^{24} = 0.237$

(iii)   Let Y be the number of puzzles which Séan fails to solve out of 52. Then Y is distributed Binomially, $Y \sim B(52, 0.05)$. For this model, $n = 52$, $p = 0.05$ and $np = 52 \times 0.05 = 2.6$. A Poisson approximation may be used because $n > 50$, $p < 0.1$ and np is not too big.

(iv)   Using $Po(2.6)$

$$P(Y = 0) = \frac{e^{-2.6} \times 2.6^0}{0!} = 0.0743$$

> Using $B(52, 0.05)$ the probability would have come to 0·0694

Exercise 3.4

In questions **A1** to **A10** you are given various Binomial distributions. State with reasons whether each one meets the guidelines for a Poisson approximation; if so then state also the parameter of the approximating Poisson distribution.

A1 B(55,0·01)

A2 B(55,0·4)

A3 B(25,0·25)

A4 B(100,0·045)

A5 B(80,0·34)

A6 B(60,0·08)

A7 B(14,0·1)

A8 B(400,0·01)

A9 B(6000,0·01)

A10 B(1000,0·0025)

B1 A variable X is distributed B(120,0·03). Using a suitable Poisson approximation, calculate:

(i) P($X = 0$);   (ii) P($X = 1$);
(iii) P($X = 3$);   (iv) P($X = 4$).

B2 A variable X is distributed B(80,0·04). Using a suitable Poisson approximation, calculate:

(i) P($X = 0$);   (ii) P($X = 1$);
(iii) P($X = 2$);   (iv) P($X \le 2$).

B3 A variable X is distributed B(450,0·01). Using a suitable Poisson approximation, calculate:

(i) P($X = 0$);   (ii) P($X = 1$);
(iii) P($X = 2$);   (iv) P($X > 2$).

B4 A variable X is distributed B(50,0·06). Using a suitable Poisson approximation, calculate:

(i) P($X = 0$);   (ii) P($X = 1$);
(iii) P($X = 2$);   (iv) P($X \ge 2$).

B5 A small company produces screens for electronic calculators. 1% of all the calculator screens produced contain a defect.

(i) Calculate the probability that a random sample of ten screens contains exactly one defective screen.

(ii) Using a suitable approximating distribution, calculate the probability that a random batch of 80 screens contains exactly one defective screen.

B6 A manufacturer of potato crisps places a special prize inside 2% of the packets produced.

(i) Calculate the probability that a random sample of 40 packets contains exactly two special prizes.

Gigi buys 80 packets from her local shop.

(ii) Using a suitable approximating distribution, calculate the probability that Gigi finds at least one prize.

(iii) Comment briefly on the reliability of this calculation, with regard to the way in which Gigi has obtained her 80 packets.

B7 Hugh has been told by his statistics teacher that a Binomial distribution B(n, p) may be approximated by a Poisson distribution Po(λ) under certain circumstances. He decides to investigate this claim by considering the Binomial distribution $X \sim$ B(60,0·03).

(i) State the conditions for the approximation to be valid, and show that this particular distribution meets these conditions.

(ii) Calculate the probability that $X = 2$ using (a) the given Binomial distribution; (b) the corresponding Poisson approximation. Comment briefly on the extent to which these two answers agree.

continued   **59**

Exercise 3.4 *continued*

B8 A paramedic team answers a large number of calls each year. The team reckons that 6% of all calls are false alarms, and 30% of all calls are critical.

 (i) Using a suitable approximating distribution, calculate the probability that a random sample of 60 calls contains exactly three false alarms.

 In any one week the paramedic team reckons that it answers 85 independent calls.

 (ii) Calculate the probability that the team answers exactly 20 critical calls in a given week. Explain carefully why it is not possible to use an approximating Poisson distribution in this case.

B9 On average approximately one birth in every 100 results in a set of twins. A maternity ward in a hospital expects to handle eight births next week.

 (i) Write down a Binomial model for the number of sets of twins born next week. Use this model to calculate the probability that exactly one birth out of the eight will result in twins.

 The maternity ward expects to handle 400 births next year.

 (ii) Write down a Binomial model for the number of sets of twins born next year. Use a suitable approximation to calculate the probability that exactly four births out of the 400 will result in twins.

B10 A poultry farmer supplies eggs to a retailer. To begin with all of the eggs are in perfect condition, but by the time the eggs have been delivered to the retailer there is a probability of 0·1 that a randomly chosen egg has cracked. The retailer then packs the eggs, at random, into boxes of six.

 (i) A shopper selects one box of six eggs. Using an appropriate Binomial distribution, which should be stated clearly, show the probability that at least three of the eggs are cracked is approximately 0·016.

 A quality control worker takes a random sample of 60 boxes, and counts the number of boxes containing at least three cracked eggs. If there are more than three such boxes in the sample then the farmer's entire consignment is rejected.

 (ii) Using a suitable approximating distribution, which should be explained clearly, calculate the probability that the consignment is rejected.

3.5 Hypothesis test: mean of a Poisson distribution

Key points

The hypothesis test is very similar to that for a Binomial distribution in Section 3.2. Cumulative Poisson tables will normally be used to establish the critical region for the test.

This is the usual pattern for the test:

- **Step 1**   State the model to be tested

    e.g. Let $X \sim \text{Po}(\lambda)$, λ is only symbolic at this stage.

- **Step 2**   State null and alternative hypotheses

    Use H_0 and H_1 notation, H_0 is always 'λ = a value'.

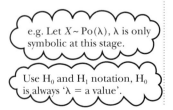

- **Step 3**   Check the significance level to be used

  > Usually given in the question. If you need to set your own level then tell the examiner you are doing so. 5% is a standard choice.

- **Step 4**   Establish the type of tail

  > One tail upper, one tail lower or two tail.

- **Step 5**   Restate the model using the value of λ supplied by H_0

  > e.g. 'Under H_0 $X \sim Po(1.5)$'

- **Step 6**   Identify the critical region(s), usually by using cumulative Poisson tables

  > State the critical region(s); either list the values or use an inequality.

- **Step 7**   Compare the test value X_{test} with the critical region(s)

  > If X_{test} is not within the critical region then accept H_0, otherwise reject H_0 in favour of H_1.

- **Step 8**   Draw a diagram or write an inequality to show the comparison

  > Warning! Poisson models are discrete so don't use continuous curves in your diagram.

- **Step 9**   State the conclusion formally

  > State 'Accept H_0', or 'Reject H_0 in favour of H_1'.

- **Step 10**   Restate it in plain English

  > e.g. 'There is evidence (at 5% level) that the mean is less than 1.5.'

Example 1

A fisherman keeps careful records over a long period of time, and reckons that the number of fish he catches per day, using one particular type of bait, can be modelled by a Poisson distribution with mean 9.

He hopes to improve his average catch by adopting a new type of bait, and on the first day with this new bait he catches 14 fish.

(i)   Write suitable null and alternative hypotheses.

(ii)   Explain why your alternative hypothesis takes this form.

(iii)   Carry out the test at the 5% level, stating your conclusion clearly.

Solution

(i)   Let the number of fish caught per day be X.

      Then $X \sim Po(\lambda)$

$H_0: \lambda = 9$

$H_1: \lambda > 9$

H_1 takes this form because he hopes to improve his average catch.

5% significance level, one-tail test

Under H_0 $X \sim \text{Po}(9)$

Using cumulative tables of $\text{Po}(9)$,

$P(X \le 13) = 0.9261$

$P(X \le 14) = 0.9585$ ← The cumulative tables show that 14 is the last value in the non-critical region.

∴ Critical region = {15, 16, 17, ...}

$X_{\text{test}} = 14$ does not lie in the critical region.

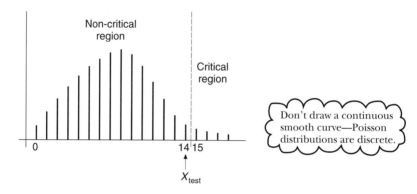

Don't draw a continuous smooth curve—Poisson distributions are discrete.

Accept H_0. There is no evidence (at 5% level) that the average catch has improved.

Exercise 3.5

In questions **A1** to **A6** list the values which would make up the critical region for the test at the indicated significance level.

A1 Under H_0 $X \sim \text{Po}(7)$. One tail (lower tail). 5% significance level.

A2 Under H_0 $X \sim \text{Po}(2.5)$. One tail (upper tail). 5% significance level.

A3 Under H_0 $X \sim \text{Po}(6)$. Two tail. 5% significance level.

A4 Under H_0 $X \sim \text{Po}(3.5)$. Two tail. 10% significance level.

A5 Under H_0 $X \sim \text{Po}(4)$. Two tail. 5% significance level.

A6 Under H_0 $X \sim \text{Po}(1.5)$. One tail (upper tail). 1% significance level.

In questions **A7** to **A10** you are given a Poisson model, null (H_0) and alternative (H_1) hypotheses, a significance level and a test value (X_{test}). List the values comprising the critical

Exercise 3.5 *continued*

region, and state whether H_0 should be accepted or rejected.

A7 $X \sim \mathrm{Po}(\lambda)$

H_0: $\lambda = 6.2$

H_1: $\lambda \neq 6.2$

10% significance level

$X_{\mathrm{test}} = 12$

A8 $X \sim \mathrm{Po}(\lambda)$

H_0: $\lambda = 2 \cdot 4$

H_1: $\lambda > 2 \cdot 4$

5% significance level

$X_{\mathrm{test}} = 4$

A9 $X \sim \mathrm{Po}(\lambda)$

H_0: $\lambda = 5 \cdot 5$

H_1: $\lambda < 5 \cdot 5$

2% significance level

$X_{\mathrm{test}} = 1$

A10 $X \sim \mathrm{Po}(\lambda)$

H_0: $\lambda = 8$

H_1: $\lambda \neq 8$

5% significance level

$X_{\mathrm{test}} = 13$

B1 The number of times that a computer system breaks down in a period of 6 months is thought to be Poisson distributed with a mean 5. To improve its reliability some new components are fitted, and over the next six months the system breaks down only twice.

You are required to set up a hypothesis test to see whether there is any evidence that the mean of this Poisson distribution has decreased.

(i) State suitable null and alternative hypotheses for the test.

(ii) Carry out your test at the 5% significance level, stating your conclusion clearly.

B2 An ice hockey team knows that over a long period of time the number of goals scored per match can be modelled by a Poisson distribution with parameter $1 \cdot 2$.

Following a change of manager the team adopts a more aggressive style. The manager decides to test whether there is any evidence of an increase in the mean number of goals scored per match.

In the first match played under the new manager the team scores 4 goals.

(i) Using this result, conduct a hypothesis test at the 5% level. State your hypotheses and conclusion clearly.

(ii) Does the fact that this was the first match played under the new manager have any bearing on the reliability of your conclusion?

B3 A certain stretch of single carriageway is notorious for the number of serious road accidents which occur. The number of serious accidents per year is modelled by a Poisson distribution with parameter $8 \cdot 2$.

In order to improve road safety this stretch of road is upgraded to dual carriageway; in the following year it is noted that two serious accidents occur.

(i) State suitable null and alternative hypotheses which might be tested.

(ii) Conduct a hypothesis test at the 5% level to see whether there is any evidence that the mean number of serious accidents has reduced following the upgrade.

B4 A recording studio buys audio tape in large reels. The tape contains a small number of minor defects; these occur randomly, and on average one defect occurs for every 100 metres of tape.

(i) Explain why the number of defects in a 500 metre reel might be modelled by a Poisson distribution, and state the value of the associated parameter.

continued

Exercise 3.5   *continued*

The studio decides to buy its tape from a new supplier, and on testing a 500 metre reel 8 defects are found.

(ii)   Conduct a hypothesis test at the 10% level, to see whether there is any evidence that the mean number of defects has changed. State your hypotheses and conclusion clearly.

B5   Chloe enjoys writing code for computer programs. She normally writes late at night, and finds that on average she makes one mistake for each 200 lines of code.

(i)   State a suitable Poisson distribution to describe the number of mistakes which Chloe makes in 500 lines of code.

Chloe now decides to write early in the morning instead, to try to reduce the frequency of mistakes. A random sample of 500 lines written in the morning is taken, and found to contain only one mistake.

(ii)   Conduct a suitable hypothesis test to see whether there is any evidence that the mean number of mistakes has reduced. Use a 10% significance level.

B6   In a large factory the number of accidents reported per month is known to be Poisson distributed with parameter 6·4. Calculate the probability that in a randomly chosen month there are

(i)   exactly four accidents;

(ii)   no more than four accidents.

Changes in procedures are introduced, with the aim of improving safety standards. In the first full month following the changes only two accidents are reported.

(iii)   Carry out a suitable hypothesis test to see whether there is any evidence, at the 5% level, that the changes have improved safety standards. State your hypotheses and conclusions clearly.

3.6   The Geometric distribution

Key points

The **Geometric distribution** is a **discrete** distribution. It is related to the Binomial distribution, and counts the number of trials up to and including the first success.

Typical situations in which the Geometric distribution is used include:
- the number of dice throws until a 'six' occurs
- the number of coins tossed until 'heads' occurs
- the number of darts thrown until a 'double' is scored.

A Geometric model relies on these modelling assumptions:
- there is a sequence of trials
- each trial results in a success or a failure (e.g. heads or tails, win or lose)
- the trials are independent
- at each trial there is a fixed probability, p, of success.

A Binomial distribution is characterised by **one parameter**, namely the probability of an individual success, p. We write $X \sim \text{Geo}(0·2)$ for example, to mean that 'the random variable X has a Geometric distribution and at any trial there is a fixed probability, $p = 0·2$, of success'.

Probabilities are computed using the formula

$$P(X = r) = (1 - p)^{r-1} \times p \text{ where } r = 1, 2, 3, \ldots$$

The mean and the variance of X are found in the following way:

$$\text{if } X \sim \text{Geo}(p) \text{ then } E(X) = \frac{1}{p}$$

$$\text{Var}(X) = \frac{q}{p^2}$$

$$\text{where } q = (1 - p)$$

Some syllabuses require knowledge of these results—i.e. they may be quoted without proof—other syllabuses expect you to be able to prove one or both of them.

Example 1

Deepak and Ravi are playing a game of Ludo. Deepak has almost finished the game; he needs only a single throw of a 1 to win, while Ravi will need a great number of turns before he is in a winning position.

(i)   Calculate the probability that Deepak will require five throws to win.

(ii) Find the expected number of throws for Deepak to win.

Solution

Let the number of throws required by Deepak be X. Then $X \sim \text{Geo}(\frac{1}{6})$

(i) $P(X = 5) = (\frac{5}{6})^4 \times \frac{1}{6} = 0\cdot0804$

(ii) $E(X) = \dfrac{1}{\frac{1}{6}} = 6$ throws.

Exercise 3.6

A1 If $X \sim \text{Geo}(0\cdot4)$ find (i) $P(X = 3)$; (ii) $P(X = 2)$; (iii) $P(X = 2 \text{ or } 3)$.

A2 If $X \sim \text{Geo}(0\cdot9)$ find (i) $E(X)$; (ii) $\text{Var}(X)$; (iii) $P(X = 4)$; (iv) $P(X = 2)$.

A3 If $X \sim \text{Geo}(\frac{1}{3})$ find (i) $P(X = 1)$; (ii) $P(X = 2)$; (iii) $P(X < 3)$.

A4 If $X \sim \text{Geo}(\frac{2}{7})$ find (i) $E(X)$; (ii) $\text{Var}(X)$; (iii) $P(X = 4)$; (iv) $P(X = 5)$.

A5 If $X \sim \text{Geo}(0\cdot35)$ find (i) $P(X = 1)$; (ii) $P(X = 2)$; (iii) $P(X \geq 3)$.

A6 If $X \sim \text{Geo}(0\cdot62)$ find (i) $E(X)$; (ii) $\text{Var}(X)$; (iii) $P(X = 4)$; (iv) $P(X = 5)$.

A7 If $X \sim \text{Geo}(\frac{3}{8})$ find (i) $P(X = 6)$; (ii) $P(X = 4)$; (iii) $P(X \geq 3)$.

A8 If $X \sim \text{Geo}(\frac{4}{9})$ find (i) $E(X)$; (ii) $\text{Var}(X)$; (iii) $P(X = 2)$; (iv) $P(X \leq 3)$.

Exercise 3.6 *continued*

B1 A cereal manufacturer puts a toy car inside each packet. 30% of these toys are red. Find the probability that Liz obtains her first red toy car when opening her fourth packet.

B2 George reckons that the probability of his obtaining an A grade in a Pure 1 exam is 0·8. He decides to keep taking the exam until an A grade is obtained. Calculate the probability that he obtains an A at his fourth attempt.

B3 10% of the eggs in a large batch are of size 1. Anton checks a random sample of 12 eggs. Calculate the probability that the only size 1 egg he sees is the last one he checks.

B4 The random variable X follows a Geometric distribution $X \sim \text{Geo}(0·4)$.

    (i)   Explain why X cannot take the value 0.

    (ii) Calculate $P(X = 1)$.

    (iii) Find $E(X)$ and $Var(X)$.

B5 The probability that Reggie is late for work on any given day from Monday to Friday is 0·15. Find the probability that next week he is late only on Friday.

B6 42% of the pupils at a large school are boys. Ten pupils are chosen at random to form a student council. Find the probability that the third pupil to be chosen is the first girl.

B7 The probability that a certain space rocket launches successfully is 0·85. Ten launches are planned.

    (i)   Find the probability that all ten launches are successful.

    (ii) Find the probability that the tenth launch is the first unsuccessful one.

B8 A darts player can hit a double with probability 0·24. Calculate the probability that he requires three throws in order to hit his first double. Find also the expected number of throws until the first double is obtained.

Revision questions

C1 A company sells a large number of chocolate eggs, 10% of which contain a toy chicken. The eggs are packed into boxes containing 12 eggs.

    (i)   Explain carefully why the number of toy chickens to be found in a box of 12 eggs can be expected to follow a Binomial distribution $B(n, p)$, and give values for n and p. State any assumptions you are making.

Calculate the probability that a box of 12 eggs contains

    (ii) exactly 2 chickens; (iii) at least 2 chickens.

The company claims that 5% of the boxes contain a money-back voucher. Calculate the probability that 40 boxes chosen at random contain

    (iv) no vouchers; (v) exactly 1 voucher;
    (vi) at least 3 vouchers.

C2 A game of ten-pin bowling consists of a series of frames. In each frame two balls are available; the bowler scores a strike if all ten pins are knocked over with the first ball in a frame.

Winston enjoys bowling. Over a long period of time he achieves a strike in 15% of all frames played. Calculate the probability that in 16 frames Winston scores

    (i)   exactly 1 strike; (ii) exactly 2 strikes;
    (iii) no more than 2 strikes.

Winston's cousin Eugene claims that he has a higher strike rate than Winston. To demonstrate this claim Eugene bowls 18 frames, scoring strikes in exactly 5 of them.

    (iv) Carry out a hypothesis test to see whether this figure provides any evidence, at the 5% level, of support for Winston's claim. State your hypotheses and conclusions clearly.

C3 Mark enjoys rock climbing in Scotland during the summer. He occasionally falls (though he is protected from serious injury by a safety rope). Mark reckons that on average he falls once each summer.

    (i) Explain the necessary assumptions in order that the number of falls which Mark experiences in any given summer can be modelled by a Poisson distribution.

    (ii) Find the probability that Mark falls exactly twice in a given summer.

One summer Mark decides to climb in the Alps instead, and he falls three times.

    (iii) Carry out a hypothesis test, at the 5% level, to see whether there is any evidence that the mean number of falls per summer has increased.

C4 When a pack of cards is cut the probability that an Ace is revealed is $\frac{1}{13}$. The pack is cut eight times. Find the probability that an Ace is revealed

    (i) exactly once;   (ii) exactly twice.

The pack is now cut a total of 52 times.

    (iii) Write down a distribution to describe the number of times on which an Ace is revealed. Write down also a suitable approximating distribution.

    (iv) Use the approximating distribution to find the probability that exactly 5 Aces are revealed when the pack is cut 52 times.

C5 A shop sells peaches, some of which have blemishes on the skin. The number of blemishes per peach has a Poisson distribution with parameter 0·8.

    (i) Calculate the probability that a randomly chosen peach contains no blemishes.

    (ii) Four peaches are chosen at random. Calculate the probability that the fourth peach chosen is the only one which has a blemished skin.

    (iii) State the expected number of blemished peaches in a random sample of 12.

The shop also sells nectarines. The number of blemishes per nectarine has a Poisson distribution with parameter 1·2.

Carl buys one peach and one nectarine from the shop.

    (iv) Write down a distribution to describe the total number of blemishes on the two fruits. Hence calculate the probability that the two fruits contain exactly three blemishes in total.

C6 Gita has been teaching an A-level linear mathematics course for many years, and has observed that 10% of her students do not succeed in passing the course.

    (i) Using a model $X \sim B(28, 0{\cdot}1)$ calculate:

        (a) $P(X = 0)$; (b) $P(X = 1)$;
        (c) $P(X = 2)$; (d) $P(X = 3)$.

Gita changes to a modular scheme, hoping that the style of assessment will provide higher motivation, leading to an increase in the pass rate. In the first year of the new modular scheme Gita enters 28 candidates for the A-level, and they all pass.

    (ii) Using your results from (i) construct the first four entries in a cumulative table for $B(28, 0{\cdot}1)$.

    (iii) Carry out a hypothesis test to see whether there is evidence, at the 10% level, of an increase in the pass rate. State your conclusion clearly.

C7 Delia's Patisserie produces exceedingly good cherry cakes. The number of cherries per cake is known to follow a Poisson distribution with mean 5·5. Calculate the probability that a randomly chosen cake contains

continued   **67**

(i)   no cherries;

(ii)   exactly four cherries;

(iii)   at least four cherries.

Lenny's Bakery claims to produce identical cakes but sells them at a lower price. A food journalist suspects that Lenny's is, in fact, using less cherries than Delia's, so he buys a cake at random from Lenny's shop. This cake is found to contain only two cherries.

(iv)   State suitable null and alternative hypotheses which may be tested by the journalist. Explain carefully why your alternative hypothesis takes the form it does.

(v)   Carry out the hypothesis test at the 5% level. State your conclusion clearly.

C8   A certain blood disorder is believed to be carried by 1 person in every 50 000. The disorder is not hereditary, so occurrences may be assumed to be independent.

A health authority wishes to examine the likely number of people carrying the disorder within its district of 300 000 inhabitants.

(i)   Write down the expected number of people within the district carrying the disorder.

(ii)   Explain briefly why the number of carriers may be modelled by a Binomial distribution, giving values for the parameters n and p.

(iii)   State three conditions in order that this distribution may be approximated by a Poisson distribution. Show that these three conditions are met in this case, and state a suitable value for the parameter λ.

(iv)   Use the Poisson approximation to find the probability that the number of carriers of the disorder within the district will be:

(a)   exactly five;

(b)   no more than 6.

C9   The number of letters I receive each working day is Poisson distributed with parameter 1·2. Calculate the probability that, on a randomly chosen working day, I receive

(i)   exactly two letters;

(ii)   at least four letters.

My next-door neighbour receives, on average, 2·2 letters each working day. Calculate the probability that, in a randomly chosen week,

(iii)   we receive ten letters each;

(iv)   we receive a total of 20 letters between us.

(In parts (iii) and (iv) a week should be taken to be six days as there is no delivery on a Sunday.)

C10   A county police force places a large number of speed cameras around the edge of residential areas. The intention is that any vehicle exceeding the 30 mph speed limit will be flash photographed as it passes the camera, and the driver will subsequently be prosecuted.

Court costs are expensive, and in practice the county police force can only afford to prosecute 1 in every 8 of the motorists who think they have been photographed in this way.

Damion has been flashed by 20 cameras in the last year. Find the probability that he is prosecuted

(i)   exactly once;   (ii)   exactly twice;
(iii)   at least twice.

Jane has been delayed on her way to an important business appointment. She decides, somewhat foolishly, to break the speed limit in order to catch up lost time. As a consequence Jane is flashed by six cameras. Calculate:

(iv)   the probability that Jane is prosecuted exactly three times;

(v)   the probability that the last camera to flash her is the first one which results in a prosecution.

Chapter 4

THE NORMAL DISTRIBUTION I

Key points

The Normal distribution is an example of a **continuous distribution**. Probabilities are calculated by finding the area under a standard curve, using tables or a graphics calculator. The Normal distribution is widely used as a distribution in its own right, and under certain circumstances, can be used as an approximation to a Binomial or Poisson distribution. This section deals with the Normal distribution in its own right.

Examples of variables which might be Normally distributed include:
- the height of an adult male
- the weight of a sack of potatoes
- the time taken for a journey to school.

A Normal distribution is characterised by two parameters: the **mean μ** and the **variance σ^2**. For example, we write $X \sim N(30, 16)$ to mean that 'the random variable X has a Normal distribution with mean $\mu = 30$ and variance $\sigma^2 = 16$'. You may prefer to write $X \sim N(30, 4^2)$ as a reminder that the standard deviation is $\sigma = 4$.

There are infinitely many different Normal distributions, but only one is tabulated: the **standardised Normal distribution N(0, 1)**. Before any probabilities are calculated the variable must be standardised:

$$\text{If } X \sim N(\mu, \sigma^2) \text{ then } Z = \frac{X - \mu}{\sigma} \sim N(0, 1)$$

i.e. to standardise, subtract the mean and divide by the standard deviation.

The required probability may then be found using tables or a graphics calculator. There are several different notations used, for example:

The probability that z is less than $1\cdot2$ is $P(z < 1\cdot2)$, often denoted by $\Phi(1.2)$, and is given by the shaded area under the curve:

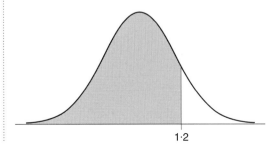

1·2

Most syllabuses use $\Phi(1.2)$ for this area; Casio fx graphics calculators use $P(1.2)$

The Normal distribution is **reproductive**, that is if two independent Normal variables are added (or subtracted) the result is another Normal variable.

> If $X \sim \mathrm{N}(\mu_1, \sigma_1^2)$ and $Y \sim \mathrm{N}(\mu_2, \sigma_2^2)$, and $T = X + Y$, $U = X - Y$
> then $T \sim \mathrm{N}(\mu_1 + \mu_2, \sigma_1^2 + \sigma_2^2)$
> and $U \sim \mathrm{N}(\mu_1 - \mu_2, \sigma_1^2 + \sigma_2^2)$

> Even when subtracting, you still **add** the variances.

A question will tell you that a variable is Normally distributed. If it doesn't you must make it clear that you are making this assumption.

Example 1

The random variable X is Normally distributed $\mathrm{N}(3, 2^2)$. Find the probability that X is

(i) less than 4; (ii) greater than 5; (iii) between 2 and 4·5.

Solution

(i) $z = \dfrac{4 - 3}{2} = 0 \cdot 5$

$P(z < 0 \cdot 5) = \Phi(0 \cdot 5)$

$\qquad = 0 \cdot 6915$

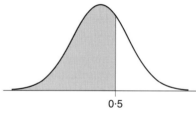

(i) $z = \dfrac{5 - 3}{2} = 1$

$P(z > 1) = 1 - P(z < 1)$

$\qquad = 1 - 0 \cdot 8413$

$\qquad = 0 \cdot 1587$

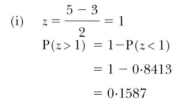

(iii) Lower tail: $z = \dfrac{2 - 3}{2} = -0 \cdot 5$

Upper tail: $z = \dfrac{4 \cdot 5 - 3}{2} = 0 \cdot 75$

$P(-0 \cdot 5 < z < 0 \cdot 75) = \Phi(0 \cdot 75) - \Phi(-0 \cdot 5)$

$\qquad = 0 \cdot 7734 - (1 - 0 \cdot 6915)$

$\qquad = 0 \cdot 7734 - 0 \cdot 3085$

$\qquad = 0 \cdot 4649$

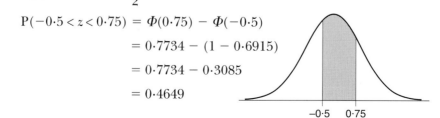

In this example, we used tables of Φ which give lower tail probabilities, and are tabulated only for positive values of z. To evaluate $\Phi(-0{\cdot}5)$ we had to use the result that $\Phi(-z) = 1 - \Phi(z)$. This problem does not arise with graphics calculators—they tabulate both ends of the distribution.

Exercise 4.1

In questions **A1** to **A10**, sketch the given Normal distribution. Replace the values marked on the x-axis with the matching standardised z-values, then use tables of N(0, 1) or a graphics calculator to find the probability corresponding to the shaded region.

A1 $X \sim \mathrm{N}(10, 2^2)$

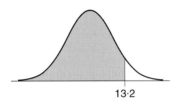

13·2

A2 $X \sim \mathrm{N}(100, 5^2)$

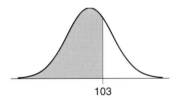

103

A3 $X \sim \mathrm{N}(150, 5^2)$

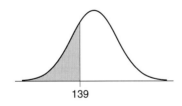

139

A4 $X \sim \mathrm{N}(60, 10^2)$

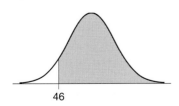

46

A5 $X \sim \mathrm{N}(2{\cdot}5, 0{\cdot}1^2)$

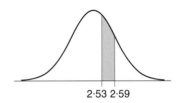

2·53 2·59

A6 $X \sim \mathrm{N}(540, 20^2)$

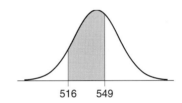

516   549

A7 $X \sim \mathrm{N}(140, 100)$

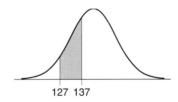

127 137

A8 $X \sim \mathrm{N}(80, 16)$

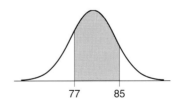

77   85

continued

Exercise 4.1 continued

A9 $X \sim N(-5, 3^2)$

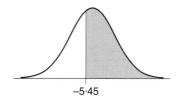

-5.45

A10 $X \sim N(2, 0.04)$

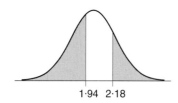

$1.94 \quad 2.18$

B1 The heights of university students are Normally distributed with mean 175 cm and standard deviation 15 cm. The doorframe to the student bar is 185 cm high. Find the probability that a student selected at random can pass through the doorway without ducking.

B2 The wrapper of a chocolate bar claims that the weight of the bar is 65 grams. In fact the weight of a bar is a Normal variable with mean 67 grams and standard deviation 3 grams. Find the probability that a randomly chosen bar:

(i) has a weight of over 66 grams
(ii) has a weight of under 70 grams.

What percentage of bars sold weigh less than 65 grams?

B3 A radio station has a large collection of '3-minute' pop songs. The lengths of the songs are Normally distributed with a mean length of 175 seconds and a standard deviation of 25 seconds. A song is selected at random. Find the probability that it lasts

(i) over 165 seconds;
(ii) between 170 and 190 seconds.

What percentage of songs in the collection last three minutes or less?

B4 Karl arrives at school T minutes after 08:20, where T is Normally distributed with mean 6 and variance 25. His arrival time on any given day is assumed to be independent of that on any other day. Find

(i) the probability that he arrives before 08:25 on Monday;

(ii) the probability that he arrives between 08:25 and 08:30 on Tuesday.

Karl's teacher marks him as late if he arrives after 08:30.

(iii) Find the probability that Karl is late on Wednesday.

(iv) Find the probability that Karl is late exactly once in a school week of five days.

B5 A drinks machine is supposed to dispense cups containing 220 ml of orange juice. In fact the amount dispensed in each cup follows a Normal distribution with mean 225 ml and variance 9 ml². Find the probability that a randomly chosen cup contains

(i) at least 222 ml;

(ii) no more than 230 ml;

(iii) between 222 and 230 ml.

What percentage of the cups dispensed contain less than 220 ml of orange juice?

Questions **B6** to **B10** require the reproductive property of the Normal distribution.

B6 Bags of potatoes weigh W kg, where W is distributed Normally with mean 2·5 and variance 0·04. One bag is selected at random. Find the probability that it weighs

(i) less than 2·4 kg;

(ii) between 2·4 and 2·6 kg.

Peter chooses two bags of potatoes at random.

(iii) Write down the distribution of T, the total weight in kg of the two bags.

(iv) Find the probability that the total weight of the two bags exceeds 5·2 kg.

B7 A machine produces pork sausages with a mean weight of 55 grams and a standard deviation of 5 grams. They are sold in packs of 8 sausages.

Roxanne wants to describe the distribution of weights of the packs, and so she assumes the weights of individual sausages can be described by a Normal distribution. She says 'the weights of individual sausages are N(55, 5) so the weights of packs of 8 must be N(440, 40)'.

(i) Where has Roxanne's arithmetic gone wrong?

(ii) What other assumption is she making about the weights of individual sausages?

(iii) Calculate the probability that the weight of a randomly chosen pack lies between 425 and 445 grams.

B8 The body length of a certain type of stick insect is known to be Normally distributed with mean 12 cm and standard deviation 1·2 cm; the head length follows an independent Normal distribution with mean 25 mm and standard deviation 6 mm.

Find the probability that a stick insect chosen at random has

(i) a body length of more than 11 cm;

(ii) a head length of more than 20 mm.

Write down the distribution for the overall length (head plus body) in cm. Hence find the probability that a randomly chosen stick insect has an overall length of more than 13 cm.

B9 A machine produces stickers of famous Olympic athletes. The stickers are meant to be square, but in fact the length, L, is Normally distributed with mean 55 mm and standard deviation 5 mm, and the breadth, B, is Normally distributed with

mean 58 mm and standard deviation 6 mm. A sticker is selected at random. Find the probability that

(i) its length exceeds 58 mm;

(ii) its breadth is between 55 mm and 60 mm.

The variable D is defined as the difference between the length and the breadth of a randomly chosen sticker.

(iii) Write down the distribution of D. What additional assumption are you making about the two Normal variables L and B?

(iv) Find the probability that a randomly chosen sticker has a length greater than its breadth.

B10 Beatrice and Greg are keen cyclists. They decide to race over a measured 8 km course. During training Beatrice discovers that she can cycle 8 km in a mean time of 21 minutes with a standard deviation of 1 minute. Greg can cycle 8 km in a mean time of 22 minutes, with a standard deviation of 2 minutes. Assuming that Beatrice's and Greg's times may be taken to be Normally distributed, find the probability that in a randomly chosen 8 km training cycle

(i) Beatrice takes between 21 and 22 minutes;

(ii) Greg takes between 21 and 22 minutes.

Assume further that the two racers' times are independent.

(iii) Write down the distribution for T, the amount by which Beatrice's time is faster than Greg's.

(iv) Hence find the probability that Beatrice wins the race.

4.2 Using Normal tables in reverse

In the last section, the mean and variance were known, and Normal tables were used to calculate probabilities. Sometimes probabilities are given, and the tables are used in reverse to deduce the mean and variance.

This section covers the use of inverse tables of the Normal distribution $N(0, 1)$.

Example I

It is believed that the heights of 17-year-old girls are Normally distributed. 25% are known to be over 170 cm, while 33% are under 160 cm. Using inverse Normal distribution tables obtain values for the mean and standard deviation, correct to 3 significant figures.

Solution

Let $X \sim N(\mu, \sigma^2)$

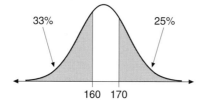

33%   25%

160   170

Always draw a sketch.

For the left tail:

$$\Phi(z) = \Phi\left(\frac{160 - \mu}{\sigma}\right) = 0.33$$

Using inverse tables,

$$\frac{160 - \mu}{\sigma} = -[\Phi^{-1}(1 - 0.33)]$$

$$= -\Phi^{-1}(0.67)$$

$$= -0.4399$$

For the right tail:

$$\Phi(z) = \Phi\left(\frac{170 - \mu}{\sigma}\right) = 0.75$$

Using inverse tables,

$$\frac{170 - \mu}{\sigma} = \Phi^{-1}(0.75) = 0.6745$$

So we have two simultaneous equations:

$$160 - \mu = -0.4399\sigma$$

$$170 - \mu = 0.6745\sigma$$

You will always get two equations containing $-\mu$ at this stage, so subtract them and solve for σ.

Subtracting,

$-10 = -1.1144\sigma$

Therefore $\sigma = \dfrac{10}{1.1144} = 8.973$

Then $\mu = 160 + 0.4399\sigma$

$= 160 + 0.4399 \times 8.973$

$= 163.95$

And so, to 3 significant figures, the values are $\mu = 164$ cm and $\sigma = 8.97$ cm.

Exercise 4.2

In questions **A1** to **A10** a Normal distribution curve is drawn, with two values on the x-axis, and the areas of the regions under the curve are given. Use inverse Normal tables to set up two simultaneous equations in μ and σ, and solve them to a sensible level of accuracy.

A1

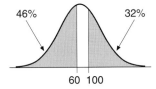

A2

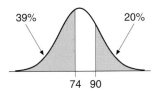

A3

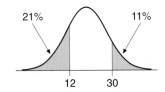

A4

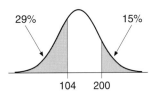

A5

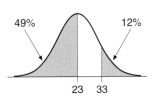

A6

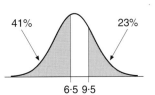

continued

Exercise 4.2   *continued*

A7

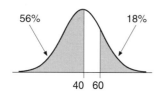

56%   18%

40 60

A8

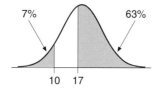

7%   63%

10 17

A9

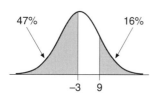

47%   16%

−3 9

A10

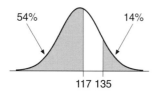

54%   14%

117 135

B1 Nick is studying the lengths of leaves of his favourite species of potted plant. He believes that the lengths are Normally distributed with mean 12·5 cm, and in a random sample of 40 leaves he notices that 35% are over 14 cm in length.

(i) Show that σ may be estimated by the result $\dfrac{14 - 12\cdot5}{\sigma} = 0\cdot3853$, and so

obtain an estimate of σ correct to three significant figures.

(ii) Explain why your answer to (i) is only an estimate.

(iii) Further research reveals that in fact σ is exactly 3·5 cm. Using this result, calculate the proportion of leaves within the population which are over 14 cm in length.

B2 A firework company manufactures Roman Candles. When lit these burn for a time T seconds, which can be modelled by a Normal distribution. It is known that 15% of the Roman Candles burn for less than 45 seconds, while 25% burn for over one minute.

(i) Given that $T \sim N(\mu, \sigma^2)$, show that
$$\frac{45 - \mu}{\sigma} = -1\cdot036$$

(ii) Write down a second equation containing μ and σ.

(iii) Solve these two equations to show that σ is approximately 8·8 seconds, and find μ.

B3 A school fête includes a 'Guess the Weight of the Cake' stall. Large numbers of guesses are made, and these are modelled by a Normal distribution $N(\mu, \sigma^2)$. 40% of the guesses were under 3·8 kg, while 25% were over 5·35 kg.

(i) Set up two simultaneous equations in μ and σ.

(ii) Solve these equations to show that σ is approximately 1·67 kg, and find the value of μ in kg, correct to the nearest 10 g.

B4 A shop sells hand-made Easter eggs, the weights of which may be assumed to follow a Normal distribution. 35% of the eggs weigh less than 450 grams, while 17% weigh over 550 grams.

(i) Set up two simultaneous equations for the mean μ and standard deviation σ.

Exercise 4.2   *continued*

(ii)   Find the values of μ and σ in grams, correct to 3 significant figures.

(iii)   What percentage of the eggs weigh over 500 grams?

B5   A machine fills plastic trays with Chicken Balti for sale in a supermarket. The packaging says: 'This pack contains 400 grams.'

In fact, the weight of the contents varies from one container to another, according to a Normal distribution with mean 410 grams. 6% of the containers actually weigh less than the stated figure of 400 grams.

(i)   Calculate the standard deviation of the weights, in grams.

(ii)   Following complaints from the supermarket, the standard deviation is reduced so that only 4% of the containers weigh less than 400 grams. Calculate the new value of the standard deviation.

4.3   Normal approximation to a Binomial distribution

Key points

When dealing with a large Binomial distribution, it is often easier to use an approximating Normal distribution instead. Provided certain conditions are satisfied, the approximation is remarkably accurate, and the calculations are greatly simplified.

The Normal distribution is **continuous** but the Binomial distribution is **discrete**, so a continuity correction must always be applied.

A Binomial distribution, $\text{B}(n, p)$, can be approximated by a Normal distribution, $\text{N}(\mu, \sigma^2)$, with $\mu = np$ and $\sigma^2 = npq$ provided:

- n is large
- p is not too close to 0 or 1

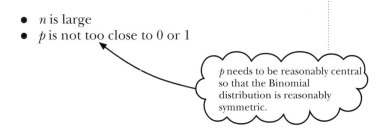

p needs to be reasonably central so that the Binomial distribution is reasonably symmetric.

Example 1

The random variable $X \sim \text{B}(50, 0\cdot3)$.

(i)   Write down the mean and variance of a suitable approximating Normal distribution.

(ii)   Explain briefly why this approximation is valid.

(iii)   Use the approximation to find the probability that X lies between 10 and 18 inclusive.

Solution

(i)   Mean: $\mu = np = 50 \times 0{\cdot}3 = 15$

      Variance: $\sigma^2 = npq = 15 \times 0{\cdot}7 = 10{\cdot}5$

(ii)   The approximation is valid because n (50) is large and p (0·3) is not too close to 0 or 1.

(iii) Now $X \sim B(50, 0{\cdot}3)$ is approximately $\sim N(15, 10{\cdot}5)$

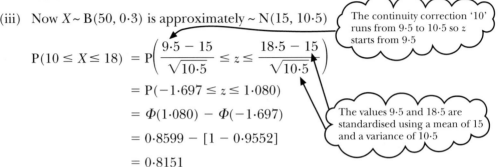

The continuity correction '10' runs from 9·5 to 10·5 so z starts from 9·5

$$P(10 \le X \le 18) = P\left(\frac{9{\cdot}5 - 15}{\sqrt{10{\cdot}5}} \le z \le \frac{18{\cdot}5 - 15}{\sqrt{10{\cdot}5}} \right)$$

$$= P(-1{\cdot}697 \le z \le 1{\cdot}080)$$

$$= \Phi(1{\cdot}080) - \Phi(-1{\cdot}697)$$

The values 9·5 and 18·5 are standardised using a mean of 15 and a variance of 10·5

$$= 0{\cdot}8599 - [1 - 0{\cdot}9552]$$

$$= 0{\cdot}8151$$

Example 2

A fair die is thrown 180 times, and the number of sixes, X, is recorded.

(i)   Write down the distribution of X.

(ii)   Write down a suitable approximating distribution, and use it to find the probability of obtaining at least 25 but less than 32 heads.

Solution

(i) $X \sim B(180, \frac{1}{6})$

(ii)   Mean: $\mu = np = 180 \times \frac{1}{6} = 30$

      Variance: $\sigma^2 = npq = 30 \times \frac{5}{6} = 25$

      So a suitable approximating distribution is $N(30, 25)$

(iii) Using $N(30, 25)$

'Less than 32' means '31 or less' so 31·5 is the upper limit with the continuity correction.

$$P(25 \le X \le 31) = P\left(\frac{24{\cdot}5 - 30}{\sqrt{25}} \le z \le \frac{31{\cdot}5 - 30}{\sqrt{25}} \right)$$

$$= P(-1{\cdot}1 \le z \le 0{\cdot}3)$$

$$= \Phi(0{\cdot}3) - \Phi(-1{\cdot}1)$$

$$= 0{\cdot}6179 - [1 - 0{\cdot}8643]$$

$$= 0{\cdot}4822$$

Exercise 4.3

In questions **A1** to **A10** you are given a Binomial distribution and asked to find a corresponding probability. For each question you should decide whether a Normal approximation is appropriate; if so, use it to compute the required probability. If a Normal approximation is not appropriate then briefly explain why it is not.

A1 $X \sim B(70, 0.4)$. Find the probability that $25 \leq X \leq 29$.

A2 $X \sim B(10, 0.33)$. Find the probability that $3 \leq X \leq 5$.

A3 $X \sim B(60, 0.35)$. Find the probability that $22 \leq X < 24$.

A4 $X \sim B(50, 0.2)$. Find the probability that $9 \leq X < 13$.

A5 $X \sim B(50, 0.02)$. Find the probability that $0 \leq X \leq 3$.

A6 $X \sim B(160, 0.25)$. Find the probability that $35 < X < 42$.

A7 $X \sim B(120, 0.7)$. Find the probability that X is at least 90.

A8 $X \sim B(85, 0.99)$. Find the probability that $75 \leq X < 80$.

A9 $X \sim B(4, 0.5)$. Find the probability that $1 \leq X \leq 4$.

A10 $X \sim B(300, \frac{2}{3})$. Find the probability that $192 < X \leq 197$.

B1 A spinner scores 1, 2, 3 or 4, each with probability 0.25. The spinner is spun 100 times. Using a suitable approximating distribution, calculate the probability that the number of 1s lies between 22 and 27 inclusive.

B2 A police force reckons that one third of all vehicles driving within its district are faulty in some way. One morning, a patrol car stops 10 vehicles at random and examines them.

  (i) Write down a suitable distribution to describe the number of faulty vehicles in the sample of 10.

  (ii) Calculate the probability that exactly four vehicles are faulty.

During one week the police force examines a total of 528 vehicles.

  (iii) Write down a suitable distribution to describe the number of faulty vehicles in the sample of 528. Write down also a suitable approximating distribution.

  (iv) Use the approximating distribution to calculate the probability that between 160 and 170 vehicles (inclusive) are found to be faulty. State any necessary assumptions about the way in which the 528 vehicles were selected.

B3 D'Arcy the dog likes to collect balls from a local school's grounds. There is a probability of 0.35 that a randomly collected ball is actually a golf ball.

  (i) D'Arcy collects six balls at random. Use a suitable Binomial model to calculate the probability that at least three of them are golf balls.

  (ii) During a whole year D'Arcy collects 200 balls. Use a suitable approximating distribution to find the probability that at least 60 of them are golf balls.

B4 A mountain rescue team knows that, on average, 35% of the calls it receives are due to accidents caused by slipping. The team answers 76 calls during January.

  (i) Assuming that the number of calls due to slips may be modelled by the Binomial distribution $B(76, 0.35)$, state a suitable approximating Normal distribution, and explain why this particular approximation is valid.

  (ii) Use the approximating distribution to calculate the probability that between 20 and 30 of the calls (inclusive) were due to accidents caused by slipping.

  (iii) Hamish says, 'I'm not convinced that the Binomial model in part (i) is appropriate anyway.' Suggest one reason to support Hamish's comment.

continued

Exercise 4.3 *continued*

B5 Hugh has been told by his statistics teacher (without proof) that a Binomial distribution B(n, p) may be approximated by a Normal distribution N(np, npq) provided that the value of n is quite large and the value of p is not too close to 0 or 1. To test this claim Hugh decides to compare the distributions $X \sim$ B(48, 0·1) and $Y \sim$ B(100, 0·6) with their respective Normal approximations.

(i) Hugh thinks the Normal approximation will work well for one of these two distributions and less well for the other. Explain, with reasons, whether you agree with Hugh.

(ii) Hugh decides to calculate P($X = 5$) using both the given distribution and its Normal approximation. Show that the approximation produces a relative error of about 2·6%.

(iii) Hugh also decides to calculate P($Y = 56$) using both the given distribution and its Normal approximation. Calculate the relative error in using the Normal approximation.

(iv) Comment briefly on the quality of each of the two approximations.

4.4 Normal approximation to a Poisson distribution

Key points

A Poisson distribution with a large mean is reasonably symmetric, and so can be approximated quite well by a Normal distribution, in order to simplify the resulting calculations.

The Normal distribution is **continuous** but the Poisson distribution is **discrete**, so a continuity correction must always be applied.

A Poisson distribution, Po(λ), can be approximated by a Normal distribution, N(μ, σ^2), with $\mu = \lambda$ and $\sigma^2 = \lambda$, provided **λ is large** (at least 10, say).

Example 1

Oliver is playing the computer game Minesweeper. He wins a game by successfully sweeping all the mines, and Oliver reckons he does this, on average, once every three days.

(i) Oliver plays Minesweeper for 12 days. Write down the distribution of the number of games he wins. Calculate the probability that he wins exactly three games.

Oliver's sister Olivia is a better player; she reckons she wins, on average, once every 2·5 days.

(ii) Olivia plays for 40 days. Write down the distribution of the number of games she wins, and state a suitable approximating distribution.

(iii) Use the approximation to find the probability that Olivia wins between 14 and 19 games inclusive.

Solution

(i) Let Oliver win X games. Then $X \sim \text{Po}(4)$

$$P(X = 3) = \frac{e^{-4} \times 4^3}{3!} = 0 \cdot 1954$$

[cloud: $12 \div 3 = 4$]

(ii) Let Olivia win Y games. Then $Y \sim \text{Po}(16)$

Po(16) may be approximated by N(16, 16)

[cloud: $40 \div 2 \cdot 5 = 16$]

[cloud: 16 is then used as the mean and the variance.]

(iii) $P(14 \leq Y \leq 19) = P\left(\dfrac{13 \cdot 5 - 16}{\sqrt{16}} \leq z \leq \dfrac{19 \cdot 5 - 16}{\sqrt{16}} \right)$

$$= P(-0 \cdot 625 \leq z \leq 0 \cdot 875)$$

$$= \Phi(0 \cdot 875) - \Phi(-0 \cdot 625)$$

$$= 0 \cdot 8092 - [1 - 0 \cdot 7340]$$

$$= 0 \cdot 5432$$

Exercise 4.4

In questions **A1** to **A8** you are given a Poisson distribution and asked to find a corresponding probability. For each question you should decide whether a Normal approximation is appropriate. If it is, use it to compute the required probability; if it is not appropriate, briefly explain why not.

A1 $X \sim \text{Po}(14)$. Find the probability that $10 \leq X \leq 14$.

A2 $X \sim \text{Po}(2 \cdot 5)$. Find the probability that $2 \leq X \leq 5$.

A3 $X \sim \text{Po}(60)$. Find the probability that $50 \leq X \leq 65$.

A4 $X \sim \text{Po}(4 \cdot 2)$. Find the probability that $3 \leq X < 10$.

A5 $X \sim \text{Po}(11)$. Find the probability that X is at least 14.

A6 $X \sim \text{Po}(25)$. Find the probability that $18 < X < 29$.

A7 $X \sim \text{Po}(20 \cdot 25)$. Find the probability that X is less than 28.

A8 $X \sim \text{Po}(6)$. Find the probability that $5 \leq X < 7$.

In questions **A9** and **A10** you should calculate the required probability twice: (i) exactly, using the given Poisson distribution, and (ii) approximately, using a Normal approximation. Comment on the quality of the agreement between the two answers in each case.

A9 $X \sim \text{Po}(14)$. Find the probability that X is between 14 and 16 inclusive.

A10 $X \sim \text{Po}(17)$. Find the probability that X is exactly 18.

B1 Adrian enjoys walking along footpaths in the English countryside. He reckons that he encounters a stile on average once every 2 kilometres. Adrian plans a high-level mountain walk 25 kilometres long. He assumes that the number of stiles encountered may be modelled by a Poisson distribution Po(12·5).

(i) Explain how Adrian arrived at the parameter 12·5.

continued

Exercise 4.4 *continued*

(ii) Use a suitable approximation to calculate the probability that he encounters no more than 8 stiles.

(iii) Give one reason why Po(12·5) might not actually be a valid model.

B2 Anna is a travelling sales executive. She drives a great number of miles in the course of a year, and does not always respect the national speed limit. She reckons that on average she is given two speeding tickets in a year.

(i) Explain why the number of tickets she receives in a year might reasonably be modelled by a Poisson distribution. Using such a distribution, calculate the probability that she actually receives no tickets at all in a randomly chosen year.

(ii) Write down the distribution for the number of tickets she receives over a six-year period. Use a suitable approximating distribution to calculate the probability that Anna receives no more than nine speeding tickets over a six-year period.

B3 An office fax machine receives on average one 'wrong number' call per day.

(i) Using a suitable distribution, which should be clearly stated, calculate the probability that on a randomly chosen day the machine receives:

(a) no 'wrong number' calls;
(b) at least three 'wrong number' calls.

(ii) Using a suitable approximating distribution, which should be clearly stated, calculate the probability that in a randomly chosen month of 20 working days the machine receives between 10 and 18 'wrong number' calls (inclusive).

B4 The number of spelling mistakes which a typist makes in a 5000-word document can be modelled by a Poisson distribution. The probability that he makes no more than six mistakes is 0·4953.

(i) Use cumulative Poisson tables to find the mean number of mistakes which the typist makes in a 5000-word document.

(ii) Write down the distribution of the number of mistakes which the same typist would make in a similar document containing 12 000 words.

(iii) Use a suitable approximating distribution to calculate the probability that the typist makes at most 20 mistakes in a document of 12 000 words.

B5 A traffic warden notices that a few of the illegally parked cars which she sees each day also have no road tax. The number of such cars which she sees per day can be modelled by a Poisson distribution with parameter 1·2.

(i) Find the probability that in a given day the traffic warden sees at least two such cars.

The probability that the traffic warden sees at least one such car in a period of n days is greater than 99·95%.

(ii) Find the least value of n which meets this condition.

The traffic warden decides to record the total number of illegally parked cars with no road tax seen during a period of 14 days.

(iii) Write down a distribution for the number of such cars in the 14 day period. Using a suitable approximating distribution, which should be stated clearly, find the probability that the number of such cars lies between 10 and 20 inclusive.

Revision questions

C1 Sabrina leaves home at 08:20 every morning and travels to school. Her journey time may be assumed to be Normally distributed. If she arrives before 08:50 she has to wait in the playground, but if she arrives after 09:00 she is recorded as late. Over a long period of time Sabrina has noticed that she has to wait in the playground on 61% of the mornings, while she is recorded as late only 6% of the time.

(i) Set up two simultaneous equations containing the mean μ and standard deviation σ of her journey time in minutes.

(ii) Solve these equations to show that σ is approximately 8, and show that her mean arrival time is approximately 08:48.

It is the school's policy to telephone home if a child has not arrived by 09:10.

(iii) Taking the figures quoted in (ii) above to be exact, calculate the probability that the school has to telephone Sabrina's home on a randomly chosen morning. Hence find the expected number of calls the school makes to Sabrina's home during her school career of 800 such mornings.

C2 A machine produces small mirrors which are used in the manufacture of scientific instruments. Only 70% of these mirrors are of A-grade quality; the remaining 30% are of B-grade quality. The mirrors are tested and labelled 'A' or 'B' before being packaged in boxes of 10.

(i) A random box of 10 mirrors is selected. Use a suitable Binomial distribution to show that the probability that it contains no more than two B-grade mirrors is approximately 0.38.

Any box which contains no more than two B-grade mirrors is marked with a special sticker.

(ii) Write down the distribution for the number of boxes marked with special stickers in a random batch of 100 boxes. Use a suitable approximating distribution to find the probability that the number of boxes marked in this way is between 40 and 45 inclusive.

C3 John is solving a question about a Binomial distribution in which $X \sim B(120, 0.05)$. He wishes to find the probability that $X < 5$.

This is what John writes:

$X \sim B(120, 0.05)$ may be approximated by $X \sim Po(6)$

Then $X \sim Po(6)$ may be approximated by $X \sim N(6, 6)$

So $P(X < 5) = \phi\left(\dfrac{5-6}{\sqrt{6}}\right) = \phi(-0.408)$

$$= 1 - 0.6583 = 0.3417$$

Unfortunately John is not very good at statistics, and he has made several serious errors in this solution.

(i) Identify the errors that John has made.

(ii) Write out a corrected solution to John's problem.

C4 Two carpenters, Sonia and Samir, are making large numbers of jack-in-the-box toys. Sonia is making the jack—a figure on a compressed spring. The height of a jack is Normally distributed with a mean of 15 cm and standard deviation 2 cm. Samir is making the box for the jack. The internal height of the box is Normally distributed with mean 18 cm and standard deviation 1 cm.

(i) Find the probability that a jack has a height of less than 16 cm.

(ii) Find the probability that a box has an internal height of more than 16 cm.

(iii) Write down the distribution of the difference D by which the internal height of the box exceeds the height of the jack. Hence find the probability that a randomly chosen jack does not fit inside a randomly chosen box.

continued **83**

C5 The weights of cherries of a certain variety are Normally distributed with a mean of 7 grams. The probability that a randomly chosen cherry weighs less than 9 grams is 0·9087.

(i) Calculate the standard deviation of the weight of the cherries.

(ii) Show that the probability of a cherry weighing less than 6 grams is about 0·253.

Cherries are packed in boxes of 100.

(iii) State the distribution for the number of cherries in a box which weigh less than 6 grams. Using a suitable approximating distribution, find the probability that a randomly chosen box contains at least 20 cherries with weights of under 6 grams.

C6 A school buys light bulbs whose lifetimes are Normally distributed with mean 1050 hours and standard deviation 120 hours.

(i) Calculate the probability that a randomly chosen light bulb has a lifetime of no more than 1000 hours.

The manufacturer improves the quality of the bulbs so that the mean lifetime is still 1050 hours but the standard deviation is smaller. The probability of a bulb having a lifetime of no more than 1000 hours is now reduced to 25%.

(ii) Calculate the new value of the standard deviation, correct to the nearest hour.

The school dining hall is fitted with 100 of these new bulbs, and is inspected when the bulbs are 1000 hours old.

(iii) Calculate the probability that at least 70 of the bulbs are still working when inspected.

C7 An examination board models the marks earned by candidates in a statistics exam by a Normal distribution with mean 42 and standard deviation 8.

(i) Explain why it is necessary to use a continuity correction when calculating probabilities from this model.

(ii) Find the probability that a randomly chosen candidate scores less than 40 marks.

(iii) Grade A is awarded to any candidate who scores over 54 marks. Calculate the percentage of candidates who achieve a Grade A.

(iv) The markers reckon that 8% of the candidates have not achieved a pass standard. What is the pass mark for this examination?

C8 Marco is checking a batch of climbing ropes to make sure that there are no minor abrasions to the outer casing. He estimates that there are, on average, 2 abrasions per 500 metres of rope. Climbing ropes are 150 metres long.

(i) Write down a distribution for the number of abrasions in one climbing rope. Calculate the probability that a rope contains no abrasions at all.

Altogether Marco checks 40 climbing ropes.

(ii) Write down a distribution for the total number of abrasions in all 40 ropes. State also a suitable approximating distribution, and use it to find the probability that the 40 ropes contain at least 10 abrasions in total.

C9 The heights of a certain breed of dog are believed to be Normally distributed. 30% of the dogs are shorter than 23 cm, while 15% are taller than 32 cm.

(i) Set up two simultaneous equations containing the mean height μ and its standard deviation σ.

(ii) Solve these two equations, giving the values of μ and σ correct to 3 significant figures.

At a dog show, 60 dogs of this breed are assembled together.

(iii) Write down a suitable approximating distribution for the number of dogs whose heights are less than 23 cm.

Calculate the probability that no more than 25 dogs are shorter than 23 cm.

C10 Serious tailbacks occur on a certain motorway on average once a week during winter.

(i) Show that the probability of no more than three serious tailbacks occurring during a period of four weeks in the winter is approximately 0·4335.

Serious tailbacks occur on the same motorway on average once every two weeks during summer.

(ii) Show that the probability of no more than three serious tailbacks occurring during a period of four weeks in the summer is approximately 0·8571.

The traffic authorities decide to model a year as consisting of 24 weeks of summer and 28 weeks of winter.

(iii) Write down the distribution for the total number of serious tailbacks on the motorway during a whole year. Use a suitable approximating distribution to find the probability that the total number of tailbacks during the year lies between 30 and 42 inclusive.

Chapter 5

THE NORMAL DISTRIBUTION II

5.1 Sample means and the Central Limit Theorem

Key points

Samples are small sets of data which are chosen from a larger population. The **sample mean** has its own statistical distribution, with the **same mean** as the population, but a **smaller variance**.

Suppose a random variable X has a distribution with mean μ and variance σ^2. If n observations $X_1, X_2, \ldots, X_n$ of X are made, at random, then the sample mean $\bar{X}$ is defined as

$$\bar{X} = \frac{X_1 + X_2 + \ldots + X_n}{n}$$

If many such samples are taken then $\bar{X}$ can be thought of as a random variable with a statistical distribution in its own right. The following results apply:

- If X has mean μ then $\bar{X}$ has mean μ

- If X has variance σ^2 then $\bar{X}$ has variance $\dfrac{\sigma^2}{n}$

- If X has a Normal distribution then so does $\bar{X}$.

When several independent variables are added together their sum will be approximately Normal, **regardless of the shape of each individual distribution**. This remarkable result, the **Central Limit Theorem**, helps to explain why so many Normal distributions arise in nature. A special application of the Central Limit Theorem occurs when all of the independent variables are actually observations from the same parent distribution.

> **The Central Limit Theorem:**
>
> **If a random sample of n observations of a random variable is taken, then the distribution of the sample mean will be approximately Normal, provided n is reasonably large.**

In effect, the Central Limit Theorem lets you use tables of $N(0, 1)$ even if the parent is not Normal, **provided n is larger than about 50**.

Example I

The random variable X has mean 12 and variance 8. Find the mean and standard deviation of $\bar{X}$, the sample mean of 10 observations of X.

Solution

The mean of $\bar{X}$ is 12.

The variance of $\bar{X}$ is $\frac{8}{10} = 0.8$.

The standard deviation of $\bar{X}$ is $\sqrt{0.8} = 0.894$.

Example 2

The random variable X is Normally distributed with mean 12 and variance 8. Find the probability that the mean of 10 observations of X lies between 11.5 and 13.

Solution

$X \sim N(12, 8)$ so $\bar{X} \sim N(12, 0.8)$.

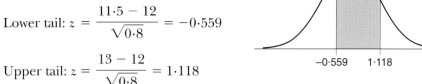

Lower tail: $z = \dfrac{11.5 - 12}{\sqrt{0.8}} = -0.559$

Upper tail: $z = \dfrac{13 - 12}{\sqrt{0.8}} = 1.118$

$$P(-0.559 < z < 1.118) = \Phi(1.118) - \Phi(-0.559)$$

$$= 0.8682 - (1 - 0.7119)$$

$$= 0.8682 - 0.2881$$

$$= 0.5801$$

Example 3

A machine produces ball bearings with masses of mean 160 grams and standard deviation 12 grams. Sixty ball bearings are selected at random and their masses are recorded.

(i) Find the probability that the mean mass of a ball bearing in this sample lies between 159 and 160 grams.

(ii) Find the probability that the total mass of all 60 balls does not exceed 9720 grams.

Solution

Let X be the mass of a single ball bearing, so $X \sim N(160, 12^2)$

Then $\bar{X} = \dfrac{X_1 + X_2 + \ldots + X_{60}}{60}$

> Under the Central Limit Theorem the distribution of $\bar{X}$ is approximately Normal.

Take $\bar{X} \sim \mathrm{N}\left(160, \dfrac{12^2}{60}\right)$

(i) To find $\mathrm{P}(159 \le \bar{X} \le 160)$ we standardise:

Lower tail: $z = \dfrac{159 - 160}{\sqrt{12^2/60}} = -0\cdot6455$

Upper tail: $z = \dfrac{160 - 160}{\sqrt{12^2/60}} = 0$

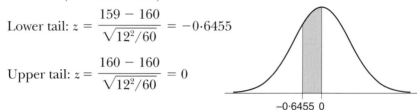

$-0\cdot6455\ \ 0$

$\mathrm{P}(-0\cdot6455 < z < 0) = \Phi(0) - \Phi(-0\cdot6455)$

$= 0\cdot5000 - (1 - 0\cdot7407)$

$= 0\cdot5000 - 0\cdot2593$

$= 0\cdot2407$

(ii) If the total mass does not exceed 9720 grams then the sample mean does not exceed $9720 \div 60 = 162$ grams.

Standardising, $z = \dfrac{162 - 160}{\sqrt{12^2/60}} = 1\cdot2910$

$\mathrm{P}(z < 1\cdot291) = \Phi(1\cdot291) = 0\cdot9017$

The probability that the total mass does not exceed 9720 grams is $0\cdot902$ (3 d.p.).

Exercise 5.1

In questions **A1** to **A6** fill in the missing values in the table:

| | Random variable X (population) | | | | Sample mean $\bar{X}$ | | |
	Mean	Variance	Standard deviation	Sample size	Mean	Variance	Standard deviation
A1	20	9		6			
A2	30	8		16			
A3	20	5		10			
A4	166		6	9			
A5	75	14		7			
A6			10		150		2

A7 The random variable X is Normally distributed with mean 22 and variance 9. Find the probability that the mean of 16 observations of X lies between 21 and 22·5.

A8 The random variable X is Normally distributed with mean 140 and variance 25. Find the probability that the mean of 4 observations of X does not exceed 143.

Exercise 5.1 *continued*

A9 The random variable X is distributed with mean 44 and variance 12. A sample of 64 observations of X is taken, and the sample mean $\bar{x}$ is computed.

(i) State the approximate shape of the distribution of $\bar{X}$, the parent distribution to which $\bar{x}$ belongs.

(ii) Find the mean and variance of $\bar{X}$, and hence describe its distribution completely.

A10 The random variable X is distributed with mean 100 and variance 90. A sample of 60 observations of X is taken, and the sample mean $\bar{x}$ is computed.

(i) State the mean and variance of $\bar{X}$, the parent distribution to which $\bar{x}$ belongs.

(ii) Find the probability that $\bar{x}$ lies between 101 and 102.

(iii) Explain how you used the Central Limit Theorem in your solution to this question.

B1 The random variable X is Normally distributed with mean 6 and standard deviation 10.

(i) Calculate the probability that a single random observation of X is positive.

Sixteen observations of X are taken, and their mean $\bar{x}$ is computed.

(ii) Write down the distribution of $\bar{X}$, the population to which $\bar{x}$ belongs.

(iii) Calculate the probability that $\bar{x}$ is positive.

B2 The random variable X is distributed with mean 52 and variance 32. A sample of 64 observations of X is taken, and the sample mean $\bar{x}$ is computed.

(i) State the approximate shape of the distribution of $\bar{X}$. State also the mean and variance of $\bar{X}$.

(ii) Find the probability that the computed value of $\bar{x}$ lies between 50 and 53.

B3 The random variable X is Normally

distributed with mean 80 and variance 90. The random variables Y and Z are obtained by finding the mean of 10 and 40 observations of X, respectively.

(i) Write down the distributions of Y and Z.

(ii) Calculate the probability that Y lies between 80 and 85.

(iii) Calculate the probability that Z lies between 80 and 85.

B4 The weights of adult baboons of a certain species are known to be distributed with mean 31·4 kg and variance 14·5 kg². Seventy of these baboons are to be flown by light aircraft as part of a wildlife management project, and the pilot is anxious that their total weight will comply with current aviation rules.

(i) The total permissible weight for the baboons is 2240 kg. Calculate the corresponding mean weight per baboon.

(ii) Write down the approximate distribution of the mean weight of the 70 baboons.

(iii) Calculate the probability that the weights of the baboons do indeed comply with the current aviation rules.

You are not expected to use any continuity correction in question **B5**.

B5 An honest gambler is playing a game using a fair die, i.e. with probability distribution given by this table:

Score, X	1	2	3	4	5	6
Probability, p	$\frac{1}{6}$	$\frac{1}{6}$	$\frac{1}{6}$	$\frac{1}{6}$	$\frac{1}{6}$	$\frac{1}{6}$

(i) Write down the expectation $E(X)$ for this distribution, and show that the value of the standard deviation of X is approximately 1·71.

The honest gambler throws the die 60 times, noting the score each time.

continued

Exercise 5.1   *continued*

(ii) Calculate the approximate probability that the mean score exceeds 3·1.

A dishonest gambler is playing the same game using a 'fixed' die, with probability distribution given by this table:

Score, Y	1	2	3	4	5	6
Probability, p	0·3	0·1	0·1	0·1	0·1	0·3

(iii) Write down the expectation $E(Y)$ for this distribution, and show that the value of the variance $Var(Y)$ is 4·25.

The dishonest gambler throws the die 60 times, noting the score each time.

(iv) Calculate the approximate probability that the mean score exceeds 3·1.

5.2 Point estimates and confidence intervals

Key points

If the mean of a population is unknown then we can estimate its value by looking at random sample of observations; this produces a **point estimate**. In the same way, the variance can be estimated from a sample, but a correction for **bias** must be applied here.

Even the best point estimate of the true mean is likely to be inaccurate, so we often prefer to indicate that the true mean probably lies within a certain range of values, called a **confidence interval**.

Some questions on this topic can be answered using Normal distribution tables, while others can be answered using the t-distribution instead. The t-distribution arises when a sample is taken from a Normal distribution whose variance is unknown. t-tables are very similar to those for the Normal distribution $N(0, 1)$, but contain a different row for each value of the sample size n and are indexed by the value of $\nu = n - 1$. So for a sample of size $n = 10$, you would use tables of t_9. There are five key principles which underpin this topic:

- The sample mean is an unbiased estimator of the population mean

  If you know the sample mean $\bar{x}$ then the population mean μ can be estimated as $\hat{\mu} = \bar{x}$

- The sample variance is not an unbiased estimator of the population variance: to correct for bias, multiply the sample value

  by $\dfrac{n}{n - 1}$

  If you know the sample variance s^2 then the population variance σ^2 may be estimated as

  $$\hat{\sigma}^2 = \frac{n}{n - 1} \times s^2$$

- If the population is Normal and its variance is **known** then a 95% confidence interval for the true

  mean is $\hat{\mu} \pm \dfrac{1 \cdot 96 \times \sigma}{\sqrt{n}}$

  For 90%, 99%, etc. you look in tables of $N(0, 1)$ and change the 1·96 to 1·645, 2·236, etc.

- If the population is Normal and its variance is **unknown** then a 95% confidence interval for the true mean is

$$\mu \pm \frac{(\text{t-factor}) \times \hat{\sigma}}{\sqrt{n}}$$

> The (*t-factor*) is equivalent to 1·96, 1·645, etc. found by using *t*-tables, not N(0, 1). For a sample of size n use the tables for $\nu = n - 1$.

- If the population is not Normal then you need a large sample, in order to use the Central Limit Theorem. The confidence interval is then

$$\hat{\mu} \pm \frac{1\cdot96 \times \sigma}{\sqrt{n}} \text{ or } \hat{\mu} \pm \frac{1\cdot96 \times \hat{\sigma}}{\sqrt{n}}$$

> Whether the variance is known or unknown, use of the Central Limit Theorem *always* leads to N(0, 1), never to *t*-tables.

Example 1

A machine is set up to produce components with Normally distributed lengths. The machine has been adjusted during a service, and the mean is thought to have changed, though the variance has remained at $0\cdot4 \text{ cm}^2$.

A test engineer takes a random sample of 10 components. Their lengths are:

33·0   33·3   32·8   32·9   32·8   33·7   33·4   33·6   33·5 and 34·0 cm.

(i)   Calculate an estimate for the population mean.

(ii)   Construct a symmetric 95% confidence interval for the population mean.

Solution

For this sample, $n = 10$, $\Sigma x = 333$, $\bar{x} = 333 \div 10 = 33\cdot3$

(i)   Estimated population mean is $\hat{\mu} = \bar{x} = 33\cdot3$

> This comes from N(0, 1) tables because the population is Normal and the variance is known.

(ii)   Symmetric 95% confidence interval is $33\cdot3 \pm \dfrac{1\cdot96 \times \sqrt{0\cdot4}}{\sqrt{10}}$

> σ here

> $\sqrt{n}$ here

$$= 33\cdot3 \pm 0\cdot392$$

So $32\cdot91 \le \mu \le 33\cdot69$

Example 2

The masses of confectionery bars may be assumed to be Normally distributed. Eight bars are taken at random, and their masses are found to be

67·5   66·0   66·2   67·1   66·8   66·9   67·5 and 66·8 grams.

(i)   Compute unbiased estimates for the mean and variance of the mass of a confectionery bar.

(ii)   Construct a symmetric 95% confidence interval for the mean mass of a bar.

Solution

For the sample,

$n = 8$, $\Sigma x = 534\cdot8$, $\Sigma x^2 = 35\ 753\cdot44$, $\bar{x} = 534\cdot8 \div 8 = 66\cdot85$

$$s^2 = \frac{\Sigma x^2}{n} - \bar{x}^2 = \frac{35\ 753\cdot44}{8} - 66\cdot85^2 = 0\cdot2575$$

(i)   The required point estimates are:

Population mean $\hat{\mu} = \bar{x} = 66\cdot85$ grams

Population variance $\hat{\sigma}^2 = \dfrac{n}{n-1} \times s^2 = \dfrac{8}{7} \times 0\cdot2575 = 0\cdot2943$ grams^2

(ii)   The 95% confidence interval is

$$66\cdot85 \pm \frac{2\cdot365 \times \sqrt{0\cdot2943}}{\sqrt{8}} = 66\cdot85 \pm 0\cdot45$$

i.e. $66\cdot40 \leq \mu \leq 67\cdot30$

> The *t*-factor of 2.365 comes from *t*-tables with $\nu = 8 - 1 = 7$

> '95% confidence interval' means that if you repeat the process with more samples a great many times, constructing large numbers of confidence intervals, 95% of the intervals would be expected to contain the true value of the population mean.

Example 3

The heights of 60 teenagers are measured correct to the nearest centimetre. The results are summarised as: $n = 60$, $\Sigma x = 10\ 215$, $\Sigma x^2 = 1\ 743\ 275$.

(i)   Calculate the mean and variance for the sample data.

(ii)   Obtain an unbiased estimate for the population variance.

(iii) Construct a 90% confidence interval for the mean height of the population.

(iv) Explain briefly what is meant by 'the population' in this context.

Solution

(i)   For the sample, $\bar{x} = \dfrac{10\ 215}{60} = 170\cdot25$

Sample variance $s^2 = \dfrac{1\ 743\ 275}{60} - 170\cdot25^2 = 69\cdot521$

(ii)   The unbiased estimate of the population variance is

$$\hat{\sigma}^2 = \frac{60}{59} \times 69{\cdot}521 = 70{\cdot}699$$

(iii) Under the Central Limit Theorem the required 90% confidence interval is

$$170{\cdot}25 \pm \frac{1{\cdot}645 \times \sqrt{70{\cdot}699}}{\sqrt{60}}$$

$$= 170{\cdot}25 \pm 1{\cdot}79$$

So $168{\cdot}46 \le \mu \le 172{\cdot}04$

(iv) 'The population' means the set of teenagers from which the sample was drawn, which may well be local. It should not be confused with the population of all ages within the country at large.

Exercise 5.2

In questions **A1** to **A5** you are given some values which represent a random sample from a population. In each case you should calculate (i) the sample mean; (ii) the sample variance and (iii) an unbiased estimate of the population variance.

A1

12	15	12	17	14	13	14	13

A2

1	5	2	2	3	2	1
6	4	6	2	3	2	6
6	2	3	5	6	4	

A3

0·651	0·826	0·423
0·573	0·475	0·307

A4

38·6	40·5	37·2	38·5	37·6

A5

0·319	0·024	0·745	0·394
0·743	0·575	0·135	0·070
0·855	0·365		

In questions **A6** to **A10** you are given some summary statistics which describe a random sample from a population. In each case you should calculate (i) the sample mean; (ii) the sample variance and (iii) an unbiased estimate of the population variance.

A6 $n = 20$, $\sum x = 842$, $\sum x^2 = 35\,464$.

A7 $n = 79$, $\sum x = 6160$, $\sum x^2 = 481\,200$.

A8 $n = 5$, $\sum x = 31{\cdot}2$, $\sum x^2 = 221{\cdot}22$.

A9 $n = 60$, $\sum x = 852$, $\sum x^2 = 16\,016$.

A10 $n = 30$, $\sum x = 2016$, $\sum x^2 = 136\,298$.

B1 An environmental group measures the level of radiation, assumed to be distributed Normally, at 12 random sites in the French Alps. The results, in suitable units, are:

1·35	1·53	2·02	1·67	1·69	1·49
1·96	2·11	1·77	1·79	1·83	1·67

(i) Compute the mean and variance for these data.

(ii) Construct a 95% confidence interval for the mean level of radiation in the French Alps.

(iii) Explain briefly why it is not possible to construct this confidence interval without assuming that the radiation levels are distributed Normally.

B2 A school tests each pupil's swimming during the first year. Part of the test is a timed activity, and over a long period of time it is established that the pupils' times are Normally distributed with mean 45 seconds and variance 5 seconds[2].

continued

Exercise 5.2 *continued*

This year new training procedures have been introduced. A random sample of eight swimmers are assessed and their times are found to be

43·5	44·2	41·3	43·1	48·3	43·5	41·7
44·8						

(i) Compute the mean time for this sample.

(ii) Assuming that the times are still Normally distributed, with the same standard deviation as before, find a 95% confidence interval for the mean time for this year.

B3 A computer supplier buys a large set of used laptop computers from an industrial client. Fifty-five of these computers are chosen at random, and the battery life (x minutes) of each is measured. The results are summarised by

$$n = 55, \Sigma x = 3450, \Sigma x^2 = 223\ 550$$

(i) Calculate the mean and variance for these data.

(ii) Construct a 95% confidence interval for the mean battery life of the computers.

B4 The random variable X is known to be Normally distributed. Eleven random observations of X are made, and are summarised by

$$n = 11, \Sigma x = 268·1, \Sigma x^2 = 6547·15$$

(i) Compute the mean and variance for these data.

(ii) Construct a 95% confidence interval for the mean of the random variable X.

B5 Rosemarie has propagated a new variety of geranium. She wants to obtain a value for the mean height of a one-year-old plant in midsummer, and so she takes a random sample of 65 one-year-old plants and measures their heights in midsummer. The results, measured in centimetres, are summarised by

$$n = 65, \Sigma x = 928, \Sigma x^2 = 13\ 496$$

(i) Calculate the mean and variance for these data.

(ii) Assuming that the heights of the plants are Normally distributed, construct a symmetric 90% confidence interval for the population mean.

(iii) If the heights were not Normally distributed would you still be able to construct a confidence interval? Explain your reasoning.

B6 The random variable X is known to be Normally distributed. Eight observations of X are made at random, as follows:

135·5	144·2	144·3	144·9	145·0
145·5	146·7	147·8		

(i) Compute the mean and variance for these data.

(ii) Construct a 95% confidence interval for the mean of the random variable X.

B7 John and Gill, two psychology students, are examining the Intelligence Quotient (IQ) of the undergraduates at their university. IQ can be assessed by means of written tests, and a score of 100 is supposed to represent the IQ of a typical adult.

John conducts an exhaustive study to measure the IQ of all of the male first-year students at the university. He concludes that the IQ for this group is approximately Normally distributed, with a mean of 122 and a standard deviation of 11·4.

Gill assumes that the IQ scores for the female first-year students are also Normally distributed, with the same standard deviation as the males. She takes a random sample of ten first-year females, and their IQ scores are measured as follows:

107	109	117	119	122	126	127
129	135	145				

(i) Calculate the mean IQ for this sample.

(ii) Construct a symmetric 95% confidence interval for the IQ of the first-year females, assuming a Normal

Exercise 5.2 *continued*

distribution with the same standard deviation as the males.

B8 On 12 randomly-chosen occasions, the number of aircraft taking off from Heathwick Airport during one hour is recorded:

11 35 49 50 51 51 52 53 54
56 56 59

(i) Compute the mean and variance for these data.

(ii) Calculate unbiased estimates for the population mean and variance.

(iii) Show that the value of 11 is located at approximately 3 standard deviations away from the population mean.

(iv) Explain briefly whether you think that these 12 data points appear to be random observations from a Normal distribution.

(v) Explain briefly why it would be unwise to use the Central Limit Theorem in order to construct a confidence interval for the population mean.

B9 A planetary geologist is studying the craters on part of the surface of one of Jupiter's moons. She takes a random sample of 70 craters and measures their diameters d in kilometres. The results are summarised as:

$n = 70$, $\Sigma x = 1822$, $\Sigma x^2 = 51\ 252$

The geologist wishes to set up a symmetric two-sided confidence interval for the mean length of the craters on this part of this moon.

(i) Explain carefully why it is not necessary to assume that the parent distribution is Normal.

(ii) Calculate unbiased estimates for the population mean and variance.

(iii) Construct a symmetric two-sided 90% confidence interval for the mean length of the craters.

B10 A motor-cycle manufacturer wants to obtain an estimate of the number of miles which its engines can sustain before the cylinders need to be serviced. Data are collected from the manufacturer's service stations, and 90 cases are chosen at random. The number of miles, x, is noted, and 10 000 is subtracted from each value, to yield the following summary statistics:

$n = 90$, $\Sigma(x - 10\ 000) = 471\ 452$,
$\Sigma(x - 10\ 000)^2 = 2\ 680\ 711\ 664$

(i) Calculate the mean and variance of the 90 observations of $(x - 10\ 000)$.

(ii) Write down the mean and variance of the 90 observations of x.

(iii) Construct a symmetric two-sided 90% confidence interval for the mean number of miles which the engines can sustain before the cylinders need to be serviced.

5.3 Hypothesis tests for the mean

Key points

In this section we will be testing a sample to see whether it is consistent with a suggested value for the population mean. The parent distribution will often be assumed to be Normal; if not, then the sample must be large enough to enable the use of the Central Limit Theorem.

Before tackling a question on this topic we need to establish the underlying assumptions about the sample and the parent distribution:

Is this a random sample from a Normal parent of known variance?	Use the given variance.	Use Normal distribution tables.

Is this a random sample from a Normal parent of unknown variance?	Estimate the population variance from the sample variance (remembering to correct for bias).	Use t-tables.

Is this a large random sample (usually 50 or more) from a parent which need not be Normal?	The population variance might be given, but usually it must be estimated from the sample (and corrected for bias).	Even if the population variance has been estimated, this type of problem always leads to use of Normal tables.

The test procedure is summarised by the following steps:

Step 1 **Define the random variable**

> e.g. 'Let X be the mean mass of a wombat.'

Step 2 **State the distribution of X**

> e.g. '$X \sim N(\mu, \sigma^2)$'

Step 3 **State null and alternative hypotheses**

> Use H_0 and H_1 notation, H_0 is always '$\mu =$ a value'.

Step 4 **Check the significance level to be used**

> Usually given in the question. If not, set your own level and tell the examiner. 5% is a standard choice.

Step 5 **Establish the type of tail**

> One tail upper, one tail lower or two tail.

Step 6 **Compute the sample mean. If necessary, estimate the population variance from the sample variance.**

> Unbiased estimate is
> $$\hat{\sigma}^2 = \frac{n}{n-1} \times s^2$$

Step 7 **Compute the test statistic**

> $$\frac{\bar{x} - \mu}{\sigma/\sqrt{n}} \text{ or } \frac{\bar{x} - \mu}{\hat{\sigma}/\sqrt{n}}$$

Step 8 **State whether this statistic is t-distributed or Normal**

> e.g. 'Under H_0 this is approximately t-distributed with $\nu = 5 - 1 = 4$'. Mention Central Limit Theorem if appropriate.

Step 9 **Identify the critical region(s)**

> Use t-tables or $N(0, 1)$ tables.

Step 10   **Compare the test value with the critical region(s)**

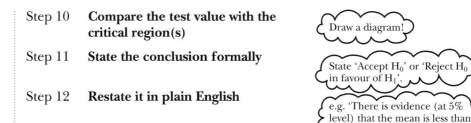

Draw a diagram!

Step 11   **State the conclusion formally**

State 'Accept H_0' or 'Reject H_0 in favour of H_1'.

Step 12   **Restate it in plain English**

e.g. 'There is evidence (at 5% level) that the mean is less than 1·5.'

Example I

A greengrocer purchases cucumbers from a certain supplier. Over a long period it has emerged that the lengths of the cucumbers may be modelled by a Normal distribution with mean 29 cm and standard deviation 2 cm.

Following a change in farming techniques, the supplier claims that the mean length of cucumbers has increased, though the lengths remain Normally distributed with the same standard deviation as before. To test this claim, the greengrocer takes a random sample of eight cucumbers, and measures their lengths as

27·8   28·9   29·4   30·6   31·6   31·8   31·9 and 34·0 cm.

(i)   State suitable null and alternative hypotheses to be tested.

(ii)   Conduct the test at the 5% level, stating your conclusion clearly.

Solution

(i)   Let X be the length of a cucumber, and $\bar{X} = \dfrac{X_1 + X_2 + \ldots + X_8}{8}$.

Then $X \sim N(\mu, 2^2)$, so $\bar{X} \sim N(\mu, 2^2/8)$.

H_0: $\mu = 29$

The null hypothesis must always supply the missing value of μ

H_1: $\mu > 29$

The alternative hypothesis will contain an inequality, either > (one tail) or < (one tail) or ≠ (two tail).

This is a one-tail 5% test.

(ii)   For the sample,

$$\bar{x} = \frac{27·8 + 28·9 + \ldots + 34·0}{8} = \frac{246}{8} = 30·75$$

Compute the test statistic

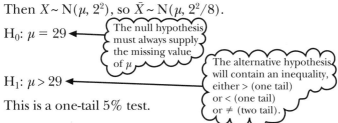

$$z_{\text{test}} = \frac{30·75 - 29}{2/\sqrt{8}} = 2·475$$

$z_{\text{test}} = \dfrac{\bar{x} - \mu}{\sigma/\sqrt{n}}$

Under H_0 this is Normally distributed as $N(0, 1)$.

From tables of $N(0, 1)$, for a 5% one-tail test, $z_{\text{crit}} = 1·645$

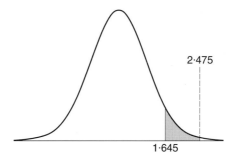

As z_{test} lies within the critical region we reject H_0 in favour of H_1. There is evidence, at the 5% level, that the mean length of the cucumbers has increased.

Example 2

The mass of strawberry jam in a *Superjammy* jam doughnut is known to follow a Normal distribution. The manufacturers claim that an average doughnut contains 25 grams of jam, but a consumer group reckons that it contains less than this. A random sample of ten doughnuts is taken, and the mass of jam in each is measured (in grams) as follows:

22·6   23·8   24·9   23·4   25·7   24·9   25·3   25·9   25·7   24·8

(i)   State suitable null and alternative hypotheses for a test on the mean mass.

(ii) Conduct the test, at the 2·5% significance level.

Solution

(i)   Let X be the mass of a doughnut, and $\bar{X} = \dfrac{X_1 + X_2 + \ldots + X_{10}}{10}$.

Then $X \sim N(\mu, \sigma^2)$, so $\bar{X} \sim N(\mu, \sigma^2/10)$.

$H_0: \mu = 25$

$H_1: \mu < 25$

This is a one-tail 2·5% test.

(ii) For the sample,

$$\bar{x} = \frac{22\cdot6 + 23\cdot8 + \ldots + 24\cdot8}{10} = \frac{247}{10} = 24\cdot7$$

$$s^2 = \frac{22\cdot6^2 + 23\cdot8^2 + \ldots + 24\cdot8^2}{10} - 24\cdot7^2 = 1\cdot08$$

> It is a good idea to show the sample variance s^2 . . .

Estimated population variance is

$$\hat{\sigma}^2 = \frac{10 \times s^2}{9} = 1\cdot2$$

> . . . as well as $\hat{\sigma}$, the unbiased estimate of the population variance.

Compute the test statistic

$$t_{test} = \frac{24 \cdot 7 - 25}{\sqrt{1 \cdot 2}/\sqrt{10}} = -0 \cdot 866$$

$$t_{test} = \frac{\bar{x} - \mu}{\hat{\sigma}\sqrt{n}}$$

Under H_0, this is t-distributed with $\nu = 10 - 1 = 9$

From tables of t_9, for a $2 \cdot 5\%$ one-tail (lower tail) test, $t_{crit} = -2.262$

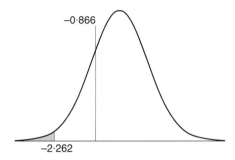

As z_{test} does not lie within the critical region we accept H_0.

There is no evidence, at the $2 \cdot 5\%$ level, to dispute the manufacturer's claim that the mean mass of jam is 25 grams.

Example 3

A large number of crossword puzzle enthusiasts attend a weekend convention. When they arrive they are given a puzzle to solve, and the mean time taken is found to be 26 minutes.

After an evening meal and a lecture on puzzle techniques the enthusiasts are given a second puzzle, of comparable difficulty to the first. The times, x, taken by a random selection of 58 enthusiasts are summarised as $n = 58$, $\sum x = 1497$, $\sum x^2 = 38\,775$. The organisers wish to test whether these data indicate that the mean time taken to solve a puzzle has changed.

(i)   State suitable null and alternative hypotheses for the test.

(ii)   Conduct the test, using a 5% significance level.

Solution

(i)   Let X be the time to solve a puzzle, and

$$\bar{X} = \frac{X_1 + X_2 + \ldots + X_{58}}{58}.$$

Resist the temptation to write $X \sim N(\mu, \sigma^2)$ at this stage—you are not told that the parent distribution is Normal.

Let X have mean μ and variance σ^2.

H_0: $\mu = 26$

H_1: $\mu \neq 26$

Two-tail 5% test

(ii)   For the sample,

$$\bar{x} = \frac{1497}{58} = 25 \cdot 81034$$

$$s^2 = \frac{38\ 775}{58} - 25 \cdot 81034^2 = 2 \cdot 361$$

> Do not cut corners with the working here—it is a good idea to show the variances both before and after the correction for bias.

$$\hat{\sigma}^2 = \frac{58 \times s^2}{57} = 2 \cdot 402$$

> Use of the Central Limit Theorem must be stated briefly.

Under the Central Limit Theorem the distribution of $\bar{X}$ is approximately Normal.

$\therefore$ Under H_0 $\bar{X} \sim N(26, \sigma^2/58)$ where σ^2 may be estimated by $\hat{\sigma}^2 = 2 \cdot 402$.

Compute the test statistic

$$z_{test} = \frac{25 \cdot 81034 - 26}{\hat{\sigma}/\sqrt{58}} = -0 \cdot 9320$$

> $z_{test} = \dfrac{\bar{x} - \mu}{\hat{\sigma}\sqrt{n}}$

From tables of $N(0,1)$, for a 5% two-tail test,

$$z_{crit} = \pm 1 \cdot 960$$

As z_{test} does not lie within the critical region we accept H_0.

There is no evidence, at the 5% level, of any change in the mean time taken to solve the crossword.

Exercise 5.3

In questions **A1** to **A5** you are given a percentage significance level for a hypothesis test. Use tables to find the critical values for the test.

A1   1% significance level, two-tail test (Normal distribution).

A2   5% significance level, one-tail (upper-tail) test (Normal distribution).

A3   10% significance level, one-tail (lower-tail) test (Normal distribution).

A4   5% significance level, two-tail test (t-distribution with $\nu = 9$).

A5   1% significance level, one-tail (upper-tail) test (t-distribution with $\nu = 7$).

In questions **A6** to **A10** you are given a percentage significance level for a hypothesis test, and a test statistic. Use tables to find the critical values for the test, and say whether the test statistic leads you to accept or reject H_0.

A6   5% significance level, two-tail test (Normal distribution), $z_{test} = 2 \cdot 553$.

Exercise 5.3 *continued*

A7 1% significance level, one-tail (upper-tail) test (Normal distribution), $z_{\text{test}} = 1 \cdot 781$.

A8 10% significance level, one-tail (lower-tail) test (Normal distribution), $z_{\text{test}} = -0 \cdot 551$.

A9 5% significance level, two-tail test (t with $\nu = 12$), $t_{\text{test}} = 1 \cdot 255$.

A10 2·5% significance level, one-tail (lower) test (t with $\nu = 8$), $t_{\text{test}} = -1 \cdot 023$.

B1 A factory produces kitchen foil in rolls whose mean length is μ metres and whose variance is $0 \cdot 25$ metres^2. The value of μ is claimed to be 10.

A random sample of 75 rolls of foil is taken, and the mean length for the sample is found to be 9·84 metres.

(i) State suitable null and alternative hypotheses in order to test whether the sample mean is consistent with the claimed value.

(ii) Conduct the test, using a 5% significance level.

(iii) Explain briefly whether it is necessary to assume that the parent distribution is Normal.

B2 Last year all the children at Greenview County Primary School took part in a survey of pocket money. The mean amount of money spent on sweets by each child (in a typical week) was found to be 70 pence, with standard deviation 9·6 pence. This year 20 children were selected and it was found that they spend (in a typical week) an average of 73 pence each. You are required to conduct a hypothesis test to see whether the mean amount spent on sweets has increased.

(i) Explain briefly why it is necessary to assume that the distribution of the amount spent on sweets is approximately Normal.

(ii) State two other necessary assumptions, one about the population and the other about the sample.

(iii) Conduct the test at the 2% significance level.

B3 A local sports shop sells fishing line in reels with a nominal length of 50 metres. It is suspected that this nominal length is incorrect, and so a sample of eight reels is taken. The actual length of fishing line, in metres, is measured for each:

49·2 49·6 50·1 50·4 51·0 50·8
52·0 51·1 50·5 48·2

You may assume that these represent random observations from a Normal distribution.

(i) Calculate the mean and variance of the lengths of the eight reels.

(ii) State suitable null and alternative hypotheses in order to test whether this sample is consistent with a population mean of 50 metres.

(iii) Conduct the test at the 2% significance level.

B4 Explain briefly what is meant by the Central Limit Theorem.

Bags of sugar are supposed to contain, on average, 2 kilograms. A quality controller suspects that they actually contain less than this amount, and so 90 bags are taken at random and the mass, x kg, of sugar in each is measured. The results are summarised by $n = 90$, $\Sigma x = 177 \cdot 9$, $\Sigma x^2 = 352 \cdot 1916$.

(i) State suitable null and alternative hypotheses for a statistical test.

(ii) Conduct the test at the 2% significance level.

B5 As part of their examination preparation A-level mathematics candidates are given a Comprehension paper. The candidates are supposed to be able to complete the paper in 20 minutes, on average, but they may take up to an hour if they wish.

A teacher suspects that the mean time taken by the candidates is greater than 20 minutes, and so she records the time, x minutes, taken by a sample of 12 pupils,

continued

Exercise 5.3 *continued*

summarised as $n = 12$, $\sum x = 322$, $\sum x^2 = 8748$. These may be assumed to be independent observations from a Normal distribution.

(i) State suitable null and alternative hypotheses for a statistical test.

(ii) Conduct the test at the 1% significance level.

B6 An office manager notices that the ink cartridges in printers need to be replaced after T working days, where T has a mean of 40 and a standard deviation of 5·5. In an effort to reduce costs he introduces an electronic mail system for internal documents, and he expects the mean value of T to increase accordingly (though he thinks the standard deviation will remain the same).

Following the introduction of the new scheme a random sample of ten newly-installed cartridges are observed to need replacement after 32, 37, 39, 42, 43, 43, 45, 48, 48 and 48 days. This sample is to be tested to see whether there is any evidence of an increase in the mean value of T.

(i) State suitable null and alternative hypotheses for a test.

(ii) Conduct the test at the 5% significance level, assuming that the standard deviation has not changed.

(iii) Use the sample to calculate an unbiased estimate of the new standard deviation. Comment briefly on this value.

B7

> For the fastest in fast food—eat at Smokey Joe's Diner
> Our average service time is only five minutes!

The management at Smokey Joe's reckon that, on average, customers will be served five minutes after ordering. I suspect that the mean waiting time is longer than this, and so I visit the Diner on eight random occasions, wearing a different disguise each time. The observed waiting times, w minutes, are summarised by $n = 8$, $\sum w = 42\cdot4$, $\sum w^2 = 227\cdot52$.

(i) Calculate an unbiased estimate for the variance of the waiting time.

(ii) Assuming that the waiting times are Normally distributed, conduct a hypothesis test to see whether there is any evidence, at the 5% level, that the mean waiting time is longer than 5 minutes.

B8 A recording studio purchases some audio cassette tapes whose lengths are supposed to be Normally distributed with a mean of 32 minutes and a standard deviation of 1 minute. The studio suspects that the mean length has been overstated, and so 18 tapes are chosen at random and their lengths measured. The mean length for the sample is found to be 31·2 minutes.

(i) State suitable hypotheses for a test on the mean length.

(ii) Conduct the test, using a 1% significance level. State your conclusion clearly.

(iii) Explain, with a reason, whether your critical value was obtained from Normal tables or from t-tables.

B9 A machine produces jars of skin cream filled to a nominal volume of 100 ml. The machine is actually supposed to be set to 105 ml, to ensure that most jars actually contain more than the nominal volume of 100 ml.

To check that the machine is correctly set 80 jars are chosen at random, and the volume, x ml, of skin cream in each is measured. The results are summarised by $n = 80$, $\sum x = 8376$, $\sum x^2 = 877\,687$.

(i) State suitable hypotheses for a test to see whether the machine appears to be set correctly.

(ii) Conduct the test, using a 2·5% significance level.

(iii) Explain carefully whether it is necessary to assume that the volume of skin cream in a jar follows a Normal distribution.

Exercise 5.3 *continued*

B10 Amanda visits a coin operated machine in order to take some passport photos. A notice on the machine claims 'Photos ready in 4 minutes'.

To test this claim Amanda watches a random sample of 11 customers, and observes the time x (in seconds) until the photos are ready. She records this information as a value above or below 4 minutes, summarising the results as follows:
$n = 11, \sum(x - 240) = 22,$
$\sum(x - 240)^2 = 1254.$

(i) Calculate the mean and variance of the observations of $x - 240$. Hence write down the mean and variance of the observations of x.

(ii) State two assumptions about the data which are necessary in order for a t-test to be valid.

(iii) Conduct a t-test to see whether these data are consistent with a mean time of 4 minutes. Use a 5% significance level.

5.4 Hypothesis tests and confidence intervals: proportion

Key points

Sometimes an attribute is possessed by a certain proportion of a population. Confidence intervals may be constructed, or hypothesis tests conducted, in a manner which is very similar to the methods of Sections 5.2 and 5.3.

The usual method is based on a Normal approximation to the Binomial distribution. Strictly speaking, a **continuity correction** should be applied; in the examples which follow this is omitted, in the interest of simplicity. Check carefully whether your own A-level syllabus requires the use of this correction.

The method is to work with a large population in which some proportion P possess a certain attribute (e.g. black hair). Then for a random sample of size n the **number** of elements within the sample possessing that attribute will be distributed Binomially with expectation nP and variance nPQ, where $Q = 1 - P$. The expectation of the sample **proportion** is described by dividing this expectation by n to leave P. The variance of the sample proportion is obtained by dividing nPQ by n^2 to leave $\dfrac{PQ}{n}$. The final result may be approximated by a Normal distribution provided n is large and P is reasonably central:

> For a population in which a proportion P possess a certain attribute, then the **sample proportion** observed within a random sample of size n can be modelled by the distribution

$$N\left(P, \frac{PQ}{n}\right)$$

Example I

A motoring organisation checks the lights on 90 vehicles chosen at random, and finds that 27 of the vehicles actually have defective lights. Obtain a symmetric 90% confidence interval for the actual proportion of vehicles within the population which have defective lights.

Solution

Within the population let a proportion P have defective lights. The sample proportion p will be used to make an estimate $\hat{P}$ of the population proportion.

For the sample, $p = \dfrac{27}{90} = 0.3$, $q = 0.7$, $n = 90$. Thus $\hat{P} = 0.3$, $\hat{Q} = 0.7$ and

the 90% confidence interval is

$$\hat{P} \pm 1.645\sqrt{\frac{\hat{P}\hat{Q}}{n}}$$

This is a standard result. For other percentage levels, e.g. 95%, simply change the value of 1·645 to 1·960 for example.

i.e. $0.3 \pm 1.645\sqrt{\dfrac{0.3 \times 0.7}{90}} = 0.3 \pm 0.079$

and so $0.221 \leq P \leq 0.379$

Example 2

When President Mädler came to power in the fictitious republic of Strabo the literacy rate was 64% (i.e. only 64% of the population could read properly.) During his first year in office an adult education programme was introduced, and at the end of the year a random sample of people were tested. Of the 300 people who were tested, 201 were able to read properly.

(i)   State suitable null and alternative hypotheses for a test to see whether there is any evidence that the literacy rate has increased during President Mädler's first year in office.

(ii) Conduct the test at the 5% significance level.

Solution

(i)   Let the population proportion who can read properly be P.

H_0: $P = 0.64$

H_1: $P > 0.64$ One-tail 5% test.

(ii) For the sample $p = \dfrac{201}{300} = 0.67$, $q = 0.33$, $n = 300$.

Under H_0 this is distributed approximately as $N\left(0.64, \dfrac{0.64 \times 0.36}{300}\right)$

Compute the test statistic:

$$z_{\text{test}} = \frac{p - P}{\sqrt{\dfrac{PQ}{n}}}$$

This is a standard result for hypothesis tests on proportion—it produces a test statistic which is standardised so that it may be compared with tables of N(0, 1).

$$= \frac{0{\cdot}67 - 0{\cdot}64}{\sqrt{\dfrac{0{\cdot}64 \times 0{\cdot}36}{300}}}$$

$$= 1{\cdot}083$$

Under H_0 this is distributed approximately as N(0, 1).

From tables the critical value is $z_{\text{crit}} = 1{\cdot}645$

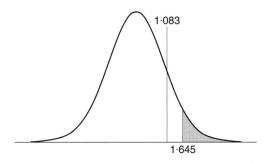

Accept H_0. There is no evidence that the literacy rate has improved during the President's first year in office.

Exercise 5.4

A1 An aircraft corporation is concerned that some of its flights are delayed. From a random sample of 90 flights it was noticed that exactly 12 of them were delayed. Construct a symmetric 90% confidence interval for the proportion of flights which are actually delayed.

A2 200 nine-year-olds are asked whether they believe in Father Christmas; 140 say that they do. Assuming that this is a random sample, construct a symmetric 90% confidence interval for the proportion of all nine-year-olds who believe in Father Christmas.

A3 A librarian notices that out of 260 book loans (chosen at random) 47 of them resulted in overdue returns. Construct a symmetric 90% confidence interval for the proportion of book loans which result in overdue returns.

A4 In clinical trials a research team notes that 44 people out a random sample of 380 suffer an allergic reaction to a new drug. Obtain a 90% confidence interval for the proportion of people within the population likely to suffer an allergic reaction to the drug.

continued

Exercise 5.4 *continued*

A5 144 university students are asked to name Britain's Prime Minister at the start of 1939. 54 of them reply correctly that it was Neville Chamberlain.

  (i) Construct a 95% confidence interval for the population proportion, assuming that the 144 students have been chosen randomly.

  (ii) Explain carefully the meaning of 'population' in this context.

A6 A supermarket chain is considering extending its trading hours to include Sundays. Ninety employees are asked whether they would be prepared to work on Sundays, and 34 reply that they would be.

Assuming that the 90 employees represent a random sample from the available workforce within the chain, construct a 95% confidence interval for the proportion of employees who would be prepared to work on Sundays.

A7 A Year 8 class is conducting some practical work on probability theory. The 25 children in the class are each given an identical drawing pin, and each pin is thrown 20 times. The pin lands either point up or point down; of the 500 throws exactly 140 landed point up.

  (i) Calculate the experimental probability that a single throw of one of these drawing pins will result in landing point down.

  (ii) Obtain a symmetric 99% confidence interval for the probability that a drawing pin will land point down.

A8 One of the stalls at a garden fete is a Treasure Hunt. Players choose a ticket from a map drawn on a pegboard; most of the tickets are marked 'Hard luck—you lose', while the rest are marked 'Well done—instant prize'. George watches 60 people play Treasure Hunt; exactly eight of the tickets result in an instant prize.

  (i) Using George's data, construct a symmetric 90% confidence interval for the proportion of tickets which result in instant prizes.

  (ii) State clearly an important assumption about the way in which George has collected his data.

B1 A new scratch card game is to be introduced, and the intention is that 10% of all cards should be winners. 250 cards are chosen at random, and it is found that 19 of them are winners.

  (i) State suitable hypotheses for a test to see whether the proportion of winning cards has been set correctly.

  (ii) Conduct the test, at the 1% significance level.

B2 A zoo is breeding a certain species of lizard. From past experience it is known that 15% of all the eggs laid are infertile. Following the introduction of a new incubation procedure a random sample of lizard eggs is studied. Of the 96 eggs only eight of them are found to be infertile.

  (i) State suitable hypotheses for a test to see whether the proportion of infertile eggs appears to have decreased.

  (ii) Conduct the test, at the 2% significance level.

B3 A GCSE Examining Board decides to set the last question on its Mathematics paper at a level of difficulty so that 12% of all the candidates will be able to answer it correctly. When the scripts are received a random sample of 240 is taken, and it is found that exactly 23 candidates have answered the question correctly.

  (i) State suitable hypotheses for a test to see whether the question has been set at the right level of difficulty.

  (ii) Conduct the test, at the 5% significance level.

B4 Arthur has set up a weather station on the balcony of his flat. Each evening he forecasts whether the following day will be dry or wet. Arthur's mum thinks he is guessing, i.e. that his forecasts will be right 50% of the time.

To convince his mum that he is not just guessing Arthur records the results of 365 forecasts made throughout the year, and notices that 220 of these were right.

(i) State suitable hypotheses for a test to see whether there is any evidence that Arthur's forecasts are better than the result of guesswork.

(ii) Conduct the test, at the 5% significance level.

B5 The manufacturers of *Snowy Flakes* breakfast cereal decide to put a plastic model of a winter sports figure in each box of cereal. There are eight different models in all, but they are not distributed in equal numbers.

120 boxes of *Snowy Flakes* are chosen at random, and it is found that 36 of them contain a model of a downhill ski racer.

(i) Construct a symmetric 95% confidence interval for the proportion of boxes of *Snowy Flakes* which contain a model of a downhill ski racer.

In another random sample of 80 boxes it is found that 5 boxes contain a model of a speed skater. The manufacturers claim that 10% of the boxes contain a model of a speed skater.

(ii) State suitable hypotheses for a test to see whether the manufacturer's claimed proportion is correct.

(iii) Conduct the test, at the 5% significance level.

5.5 Testing for the difference of two means

Key points

Sometimes we will wish to test whether two samples appear to come from the same Normal distribution. The method is to assume that both distributions have the same variance, but that their means might differ. If the common variance is given then the test statistic will be Normal; if the variance has been estimated then a t-distribution arises instead.

The data sets $x_1, x_2, \ldots, x_{n_1}$ and $y_1, y_2, \ldots, y_{n_2}$ are assumed to come from two Normal distributions $N(\mu_X, \sigma^2)$ and $N(\mu_Y, \sigma^2)$ respectively. The test statistic to be calculated is

$$z_{\text{test}} = \frac{\bar{x} - \bar{y}}{\sigma \sqrt{\dfrac{1}{n_1} + \dfrac{1}{n_2}}}$$

Provided σ is known then (under the null hypothesis $H_0: \mu_X = \mu_Y$) this will be distributed as a standardised Normal variable $N(0, 1)$.

If σ is *not* known then two extra factors come into play:

- the common variance must be estimated, using

$$\hat{\sigma}^2 = \frac{n_1 \times s_X^2 + n_2 \times s_Y^2}{n_1 + n_2 - 2}$$

- the test statistic $t_{test} = \dfrac{\bar{x} - \bar{y}}{\hat{\sigma}\sqrt{\dfrac{1}{n_1} + \dfrac{1}{n_2}}}$ is now t-distributed with $n_1 + n_2 - 2$

degrees of freedom.

Example I

Over a long period of time it is known that the heights of a certain species of dwarf tomato plant are Normally distributed with variance 3.5 cm². Eight plants are grown indoors, and their heights are measured as 19.8, 18.2, 15.6, 18.4, 21.1, 16.2, 20.3 and 17.9 cm. Six other plants are grown outdoors, and their heights are measured as 14.3, 16.4, 15.5, 15.8, 11.8 and 16.7 cm. It is desired to test whether there is any evidence that the indoor plants have a taller mean height than the outdoor plants.

(i) State suitable hypotheses for a test for a difference in the means.

(ii) State briefly any assumptions which need to be made.

(iii) Conduct the test, using a 5% significance level.

Solution

Let the height of an indoor plant be X and that of an outdoor plant be Y.

Let $X \sim N(\mu_X, \sigma^2)$ and $Y \sim N(\mu_Y, \sigma^2)$.

(i) H_0: $\mu_X = \mu_Y$

   H_1: $\mu_X > \mu_Y$ One-tail 5% test

(ii) It is assumed that the two data sets represent independent observations from two Normal distributions with a common variance of 3.5 cm².

(iii) For the indoor plants the mean height is

   $\bar{x} = \dfrac{19.8 + \ldots + 17.9}{8} = 18.4375$

   For the outdoor plants the mean height is

   $\bar{y} = \dfrac{14.3 + \ldots + 16.7}{5} = 15.0833$

   Compute the test statistic $z_{test} = \dfrac{18.4375 - 15.0833}{\sqrt{3.5} \times \sqrt{\frac{1}{8} + \frac{1}{6}}} = 3.320$

   Under H_0 this is distributed as $N(0, 1)$. *Normal distribution is used because the population variance is known.*

   From tables, $z_{crit} = 1.645$

As z_{test} lies within the critical region we reject H_0 in favour of H_1.

The mean height of the indoor plants does appear to be greater than the mean height of those grown outdoors.

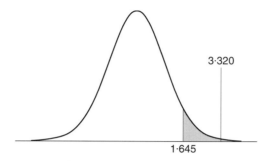

Example 2

A physiology student is investigating differences in response times for males and females. She devises a simple task, and asks 20 volunteers to take part. Twelve males are able to complete the task in a mean time of 55 seconds, with a standard deviation of 8·6 seconds, while the eight females have a mean time of 53 seconds and standard deviation 8·1 seconds.

(i) State three necessary assumptions in order that the difference in means may be tested using a two-sample t-test.

(ii) State suitable null and alternative hypotheses for the test.

(iii) Conduct the test at the 5% significance level.

Solution

(i) It must be assumed that the data points represent
  • independent observations
  • from two Normal distributions
  • with a common variance.

(ii) H_0: $\mu_X = \mu_Y$

  H_1: $\mu_X \neq \mu_Y$ Two-tail 5% test

(iii) Estimate the common variance:

$$\hat{\sigma}^2 = \frac{12 \times 8 \cdot 6^2 + 8 \times 8 \cdot 1^2}{12 + 8 - 2} = 78 \cdot 466667 \text{ and so } \hat{\sigma} = 8 \cdot 8581.$$

Compute the test statistic $t_{\text{test}} = \dfrac{55 - 53}{8 \cdot 8581 \times \sqrt{\frac{1}{12} + \frac{1}{8}}} = 0 \cdot 495$

t-distribution is used because the population variance is unknown.

Under H_0 this is t-distributed with $12 + 8 - 2 = 18$ degrees of freedom.

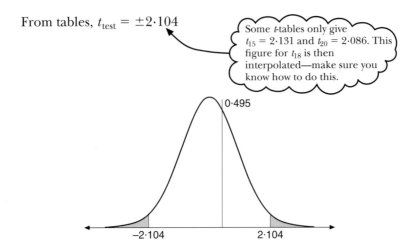

From tables, $t_{\text{test}} = \pm 2 \cdot 104$

Some t-tables only give $t_{15} = 2 \cdot 131$ and $t_{20} = 2 \cdot 086$. This figure for t_{18} is then interpolated—make sure you know how to do this.

0·495

−2·104   2·104

Accept H_0. There is no evidence of any difference in the mean time for males compared with that for females.

Exercise 5.5

In questions **A1** to **A5** you are given two sample means, the sample sizes and a known common variance; the samples are assumed to come from Normal populations. Calculate the value of the test statistic which would be used to conduct a hypothesis test for the difference of the two means.

A1 $\bar{x} = 12 \cdot 5$, $n_1 = 10$, $\bar{y} = 10 \cdot 2$, $n_2 = 12$, $\sigma^2 = 1 \cdot 44$

A2 $\bar{x} = 113$, $n_1 = 8$, $\bar{y} = 121$, $n_2 = 7$, $\sigma^2 = 25$

A3 $\bar{x} = 64 \cdot 16$, $n_1 = 25$, $\bar{y} = 59 \cdot 21$, $n_2 = 15$, $\sigma^2 = 75$

A4 $\bar{x} = 104 \cdot 1$, $n_1 = 12$, $\bar{y} = 101 \cdot 7$, $n_2 = 9$, $\sigma^2 = 14 \cdot 4$

A5 $\bar{x} = 8 \cdot 83$, $n_1 = 10$, $\bar{y} = 9 \cdot 11$, $n_2 = 10$, $\sigma^2 = 0 \cdot 49$

In questions **A6** to **A10** you are given two sample means, the corresponding sample variances and the sample sizes. Assuming that the two samples come from Normal distributions with a common variance, calculate an unbiased estimate for the value of the common variance.

A6 $\bar{x} = 14 \cdot 5$, $s_X^2 = 8 \cdot 85$, $n_1 = 8$, $\bar{y} = 11 \cdot 2$, $s_Y^2 = 10 \cdot 04$, $n_2 = 10$

A7 $\bar{x} = 144 \cdot 45$, $s_X^2 = 78 \cdot 44$, $n_1 = 11$, $\bar{y} = 151 \cdot 26$, $s_Y^2 = 66 \cdot 75$, $n_2 = 8$

A8 $\bar{x} = 3 \cdot 51$, $s_X^2 = 77 \cdot 23$, $n_1 = 12$, $\bar{y} = -2 \cdot 72$, $s_Y^2 = 80 \cdot 13$, $n_2 = 11$

A9 $\bar{x} = 22 \cdot 66$, $s_X^2 = 13 \cdot 86$, $n_1 = 7$, $\bar{y} = 26 \cdot 62$, $s_Y^2 = 15 \cdot 99$, $n_2 = 10$

A10 $\bar{x} = 47 \cdot 5$, $s_X^2 = 58 \cdot 23$, $n_1 = 6$, $\bar{y} = 61 \cdot 2$, $s_Y^2 = 62 \cdot 44$, $n_2 = 5$

B1 The mean lengths of leaves of a certain species of tree may be taken to be Normally distributed with a standard deviation of $1 \cdot 2$ cm. A random sample of 20 leaves on the north-facing side of such trees yields a mean length of $12 \cdot 2$ cm, while another random sample of 16 leaves taken from the south-facing side yields a mean length of $14 \cdot 2$ cm.

You are required to test whether the leaves from the south-facing sides appear to be longer than those from north-facing sides.

(i)   State suitable null and alternative hypotheses for your test.

(ii) Conduct the test using a $2 \cdot 5\%$ significance level.

Exercise 5.5 continued

B2 Ten toffees have a mean mass of 22·4 grams; 14 eclairs have a mean mass of 26·7 grams. It may be assumed that both figures have been obtained from random samples drawn from two Normal distributions with a common variance of 9 grams^2.

Conduct a two-sample test, at the 1% significance level, to see whether there is any evidence that the mean mass of the toffees is lower than that of the eclairs.

B3 A company manufactures bricks in two colours, red and yellow. An engineer wishes to see whether both colours of brick have the same mean length.

Seventeen red bricks are chosen at random; they are found to have a mean length of 20·5 cm and standard deviation 0·48 cm. Fifteen yellow bricks similarly chosen are found to have a mean length of 20·9 cm and standard deviation 0·55 cm.

(i) State suitable null and alternative hypotheses for a two-sample t-test.

(ii) State briefly any necessary distributional assumptions in order for the test to be valid.

(iii) Conduct the test, using a 2% significance level.

B4 The midday temperature in January at a particular Alpine ski resort may be taken to be Normally distributed with a standard deviation of 2 °C.

A meteorologist looks back at records for the 1960s and the 1980s. A random selection of eight January temperatures from the 1960s yields temperatures of 3, 1, 0, −2, 0, −2, −4, −1, while another random sample of ten January temperatures from the 1980s are 3, 1, 0, 3, 1, 3, 2, −2, 3, 1.

(i) Calculate the value of a test statistic which may be used to test the hypothesis that the mean temperatures were higher in the 1980s than in the 1960s.

(ii) State, with a reason, whether this statistic should be tested against a critical value from Normal tables or one from t-tables.

(iii) Conduct the test at the 5% level, stating your hypotheses and conclusion.

B5 A marine biologist catches a small number of adult fish of a certain species, and measures the body length of each. The six males measure 11·2, 11·5, 13·2, 10·7, 11·6 and 11·9 cm, while the seven females measure 10·4, 9·9, 11·4, 9·7, 10·5, 10·3 and 10·8 cm.

(i) Calculate the mean and standard deviation of the lengths of the males.

(ii) Calculate the mean and standard deviation of the lengths of the females.

The biologist assumes that the data represent random samples from two Normal distributions with a common variance.

(iii) Using your results from (i) and (ii) above, obtain an unbiased estimate of the common variance.

The biologist wishes to conduct a hypothesis test to see whether there is significant evidence that the males have a longer mean body length than the females.

(iv) State suitable null and alternative hypotheses for the test.

(v) Conduct the test at the 5% significance level, stating your conclusion clearly.

B6 An Examinations Board believes that marks in its Pure 1 and Statistics 1 modules may be modelled by two independent Normal distributions.

Nineteen candidates from Pure 1 were chosen at random, and found to have a mean mark of 38·5, with standard deviation 6·4. Thirteen candidates from Statistics 1 were chosen at random, and found to have a mean mark of 41·6, with standard deviation 8·5. The Board wants to conduct a two-sample t-test to see whether the mean marks for the two modules appear to be different. *continued*

Exercise 5.5 *continued*

(i) State one further assumption which must be made about the standard deviation of the marks obtained in the two modules.

(ii) State suitable null and alternative hypotheses in order to test whether the mean marks for the two modules appear to be different.

(iii) Conduct the test, at the 5% significance level.

(n.b. Although the Normal distribution is continuous and exam marks are discrete the statement '... may be modelled by two independent Normal distributions ...' should be taken literally—*do not* attempt to use any kind of continuity correction.)

B7 Mario is studying the incubation periods of two different species of gull. He observes a random sample of 10 eggs from gulls of species A, and records the number of days x until each egg hatches. The results are summarised by $\sum x = 255$, $\sum x^2 = 6545$, $n_1 = 10$.

Corresponding results from a random sample of 12 eggs belonging to species B are summarised by $\sum y = 314$, $\sum y^2 = 8291$, $n_2 = 12$.

Mario decides to conduct a two-sample hypothesis test to see whether there is any evidence of a difference between the mean times for the two species.

(i) State any necessary assumptions about the nature of the parent distributions.

(ii) Calculate the sample mean and sample variance for each of the two species. Hence compute an unbiased estimate for the common population variance σ^2.

(iii) Conduct the test at the 5% significance level, stating your hypotheses and conclusions clearly.

B8 Leonardo notices that the cheese and tomato pizzas sold by two different supermarkets are actually very similar, and he suspects that they are manufactured by the same supplier. To test this hypothesis he decides to conduct a two-sample *t*-test on the diameters of the pizzas, and to conclude that they are manufactured by the same supplier if there is no evidence of any difference in the mean diameter.

A random sample of 11 pizzas from *Superway* have a mean diameter of 22·5 cm with sample standard deviation of 1·95 cm; corresponding figures for a random sample of 11 pizzas from *Safeco* are 24·7 cm and 2·05 cm, respectively.

In order to conduct the test Leonardo assumes that both samples come from Normal distributions with a common standard deviation. He calculates an estimate of the standard deviation as 2·0 cm; this figure is incorrect.

(i) Explain how Mario might have arrived at the value of 2·0 cm.

(ii) Calculate a correct estimate for the common standard deviation.

(iii) Conduct the hypothesis test, using a 5% significance level.

Revision questions

C1 Explain briefly what is meant by the Central Limit Theorem.

An aeronautical engineer designs an aircraft which can carry passengers up to a total weight of 11 900 pounds. He assumes that the weight of an individual passenger may be thought of as a statistical variable with mean 165 pounds and standard deviation 15 pounds. He would like the aircraft to be able to carry 70 passengers.

(i) Assuming that the 70 passengers are chosen randomly, write down the mean and standard deviation of the mean weight of a passenger. State also the approximate shape of the distribution of this sample mean.

(ii)   Write down the mean weight of a passenger if the aircraft is carrying 70 passengers at a total weight of 11 900 pounds.

(iii)   Using your answers to (i) and (ii) above, calculate the probability that the aircraft is able to carry 70 passengers. Explain why there is no need to assume that the weights come from a Normal distribution.

A charter company operates a fleet of 70-seater aircraft, each of which is able to carry passengers up to a total weight of 11 900 pounds. The charter company receives a booking from a Weightlifter's club, who would like them to fly 65 members of the club to a Weightlifting Convention.

(iv)   Explain briefly whether it would be wise to fly all 65 weightlifters on a single aircraft.

C2   A doctor is studying police records of the blood alcohol level recorded when motorists are given blood tests. A reading of 80 units or more indicates that the motorist has been driving with excess alcohol in the blood.

The doctor selects 50 records at random, and notes that the blood alcohol level for that sample has a mean of 96 units, with standard deviation 16 units.

(i)   Show that an unbiased estimate for the population standard deviation is approximately 16·16 units.

(ii)   Construct a symmetric 95% confidence interval for the mean blood alcohol level for all the motorists who had been tested.

(iii)   Explain the relevance of the Central Limit Theorem in obtaining your confidence interval.

C3   The mean lifetime of a particular brand of battery is known to be Normally distributed

with mean 40 hours and standard deviation 4 hours. A modification to the design is intended to increase the mean lifetime, while leaving the standard deviation and the shape of the distribution unaltered.

A batch of batteries is produced under the modified design, and a random sample of 20 batteries are found to have a mean lifetime of 42·2 hours. Construct a symmetric 95% confidence interval for the mean lifetime of a battery produced under the modified design.

One hundred batteries are chosen at random and tested for leaks when they are three months old, and 12 of them are found to be leaking. Construct a symmetric 90% confidence interval for the proportion of batteries which leak after three months.

C4   A drinks machine dispenses cups of orange squash. The amount of squash dispensed varies from one cup to another, and can be modelled by a Normal distribution with a standard deviation of 5 ml.

The mean volume of drink per cup is supposed to be 250 ml, but an engineer suspects that this value has been set wrongly. She collects a random sample of ten cups of orange, and measures their volumes as 245, 251, 241, 244, 252, 244, 238, 241, 248 and 242 ml.

(i)   Carry out a hypothesis test, at the 5% significance level, to see if there is any evidence that the machine has been set wrongly.

The engineer adjusts the machine, and then takes a second sample of ten cups, recording their volumes as 250, 244, 249, 253, 247, 248, 255, 241, 249 and 247 ml. She assumes that these readings can still be regarded as coming from a Normal distribution with a standard deviation of 5 ml.

(ii)   Carry out a hypothesis test, at the 5% significance level, to see if there is any evidence that the machine is now set correctly.

C5 The headteacher of a primary school decides to organise a 'Fling the Wellie' competition as part of the Year 6 sports day. She is told that an average Year 6 pupil would be able to fling a wellie a distance of 10 metres, but she suspects that this figure is not correct.

To test whether the suggested mean of 10 metres is correct, the headteacher selects eight Year 6 pupils. Each child throws a wellington boot, and the distances are measured as follows:

Pupil	Distance (metres)
Annie	8.3
Morag	11.1
Dan	9.2
David	9.5
Jemma	8.9
Suzy	10.3
Ben	9.5
Linton	9.6

(i) Calculate the mean and standard deviation for these data.

(ii) State suitable null and alternative hypotheses for a test on the mean.

(iii) Assuming that these are random observations from an underlying Normal distribution, conduct the hypothesis test. Use a 5% significance level.

C6 In the run-up to an election voters are asked which party they support. From their replies statisticians attempt to predict the results of the local and national elections (which are to be held on the same day).

One hundred and twenty voters are chosen at random, locally, and asked how they will vote in the local election. Thirty of them say that they will vote for the Independent candidate.

(i) Calculate a symmetric 90% confidence interval for the proportion of voters who will vote for the Independent candidate.

A random sample of n voters chosen nationally are asked whether they will vote for the Alliance candidate. 50% of them say they will.

(ii) A 95% confidence interval is constructed, from which it is claimed that between 44·83% and 55·17% of the electorate will vote Alliance. Find n.

(iii) Explain carefully why opinion polls often take a sample of size $n = 1068$.

C7 An advertisement claims '60% of all households now use semi-skimmed milk.'

To test this figure, a researcher interviews 200 households, chosen at random; 105 of them do use semi-skimmed milk.

Conduct a hypothesis test, at the 5% level, to see whether the data is consistent with the claimed proportion of 60%.

C8 Jars of marmalade are supposed to contain, on average, 225 grams. The producer suspects that his packing machine is not putting enough marmalade into each jar, and so he takes a random sample of 12 jars, and notes the amount of marmalade (in grams) in each:

220	221	220	227	225	222	228	220
223	221	222	222				

You may assume that these values come from a Normal population.

(i) State suitable null and alternative hypotheses for a test on the mean.

(ii) Conduct the test, using a 5% significance level.

C9 A psychologist is assessing the mental agility of children by giving them a jigsaw puzzle to solve as quickly as possible.

Twelve 12-year-olds are chosen at random, and they are observed to solve the puzzle in a mean time of 12·4 minutes. Fourteen 14-year-olds are similarly chosen at random, and they complete the puzzle in a mean time of 10·2 minutes. Previous experience leads the psychologist to assume that both samples are from independent Normal distributions with a common variance of 8.25 minutes².

(i) State suitable null and alternative hypotheses for a test to see whether there is significant evidence that the mean time for the 14-year-olds is faster.

(ii) Conduct the test, using a 5% significance level.

C10 An environmental group measures the radiation level at 20 randomly-chosen sites in a National Park shortly before the construction of a large nuclear power station. The results, in suitable units, yield a

mean of 44·8 and standard deviation of 5·4.

Ten years after the construction of the power station the group again measures the radiation level, at 22 randomly chosen sites. The results now yield a mean of 49·7 and a standard deviation of 6·1. The group is anxious to determine whether this is significant evidence of an increase in the mean level of radiation since the power station was built.

(i) State two necessary distributional assumptions in order that the data may be tested by a two-sample *t*-test.

(ii) Obtain an unbiased estimate of the variance required for your test.

(iii) Conduct the test, using a 1% significance level.

Chapter 6

THE CHI-SQUARED GOODNESS-OF-FIT TEST

6.1 The basic Chi-squared Goodness-of-fit test

Key points

The χ^2 (**Chi-squared**) **test** is used to compare the **observed results** of an experiment with the **expected frequencies** predicted by some mathematical model; it tells us whether the model looks like a good one or not.

This section covers the basic test, as applied to expected frequencies which are either in a given proportion or based on uniform, Binomial or Poisson models.

The model to be tested should be stated as the **null hypothesis H_0**. The **alternative hypothesis H_1** is always that H_0 is not true.

The test works by comparing a test statistic X^2 (which is a discrete variable) against a critical value χ^2 (which comes from a tabulated continuous distribution). The distribution of X^2 will approximate to χ^2 provided:
- the observations are independent
- each expected frequency is at least 5.

The test is carried out in the following way

- **Step 1** State the model to be tested

  Use H_0 and H_1 notation.

- **Step 2** Check the significance level to be used

  Usually given in the question. If you need to set your own level then state that you are doing so. The standard choice is 5%.

- **Step 3** Use the model to produce a list of expected frequencies E

  Work to one decimal place if these are not whole numbers.

- **Step 4** Check that all Es are ≥ 5

  If not, merge cells.

- **Step 5** Compute the test statistic

  $$X^2 = \sum \frac{(O - E)^2}{E}$$

  O and E are corresponding observed and expected frequencies.

- **Step 6** Find the number of degrees of freedom, ν

  $\nu = n - 1$ for the basic test applied to n pairs of cells.

- **Step 7** Use tables to find the critical value of χ^2

- **Step 8**   Draw a diagram to compare the test value with the critical region
- **Step 9**   State the conclusion formally
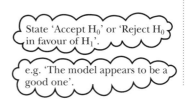

State 'Accept H_0' or 'Reject H_0' in favour of H_1'.

- **Step 10**   Restate it in plain English

e.g. 'The model appears to be a good one'.

Example 1

A gardener is planning to grow a certain variety of flower from seed. It is not possible to tell the colour until the flower blooms, but the packets carry this message:

> CONTAINS RED, BLUE, WHITE SEEDS
> IN RATIO 6:3:1 (ON AVERAGE)

Each packet contains 20 seeds.

(i)   Explain why the gardener could not carry out a χ^2 test using only one packet of seeds.

(ii)   Write down the least number of packets he must use in order to apply a χ^2 test with 2 degrees of freedom.

The gardener buys 5 packets of seeds from his local garden centre. All the seeds germinate successfully, and when they bloom he observes 51 red, 38 blue and 11 white.

(iii)   Carry out a χ^2 test to see whether the observed colours are consistent with the message on the packet.

(iv)   Comment briefly on the sampling procedure used by the gardener.

Solution

(i)   For one packet of seeds the expected frequencies would be 12, 6 and 2 respectively. As 2 is less than 5 the test cannot be conducted on this data.

(ii)   For all Es to be ≥ 5 the minimum is 30:15:5, i.e. 50 seeds, so at least 3 packets are needed.

(iii) H_0: The data may be modelled by a 6:3:1 ratio.   **(Step 1)**

H_1: The data may not be so modelled.

As no significance level is given, a 5% test will be used.   **(Step 2)**

Using ~~10~~ 5 packets the expected frequencies under H_0 are   **(Step 3)**

	Red	Blue	White
Observed	51	38	11
Expected	60	30	10

117 ·

All Es are ≥ 5 so no need to merge cells. **(Step 4)**

Compute the test statistic **(Step 5)**

$$X^2 = \frac{(51 - 60)^2}{60} + \frac{(38 - 30)^2}{30} + \frac{(11 - 10)^2}{10}$$

$$= 1\cdot35 + 2\cdot13 + 0\cdot10$$

$$= 3\cdot58$$

Under H_0 this is approximately χ^2 with $\nu = 2$ degrees of **(Step 6)**
freedom.

From tables, $\chi^2_{\text{crit}} = 5\cdot991$ **(Step 7)**

(Step 8)

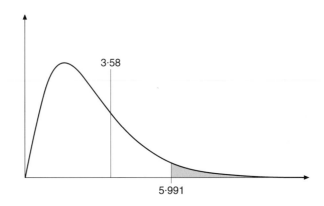

Accept H_0. **(Step 9)**

The observed frequencies are consistent with the claim on **(Step 10)**
the packet.

(iv) The gardener has not really given any thought to a sampling
procedure. All the seeds were from a small number of packets
bought at the same garden centre, so they do not constitute
independent observations; hence the conclusion to the hypothesis
test may be unsound.

Example 2

A mathematical gambler owns a set of four normal-looking dice. She wants
to see whether they are fair or not, and so she throws all four dice
together, 100 times, and records the number of 1s obtained each time.
Here are the results:

Number of 1s, X	0	1	2	3	4
Observed frequency	38	38	10	8	6

(i) Explain why the number of 1s, X, out of four fair dice may be
modelled by a Binomial distribution $B(n, p)$, stating suitable values
for n and p.

(ii) Write down suitable null and alternative hypotheses for a χ^2 test.

(iii) Under your null hypothesis show that the expected number of times on which no 1s are obtained is approximately 48·2.

(iv) Calculate corresponding expected frequencies for the other values of X.

(v) Explain why it is necessary to combine the last three cells before conducting a χ^2 test.

(vi) Carry out the test at the 10% level, stating your conclusion clearly.

Solution

(i) A Binomial distribution may be a good model because there is a fixed number n of independent trials, each with a fixed probability p of success. In this case $n = 4$ and $p = \frac{1}{6}$.

(ii) H_0: The data may be modelled by $X \sim B(4, \frac{1}{6})$

H_1: The data may not be so modelled.

(iii) Under H_0 the expected number of times on which no 1s are obtained is $100 \times {}^4C_0 \times (\frac{1}{6})^0 \times (\frac{5}{6})^4 = 48\cdot2$ (1 decimal place).

(iv) Similar calculations for the other values of X give these expected frequencies:

Number of 1s, X	0	1	2	3	4
Expected frequency	48·2	38·6	11·6	1·5	0·1

(v) The last three cells must be combined in order that all the expected frequencies are at least 5.

(vi) Combining cells we obtain

Number of 1s, X	0	1	2+
Observed frequency, O	38	38	24
Expected frequency, E	48·2	38·6	13·2

Compute the test statistic

$$X^2 = \frac{(38 - 48\cdot2)^2}{48\cdot2} + \frac{(38 - 38.6)^2}{38\cdot6} + \frac{(24 - 13\cdot2)^2}{13\cdot2}$$

$$= 11\cdot004$$

Under H_0 this is approximately χ^2 with $\nu = 3 - 1 = 2$ degrees of freedom.

From tables $\chi^2_{crit} = 4\cdot605$

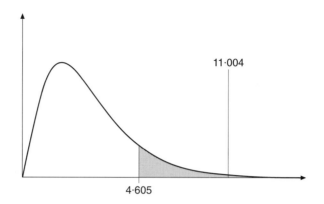

Reject H_0 in favour of H_1.

The dice do not appear to be fair.

Exercise 6.1

In questions **A1** to **A5** you are given a set of Observed and Expected frequencies. Compute the value of the test statistic X^2 in each case.

A1

Observed frequency, O	11	14	15
Expected frequency, E	10	10	20

A2

Observed frequency, O	8	35	28	9
Expected frequency, E	10	30	30	10

A3

Observed frequency, O	15	9	10	10	16
Expected frequency, E	12	12	12	12	12

A4

Observed frequency, O	10	25	68	45	12
Expected frequency, E	10	40	60	40	10

A5

Observed frequency, O	48	25	11	11
Expected frequency, E	45	30	12	8

In questions **A6** to **A10** you are given a set of Observed and Expected frequencies. Compute the value of the test statistic X^2 in each case. Also use tables to find the critical value χ^2_{crit} corresponding to the given significance level.

A6

Observed frequency, O	68	52	30
Expected frequency, E	60	50	40

5% significance level, $\nu = 2$ degrees of freedom

A7

Observed frequency, O	12	21	27	38	52
Expected frequency, E	10	20	30	40	50

5% significance level, $\nu = 4$ degrees of freedom

Exercise 6.1 *continued*

A8

Observed frequency, O	71	51	14	14
Expected frequency, E	80	40	20	10

10% significance level, $\nu = 3$ degrees of freedom

A9

Observed frequency, O	94	88	121	97
Expected frequency, E	100	100	100	100

1% significance level, $\nu = 3$ degrees of freedom

A10

Observed frequency, O	14	18	35	45	32	15	1
Expected frequency, E	10	20	30	50	30	10	10

5% significance level, $\nu = 6$ degrees of freedom

B1 Frostybix breakfast cereal contains a small toy dog in each packet. The dog is one of four breeds, and the manufacturers claim that all four breeds are packaged in equal numbers.

Ginnie decides to investigate whether the distribution is, in fact, uniform. She asks her friends to record the various dogs which they collect from Frostybix cereal packets over a two-month period. The resulting frequencies are: Labrador 24, Old English Sheepdog 17, Yorkshire Terrier 26, Poodle 21.

(i) State suitable null and alternative hypotheses for a χ^2 test.

(ii) Draw up a table of Observed and Expected frequencies.

(iii) Carry out the test at the 10% significance level. State your conclusion clearly.

B2 My bank account is with first direct™, the telephone banking division of Midland plc.

Each time I telephone the bank I have to pass a security check, during which I am asked to state two letters from my six-letter password. I will be asked, for example, for the first and fifth letters of the password.

Some time ago I noticed that the choice of letter for which I am asked does not appear to be uniform, so I noted the letters asked for during my next 24 calls:

Letter number	1	2	3	4	5	6
Number of times requested	12	10	8	7	0	11

(i) State suitable null and alternative hypotheses for a χ^2 test.

(ii) Carry out the test at the 5% level, stating your conclusion clearly.

(iii) Comment briefly on my sampling procedure for the 24 calls.

B3 A sweet shop manager claims that her mixed sweets contain toffees, nuts and eclairs in the ratio 5:3:4. A bag of 60 is purchased, and is found to contain 23 toffees, 18 nuts and 19 eclairs.

(i) State suitable null and alternative hypotheses for a χ^2 test.

(ii) Verify that there is sufficient data for a χ^2 test with 2 degrees of freedom.

(iii) Carry out the test at the 2·5% level, stating your conclusion clearly.

B4 Gemma has written a computer program to simulate a spinner with the following probability distribution:

Score, X	1	2	3	4
Probability	0·1	0·2	0·3	0·4

To check that the program is running correctly Gemma simulates the results of 100 spins, and obtains the following results:

Score, X	1	2	3	4
Frequency	11	19	32	38

continued

Exercise 6.1 continued

(i) State suitable null and alternative hypotheses for a χ^2 test.

(ii) Carry out the test at the 5% level, stating your conclusion clearly.

(iii) The 100 simulations were, in fact, consecutive, so they were not really a random sample of observations. Do you think that this is likely to invalidate your conclusion?

B5 A fairground games consists of rolling a ball, which will pass through one of four gates labelled A, B, C and D. The intention is that the probability of each of the four alternatives is as follows:

Gate	A	B	C	D
Probability	0·1	0·5	0·3	0·1

Carlos observes the results of 65 randomly chosen games to be

Gate	A	B	C	D
Frequency	11	25	15	14

(i) State suitable null and alternative hypotheses for a χ^2 test.

(ii) Draw up a table of observed and expected frequencies.

(iii) Carry out the test at the 5% level, stating your conclusion clearly.

B6 A hotel manager reckons that 25% of his guests like a continental breakfast, and the rest prefer English breakfast. To test this idea he records the number of continental breakfasts ordered by each family party of four visitors over a period of one month:

Number of continental breakfasts	0	1	2	3	4
Frequency	61	44	9	5	1

(i) Write down the total number of families of four visitors during the month.

(ii) Using a suitable Binomial distribution

show that, under the manager's model, the expected number of families ordering 1 continental breakfast is 50·6, correct to 1 decimal place.

(iii) Compute the remaining frequencies using the same model.

(iv) Carry out a χ^2 test at the 5% level, stating your conclusion clearly.

B7 The random variable X is thought to be Binomially distributed $B(5, 0·3)$. To test this belief 200 observations are made, at random, as follows:

Value, X	0	1	2	3	4	5
Frequency	30	57	59	29	11	14

(i) Using the proposed Binomial model show that the expected frequency corresponding to $X = 0$ is 33·6, correct to 1 decimal place.

(ii) Compute the remaining frequencies using the same model.

(iii) Carry out a χ^2 test at the 5% level, stating your conclusion clearly.

B8 The manager of a hockey team believes that the number of goals X per match which her team scores may be modelled by a Poisson distribution with parameter 1·2. She records the results of the last 35 matches in a table:

Number of goals, X	0	1	2	3	4	5+
Frequency	7	15	9	3	1	0

(i) Use the model $X \sim Po(1·2)$ to construct a corresponding list of expected frequencies, working to one decimal place.

(ii) State suitable null and alternative hypotheses for a χ^2 test.

(iii) Explain why it is not possible to use a χ^2 test on the data as it stands. Describe a suitable adjustment so that the data may be tested by this method.

Exercise 6.1 *continued*

(iv) Carry out the χ^2 test at the 5% level of significance.

Comment briefly on the manager's method of data collection.

B9 A scientist suspects that a certain random variable X may be modelled by a Poisson distribution with parameter 1·5. A laboratory experiment yields the following data set:

Value, X	0	1	2	3	4	5+
Observed frequency	23	33	24	12	8	0

(i) Show that the mean of this data set is close to 1·5.

(ii) Calculate the variance of the data set, and explain briefly how this value lends further support to the Poisson model.

(iii) Use the model $Po(1·5)$ to construct a corresponding set of expected frequencies.

(iv) Conduct a χ^2 test at the 5% level of significance. Explain carefully why your test is based on four degrees of freedom.

B10 James likes to play a board game in which a 6 must be thrown on a die in order to start. He thinks that the number of throws X up to and including the first 6 may be modelled by the distribution $Geo(\frac{1}{6})$ defined by:

$$P(X = r) = \left(\tfrac{5}{6}\right)^{r-1} \times \left(\tfrac{1}{6}\right) \quad r = 1, 2, 3, \ldots$$

(i) Name the distribution, and state its mean.

James records the results of 55 games, noting the following values of X:

Number of throws, X	1	2	3	4	5	6	7	9	10	11	15	19
Frequency	8	8	7	7	6	3	3	2	5	3	2	1

(ii) Show that the model $Geo(\frac{1}{6})$ produces an expected frequency of about 9·2 when $X = 1$ and obtain corresponding expected frequencies for $X = 2,3,4,5$.

James decides to compare the observed and expected frequencies by using this table:

(iii) Explain briefly why James has chosen to group the data in this way.

(iv) Copy and complete the table to show the observed and expected frequencies.

(v) Conduct a χ^2 test at the 5% level of significance, stating your conclusion.

Number of throws, x	O	E
1		
2		
3		
4		
5 or 6		
7 or 8		
9, 10 or 11		
12 or more		

6.2 Chi-squared test: contingency tables

Key points

A **contingency table** is a set of frequencies arranged in a two-way table; the idea is to see whether two factors (such as smoking and drinking) are related or not. The null hypothesis will be that the two factors are independent; we use the marginal totals to compute expected frequencies. If any of these are below 5 then cells must be combined; this is done by merging two rows (or columns).

Remember that the X^2 statistic is discrete while the χ^2 distribution is continuous; this means that we should, strictly speaking, be using a continuity correction. Most statisticians ignore this point, since it usually makes little difference, but the effect is noticeable in a 2 by 2 contingency table leading to only one degree of freedom. Example 2 illustrates the **Yates' continuity correction**—check whether your own A-level syllabus requires its use.

Example 1

In a survey a random sample of university students are asked whether they drink or smoke heavily, moderately, or rarely or never. The results are:

	Smoke heavily	Smoke moderately	Smoke rarely or never
Drink heavily	62	20	8
Drink moderately	38	20	5
Drink rarely or never	15	29	10

(i)   State suitable null and alternative hypotheses for a χ^2 test.

(ii) Draw up a list of expected frequencies, using the marginal frequencies. Explain why there is no need to combine any cells.

(iii) Conduct the test at the 5% level.

Solution

(i) H_0: Smoking and drinking are independent.

 H_1: They are not independent.

(ii) The marginal totals are as follows:

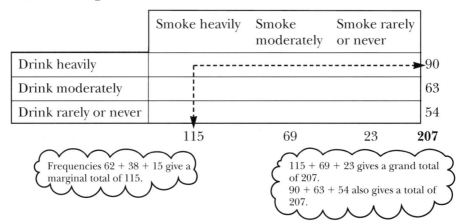

	Smoke heavily	Smoke moderately	Smoke rarely or never	
Drink heavily				90
Drink moderately				63
Drink rarely or never				54
	115	69	23	**207**

Frequencies 62 + 38 + 15 give a marginal total of 115.

115 + 69 + 23 gives a grand total of 207.
90 + 63 + 54 also gives a total of 207.

The expected frequencies are now computed as $\dfrac{115 \times 90}{207}, \dfrac{69 \times 90}{207}$ and so on to yield:

	Smoke heavily	Smoke moderately	Smoke rarely or never	
Drink heavily	50	30	10	90
Drink moderately	35	21	7	63
Drink rarely or never	30	18	6	54
	115	69	23	**207**

As all *E*s are at least 5 (the smallest is 6) there is no need to combine any cells.

(iii) Compute the test statistic

$$X^2 = \frac{(62 - 50)^2}{50} + \ldots + \frac{(10 - 6)^2}{6} = 24 \cdot 38$$

Under H_0 this is approximately χ^2 with $\nu = 4$ degrees of freedom.

From tables, $\chi^2_{\text{crit}} = 9 \cdot 488$

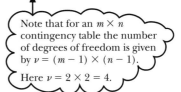

Note that for an $m \times n$ contingency table the number of degrees of freedom is given by $\nu = (m - 1) \times (n - 1)$.

Here $\nu = 2 \times 2 = 4$.

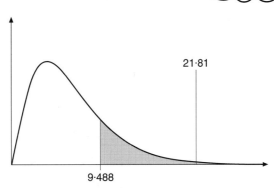

Reject H_0. Drinking and smoking do not seem to be independent.

Example 2

The pupils at a local Sixth Form College are classified as following either Arts or Science courses. The numbers of boys and girls following these courses are:

	Boys	Girls
Arts courses	45	60
Science courses	55	30

Carry out a χ^2 test at a 1% level to find out whether there is any evidence that the Arts/Science preference for boys is different from that for girls.

Solution

H_0: Arts/science preference and gender of student are independent.

H_1: They are not independent.

The marginal totals are as follows:

	Boys	Girls	
Arts courses			105
Science courses			85
	100	90	**190**

Then $\dfrac{105 \times 100}{190} = 55 \cdot 3$ and similar calculations give expected frequencies of

	Boys	Girls
Arts courses	55·3	49·7
Science courses	44·7	40·3

Compute the test statistic, using Yates' continuity correction as $\nu = 1$

$$X^2 = \frac{[(45 - 55 \cdot 3) - \frac{1}{2}]^2}{55 \cdot 3} + \ldots + \frac{[(30 - 40 \cdot 3) - \frac{1}{2}]^2}{40 \cdot 3} = 8 \cdot 201$$

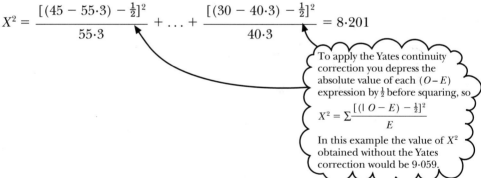

To apply the Yates continuity correction you depress the absolute value of each $(O - E)$ expression by $\frac{1}{2}$ before squaring, so

$$X^2 = \Sigma \frac{[(\mid O - E) - \frac{1}{2}]^2}{E}$$

In this example the value of X^2 obtained without the Yates correction would be 9·059.

Under H_0 this is approximately χ^2 with $\nu = 1$ degree of freedom.

From tables, $\chi^2_{\text{crit}} = 6 \cdot 635$

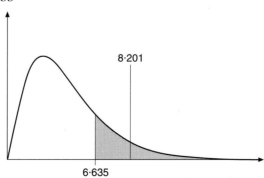

Reject H_0 in favour of H_1. There is evidence that the Arts/Science preference for boys is different from that for girls.

> The hypothesis test simply tells us there is evidence that the two factors are not independent—it **does not** go on to specify **how** the two factors are related. Often the final part of an A-level question will invite speculation on this matter.

Exercise 6.2

In questions **A1** to **A6** you are given a table of observed frequencies. For each table draw up the marginal totals, and compute the expected frequencies under the assumption that the two factors (ABC ... or PQR ...) are independent. State also the number of degrees of freedom that would be associated with the corresponding χ^2 test.

A1

	A	B	C
P	24	58	50
Q	35	80	61
R	46	51	57

A2

	A	B
P	18	42
Q	50	25
R	68	52

A3

	A	B	C	D
P	42	40	38	30
Q	42	65	39	54

A4

	A	B	C
P	12	20	23
Q	14	18	20

A5

	A	B	C
P	6	6	8
Q	22	35	23
R	12	23	25

A6

	A	B	C	D
P	10	20	40	36
Q	8	19	35	30
R	14	21	40	32

B1 A medical student is investigating the link between bedtime snacks and the occurrence of migraine. She asks a group of volunteers to eat one of three snacks at bedtime, and record whether or not a migraine attack occurs later that night. The results are:

	Type of food eaten at bedtime		
	Cheese	Chocolate	Citrus
Migraine	8	5	6
No migraine	40	59	34

(i) State suitable null and alternative hypotheses for a χ^2 test.

(ii) Carry out the χ^2 test at the 5% level of significance.

continued

B2 An off-licence carries out a survey of a random sample of its customers during the month of December. Each customer is asked to indicate their age category, and also whether their preferred drink is Beer, Wine or Spirits. The results are shown in this table:

	Age 18 to 30	Age 31 to 50	Age 51 or over
Beer	25	20	54
Wine	35	32	32
Spirits	50	48	34

The manager of the off-licence wants to see whether the preferred drink is independent of age category.

(i) State suitable null and alternative hypotheses for a χ^2 test.

(ii) Carry out the χ^2 test at the 5% level of significance.

(iii) Comment briefly on how the method of data collection affects your conclusion.

B3 A railway company decides to compare the efficiency of its services in summer and winter. A random sample of train services is taken throughout the year, and the frequencies of those on time and late are recorded:

	Summer	Winter
On time	40	26
Late	20	24

(i) State suitable null and alternative hypotheses for a χ^2 test.

(ii) Explain briefly why a Yates' continuity correction is desirable in this case.

(iii) Carry out the χ^2 test at the 5% level of significance.

B4 A small town contains three take-away restaurants, serving English, Chinese and Indian food, respectively. A local consumer group carries out a survey by randomly choosing 240 people who live in one of four residential areas, A, B, C or D, and asking which of the three restaurants they are most likely to use. The results are:

Residential area

	A	B	C	D
English	27	26	25	2
Chinese	32	18	5	5
Indian	61	16	18	5

(i) State suitable null and alternative hypotheses for a χ^2 test.

(ii) Draw up a list of expected frequencies under your null hypothesis.

(iii) Explain briefly why it would not be valid to conduct a χ^2 test on the data as it stands. Verify that the test could be conducted if columns C and D were combined into a single column.

(iv) Carry out the χ^2 test at the 5% level of significance.

B5 A mathematics teacher is investigating whether the distribution of his department's A-level grades has changed in recent years. He compiles this table of results:

Grade awarded

Year	A	B	C	D or below
1990	14	5	9	10
1993	6	5	6	17
1996	10	8	8	7

(i) State suitable null and alternative hypotheses for a χ^2 test.

(ii) Draw up a list of expected frequencies under your null hypothesis.

(iii) Explain briefly why it is not necessary to combine any rows or columns before conducting a χ^2 test on these data.

(iv) Carry out the χ^2 test at the 5% level of significance.

6.3 Chi-squared test: estimated parameters

Key points

We sometimes need to test whether a set of data appears to fit a Poisson distribution, for example, in which the value of the parameter μ is not supplied. The procedure is to calculate the **mean of the data set** and use this as an **estimate of the mean μ of the distribution**. The test then proceeds as usual, but the number of degrees of freedom ν has to be reduced by one for each estimated parameter.

Example 1

The leader of a local mountain rescue team decides to investigate whether the number of calls for help received each day follows a Poisson distribution. The number of calls received during each of 100 randomly-chosen days are as follows:

Number of calls	0	1	2	3	4	5	6 or more
Frequency	21	35	24	15	4	1	0

(i) Calculate the mean of this data set.

(ii) Construct null and alternative hypotheses based on the assumption of a Poisson distribution.

(iii) Conduct the test, at the 5% level. Explain clearly how the number of degrees of freedom is obtained.

Solution

(i) For the data set
$$\bar{x} = \frac{0 \times 21 + 1 \times 35 + 2 \times 24 + 3 \times 15 + 4 \times 4 + 5 \times 1}{100} = 1.49$$

(ii) H_0: The data may be modelled by Po(1·49).

H_1: The data may not be so modelled.

(iii) Under H_0 the expected frequencies may be computed using

$$P(X = r) = e^{-1.49} \times \frac{1.49^r}{r!}$$ and multiplying by 100, to obtain

> 100 minus the sum of all the other frequencies.

Number of calls	0	1	2	3	4	5	6 or more
Expected frequency, E	22·5	33·6	25·0	12·4	4·6	1·4	0·5

In order to maintain $E \geq 5$ it is necessary to combine the last three cells:

Number of calls		0	1	2	3	4 or more
Observed frequency, O		21	35	24	15	5
Expected frequency, E		22·5	33·6	25·0	12·4	6·5

Compute the test statistic,

$$X^2 = \frac{(21 - 22·5)^2}{22·5} + \ldots + \frac{(5 - 6·5)^2}{6·5} = 1·090$$

Under H_0 this is approximately χ^2 with $\nu = 5 - 1 - 1 = 3$ degrees of freedom (number of cells minus 1 minus an extra 1 because of the estimated parameter).

From tables, $\chi^2_{\text{crit}} = 7·815$

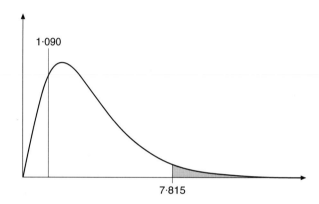

Accept H_0: The Poisson model appears to be a good one.

Example 2

When customers purchase a sound system from a certain discount warehouse they have the option of taking out an extended warranty for an extra period of 1, 2, 3 or 4 years. A sample of 180 recent sales records shows the following pattern:

Number of years of extended warranty	0	1	2	3	4
Number of customers	65	70	29	12	4

Test the hypothesis that the data may be modelled by a Binomial distribution $B(4, p)$ with the same mean as the sample. Use a 5% significance level.

Solution

The model to be tested is $B(4, p)$ where p is to be estimated from the sample.

For the data set $\bar{x} = \dfrac{0 \times 65 + 1 \times 70 + 2 \times 29 + 3 \times 12 + 4 \times 4}{180} = 1$

The mean of a Binomial distribution is np. Therefore set $np = 1$ so that $n = 4$ gives $p = \frac{1}{4}$.

H_0: The data may be modelled by $B(4, \frac{1}{4})$.

H_1: The data may not be so modelled.

Under H_0 the expected frequencies may be computed using $P(X = r) = {}^4C_r \times \left(\frac{1}{4}\right)^r \times \left(\frac{3}{4}\right)^{4-r}$ and multiplying by 180, to obtain

Number of years of extended warranty	0	1	2	3	4
Expected frequency, E	57·0	75·9	38·0	8·4	0·7

In order to maintain $E \geq 5$ it is necessary to combine the last two cells:

Number of years of extended warranty	0	1	2	3 or 4
Observed frequency, O	65	70	29	16
Expected frequency, E	57·0	75·9	38·0	9·1

Compute the test statistic,

$$X^2 = \frac{(65 - 57\cdot0)^2}{57\cdot0} + \ldots + \frac{(16 - 9\cdot1)^2}{9\cdot1} = 8\cdot945$$

Under H_0 this is approximately χ^2 with $\nu = 4 - 1 - 1 = 2$ degrees of freedom (number of cells minus 1 minus an extra 1 because of the estimated parameter).

From tables, $\chi^2_{\text{crit}} = 5\cdot991$

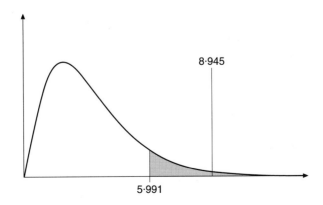

Reject H_0 in favour of H_1. The data do not appear to be consistent with a Binomial distribution.

Exercise 6.3

In questions **A1** to **A7** you are given a set of data and a suggested distribution. Calculate the mean of the data, and hence supply a suitable estimate for the missing parameter.

> Remember:
> The Poisson distribution Po(μ) has mean μ
> The Binomial distribution B(n, p) has mean np
> The Geometric distribution Geo(p) has mean $\frac{1}{p}$

A1

X	0	1	2	3	4	5 or more
Frequency	11	12	13	9	5	0

Poisson Po(μ)

A2

X	0	1	2	3	4	5	6	7 or more
Frequency	10	21	20	13	7	2	2	0

Poisson Po(μ)

A3

X	0	1	2	3
Frequency	54	54	18	2

Binomial B$(3, p)$

A4

X	1	2	3	4	5	6	7 or more
Frequency	182	56	22	6	3	1	0

Geometric Geo(p)

A5

X	0	1	2	3	4	5	6 or more
Frequency	66	75	40	13	4	2	0

Poisson Po(μ)

A6

X	1	2	3	4	5	6 or more
Frequency	180	52	12	5	1	0

Geometric Geo(p)

A7

X	0	1	2	3	4
Frequency	4	16	24	16	4

Binomial B$(4, p)$

B1 An engineering company produces components which are packed in boxes of 1000; a small number of the components contain minor defects. The company believes that the number of defective components X per box follows a Poisson distribution. A random sample of 200 boxes yields the following data:

Number of defective components, X	0	1	2	3	4	5	6 or more
Frequency	32	60	53	32	14	5	0

(i) Calculate the mean of this data set.

(ii) Construct null and alternative hypotheses for a χ^2 test, based on the assumption of a Poisson distribution.

(iii) Conduct the test at the 5% level, stating your conclusion clearly.

B2 The table shows the number of goals scored by Barchester School's First XI Hockey team in their last 120 matches:

Number of goals, X	0	1	2	3	4	5 or more
Frequency	50	44	16	8	2	0

(i) Calculate the mean of this data set.

(ii) Carry out a χ^2 test at the 5% level, to see whether the data are consistent with a Poisson distribution whose mean should be clearly stated.

B3 When racing cars stop at the pits during a motor race up to four tyres may be changed. During one season a team records its tyre changes as follows:

Number of tyres changed, X	0	1	2	3	4
Frequency	12	45	40	24	15

The team believes that the data can be modelled by a Binomial distribution B$(4, p)$.

(i) Calculate the mean of this data set, and hence determine a suitable estimate for the missing parameter p.

(ii) Construct null and alternative hypotheses for a χ^2 test.

(iii) Conduct the test at the 5% level, stating your conclusion clearly.

Exercise 6.3 *continued*

B4 The customer services desk in a large supermarket records the number of defective goods returned by its customers during one-hour periods as follows:

Number of defective items returned, X	0	1	2	3	4	5	6 or more
Frequency	40	30	12	6	1	1	0

It is suggested that the variable X is Poisson distributed.

(i) Calculate the mean of this data set.

(ii) Construct null and alternative hypotheses for a χ^2 test based on the assumption of a Poisson distribution.

(iii) Conduct the test at the 5% level, stating your conclusion clearly.

B5 The diameters of 600 beech trees are measured as follows:

Diameter (cm)	Frequency
$x < 15$	10
$15 \le x < 20$	84
$20 \le x < 25$	268
$25 \le x < 30$	205
$30 \le x$	33

The raw data had a mean of 24 cm and a standard deviation of 4 cm. You are required to carry out a χ^2 test to see if the data are consistent with a Normal distribution.

(i) Using the model $X \sim N(24, 4^2)$ show that the probability that X lies between 15 and 20 is approximately 0·146, resulting in an expected frequency of 87·9.

(ii) Construct similar expected frequencies for the other four intervals.

(iii) Explain carefully why the number of degrees of freedom for the test is only two, even though there are five pairs of cells.

(iv) Conduct the test at the 1% level, stating your conclusion clearly.

B6 The following data are thought to come from a Geometric distribution $Geo(p)$ in which probabilities are found by the expression $P(X = r) = (1 - p)^r \times p$. The mean of a Geometric distribution is $\frac{1}{p}$

X	1	2	3	4	5	6	7 or more
Frequency	62	43	28	45	25	24	0

(i) Calculate the mean of the data. Hence suggest a suitable value for the parameter p.

(ii) Using this value of p and a Geometric distribution construct a set of expected frequencies.

(iii) Carry out a χ^2 test, at the 5% significance level, to see if the data are consistent with a Geometric distribution.

B7 Six loaded dice are thrown repeatedly, and the number of fives recorded:

Number of fives, X	0	1	2	3	4	5	6
Frequency	13	35	28	14	5	3	2

It is proposed that the data can be modelled by a Binomial distribution $B(6, p)$.

(i) Calculate the mean of this data set, and hence determine a suitable estimate for the missing parameter p.

(ii) Construct null and alternative hypotheses for a χ^2 test.

(iii) Conduct the test at the 5% level, stating your conclusion clearly.

Revision questions

C1 Maria reads this headline in a national newspaper:

> Last digits in telephone numbers not random, Statistician claims!

She wants to test whether the last digit of a telephone number is truly random or not, and so Maria takes the telephone numbers of the 60 Year 12 pupils at her school, recording the last digit as follows:

Last digit	0	1	2	3	4	5	6	7	8	9
Frequency	5	7	7	4	3	7	6	7	6	8

(i) State suitable null and alternative hypotheses for a χ^2 test.

(ii) Carry out the χ^2 test at the 5% level of significance.

C2 The random variable X is thought to be Binomially distributed with parameters $n = 6$ and $p = 0.4$. The table below summarises a sample of 160 independent observations of X:

X	0	1	2	3	4	5	6
Frequency	12	27	46	41	22	7	5

(i) Assuming the Binomial model to be valid, calculate a set of corresponding expected frequencies.

(ii) Explain briefly why it is necessary to combine the last two cells in order to conduct a χ^2 goodness-of-fit test.

(iii) Carry out the test at the 5% significance level, stating your conclusion clearly.

C3 A certain newspaper contains, on average, three spelling mistakes per page.

(i) Explain why a Poisson distribution $Po(\lambda)$ might be expected to give a reasonable model for the number of errors X per page. State a suitable value for the parameter λ.

The editor records the number of errors on each of 200 pages, chosen at random from a wide selection of past issues of the paper.

(ii) Using the model from part (i) show that the expected number of pages containing exactly three mistakes is approximately 44·8.

(iii) Using the same model, complete this table of expected frequencies:

Number of errors per page	0	1	2	3	4	5+
Expected frequency				44·8		

In fact the observed results from the 200 pages were:

Number of errors per page	0	1	2	3	4	5+
Observed frequency	18	28	50	40	38	26

Carry out a χ^2 test at the 2·5% level, stating your conclusions clearly.

C4 A hotel in the west of Ireland continually surveys its customers by leaving questionnaire forms in the hotel rooms. At the end of last season the responses from American, British and German tourists were analysed, and the following frequency table shows the main reason for their visit:

Main reason for visit

	Business	Fishing	Golf	Other
American	52	36	28	39
British	42	26	23	33
German	26	22	21	24

The hotel manager wishes to investigate whether the reasons for visiting are the same for each of the three nationality groups.

(i) State suitable null and alternative hypotheses for a χ^2 test.

(ii) Carry out the χ^2 test at the 5% level of significance.

(iii) Comment briefly on the method of data collection.

C5 An estate agent has two branches, in Kentdale and Dentdale. Last month the numbers of houses sold to first-time and second-time buyers were as follows:

	First-time buyers	Second-time buyers
Kentdale branch	24	26
Dentdale branch	26	49

Carry out a χ^2 test to examine whether there is any evidence that the distribution of sales to first- and second-time buyers is different at the two branches.

C6 My office photocopying machine is getting quite old now, and seems to jam almost every day. To measure its reliability I record the number of jams per day over a three-month period as follows:

Number of jams per day	0	1	2	3	4	5 or more
Frequency	17	23	14	3	3	0

(i) Calculate the mean number of jams per day from these data.

(ii) Carry out a χ^2 test to see whether there is any evidence that the number of jams per day follows a Poisson distribution. Use a 5% significance level.

C7 At the end of a first-aid training course, the 80 candidates are given five tests. The numbers of tests successfully passed by each candidate are as follows:

Number of tests passed	0	1	2	3	4	5
Frequency	14	25	31	8	1	1

(i) Calculate the mean number of passes per candidate from this data.

(ii) Carry out a χ^2 test to see whether there is any evidence, at the 5% level, that the number of passes per candidate follows a Binomial distribution B$(5, p)$.

C8 A shop carries out a survey of all customers who purchase CDs during a given month. From the survey a random sample of responses is chosen, and the age of the customer and type of CD is noted as in the frequency table below:

	Type of CD			
	Classical	Rock/Pop	Jazz	Other
Age 16–25	23	55	16	14
Age 26–35	23	30	12	7
Age over 35	9	3	5	1

(i) Construct a set of expected frequencies under the hypothesis that age and type of purchase are independent.

(ii) Explain why it would be helpful to merge the third and fourth columns before carrying out a χ^2 test.

(iii) Perform a χ^2 test at the 5% significance level. State your hypotheses and conclusion clearly.

C9 Susan likes to play Monopoly™, in which two dice are thrown together at each turn She notices that a total score of, say, 6 or 7 is far more likely than a total of, say, 2 or 3.

(i) Make a copy of this sample space diagram and fill in the missing total scores.

	1	2	3	4	5	6
1	2	3	4			
2	3	4				
3						
4						
5						
6						

Susan decides to record the results of 180 throws of the pair of dice.

(ii) Copy and complete this list of expected frequencies, using the sample space diagram from part (i):

Total	2	3	4	5	6	7	8	9	10	11	12
Expected frequency	5					20					

In fact Susan's results were:

Total	2	3	4	5	6	7	8	9	10	11	12
Observed frequency	4	9	16	18	27	30	25	19	19	7	6

(iii) Carry out a χ^2 test at the 5% level, stating your hypotheses and conclusions clearly.

C10 The weights of 200 adult fish of a certain species are summarised in the table below:

Weight (grams)	Frequency
$x < 700$	8
$700 \leq x < 750$	25
$750 \leq x < 800$	45
$800 \leq x < 850$	52
$850 \leq x < 900$	38
$900 \leq x < 950$	18
$950 \leq x$	14

(i) Give two distinct mathematical reasons why it is difficult to calculate the mean and standard deviation of these weights without access to the original raw data.

In fact the mean and standard deviation of the raw data were 825 grams and 80 grams respectively.

(ii) Fit an appropriate Normal distribution to the given data to produce a list of expected frequencies, and examine the goodness-of-fit using a χ^2 test at the 5% level. Explain carefully how you decided on the number of degrees of freedom for the test.

Chapter 7

BIVARIATE ANALYSIS

7.1 Scatter diagrams and regression lines

Key points

In this chapter we will study **bivariate quantities**, i.e. quantities consisting of pairs of data, such as:
- the day of the week and the height of a sunflower
- scores in a French test and a German test.

A **scatter diagram** is an (x, y) plot of bivariate data. If there is an underlying linear relationship, then we can calculate the equation of the regression line of y on x. This calculation assumes that the x-values are controlled but the y-values are subject to random variation above and below the underlying linear relationship; this kind of situation is known as **random on non-random**.

The **gradient**, b, of the regression line may be calculated as

$$b = \frac{s_{xy}}{s_x^2} \text{ where } s_{xy} = \frac{1}{n}\sum x_i y_i - \bar{x} \cdot \bar{y} \text{ and } s_x^2 = \frac{1}{n}\sum x_i^2 - \bar{x}^2$$

The **intercept**, a, may then be deduced from the fact that

the regression line of y on x always passes through the mean point $(\bar{x}, \bar{y})$.

Many scientific calculators (not just graphics models) have a facility to calculate the equation of a regression line. This is usually accomplished in LR mode or STAT mode; after entering the data pairs you can read out the values of a and b, and also the pmcc r (see Section 7.2).

Exam boards usually penalise you if you rely exclusively on your calculator's LR statistical functions. The best approach is to solve the question by showing all the working anyway, and use the calculator's LR mode as a check.

A very common situation is that in which neither of the variables is controlled; both x and y are random. Provided they are also Normally distributed it turns out that the same form of the regression line applies (though for different reasons). This situation is known as **random on random**.

Example 1

The height of a seedling is measured at daily intervals as in the table:

Day number, x	1	2	3	4	5	6	7
Height, y, mm	5	7	8	11	12	14	13

(i)   Explain briefly why these data can be described as random on non-random.

(ii) Plot the data on a scatter diagram.

(iii) Calculate the equation of the regression line of y on x, and plot this line on your scatter diagram.

(iv) Explain briefly whether you think it would be wise to use your graph to predict the height of the seedling on day 8.

Solution

(i)   The day number is a controlled variable, while the height is dependent on the day, so this situation is random on non-random.

(ii)
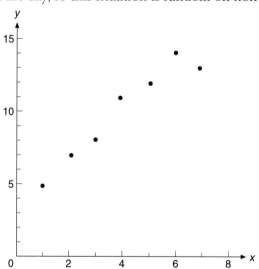

(iii) Tabulating the data:

x	x^2	y	xy
1	1	5	5
2	4	7	14
3	9	8	24
4	16	11	44
5	25	12	60
6	36	14	84
7	49	13	91
Σ 28	140	70	322

$\bar{x} = 28 \div 7 = 4$ and $\bar{y} = 70 \div 7 = 10$ so the mean point $(\bar{x}, \bar{y})$ is $(4, 10)$

$$s_{xy} = \frac{1}{n}\Sigma x_i y_i - \bar{x} \cdot \bar{y} \qquad\qquad s_x^2 = \frac{1}{n}\Sigma x_i^2 - \bar{x}^2$$

> The mean point is computed first ...

$$= \frac{1}{7} \times 322 - 4 \times 10 \qquad\qquad = \frac{1}{7} \times 140 - 4^2$$

> ... then s_{xy} and s_x^2 ...

$$= 6 \qquad\qquad\qquad\qquad\qquad = 4$$

> ... and then b.

$$\therefore b = \frac{s_{xy}}{s_x^2} = \frac{6}{4} = \frac{3}{2}$$

The equation of the regression line is $y = a + \frac{3}{2}x$.

This passes through $(4, 10)$ so $10 = a + \frac{3}{2} \times 4$, giving $a = 4$.

The required regression line is $y = 4 + \frac{3}{2}x$.

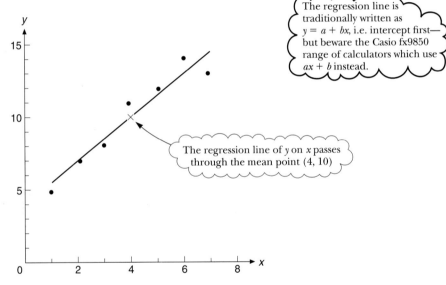

> The regression line is traditionally written as $y = a + bx$, i.e. intercept first— but beware the Casio fx9850 range of calculators which use $ax + b$ instead.

> The regression line of y on x passes through the mean point $(4, 10)$

(iv) It would not be wise to use the graph to predict the value of y when $x = 8$ as this lies beyond the end of the range of the data set. The scatter graph seems to suggest that the linear relationship might be unreliable beyond $x = 7$.

Exercise 7.1

In questions **A1** to **A5** draw a scatter diagram and calculate the regression line of y on x in each case.

A1

x	1	2	3	4	5	6
y	10	15	18	25	28	34

A2

x	10	15	20	25	30	35	40
y	99	94	90	82	79	80	71

A3

x	7	14	21	28	35
y	25	23	20	21	17

Exercise 7.1   *continued*

A4

x	30	35	40	45	50	55	60	65
y	5·1	5·6	6·0	6·1	7·1	7·8	8·6	9·0

A5

x	8	10	12	14	16	18	20
y	14·6	16·3	18·5	21·0	22·4	24·9	26·5

In questions **A6** to **A10** state whether you think the relationship between y and x is random on non-random or random on random, and calculate the equation of the regression line of y on x in each case. (To assist in the calculation of the regression line you are given relevant summary statistics.)

A6

Latitude of town, $x°$	6	17	23	44	45	70	73
Maximum temperature, $y°C$	44	41	36	29	31	15	12

$n = 7$, $\Sigma x = 278$, $\Sigma y = 208$, $\Sigma x^2 = 15\,044$, $\Sigma xy = 6386$

A7

Mass of adult dog, x kg	3·2	5·0	5·9	7·5	6·4	4·6
Tail length of adult dog, y cm	6·0	8·0	7·5	8·9	7·9	7·1

$n = 6$, $\Sigma x = 32·6$, $\Sigma y = 45·4$, $\Sigma x^2 = 188·42$, $\Sigma xy = 253·42$

A8

Latitude of town, $x°$	0	10	20	30	40	50	60
Maximum temperature, $y°C$	44	40	35	37	30	26	21

$n = 7$, $\Sigma x = 210$, $\Sigma y = 233$, $\Sigma x^2 = 9100$, $\Sigma xy = 5970$

A9

Elapsed time, x minutes	0	2	4	6	8	10	12	14
Temperature of liquid, $y°C$	100	92	84	78	69	59	50	45

$n = 8$, $\Sigma x = 56$, $\Sigma y = 577$, $\Sigma x^2 = 560$, $\Sigma xy = 3360$

A10

Actual wind speed, x mph	23	27	44	51	55	68
Measured wind speed, y mph	20	25	43	50	52	60

$n = 6$, $\Sigma x = 268$, $\Sigma y = 250$, $\Sigma x^2 = 13\,444$, $\Sigma xy = 12\,517$

B1   In an electroplating experiment the thickness of the coating is measured at regular time intervals as in the table:

Time, t minutes	0	20	40	60	80	100	120
Thickness, y microns	0	4	7	12	16	18	22

(i)   Calculate the equation of the regression line of y on t.

(ii)   Use your equation to estimate the thickness of the coating after 30 minutes.

B2   Nine of the couples in a local dance group are married. The ages of each couple when they got married were as follows:

Couple	A	B	C	D	E	F	G	H	I
Age, x, of husband	22	23	27	27	28	31	33	34	41
Age, y, of wife	23	21	25	26	31	31	32	30	29

(i)   Plot these data on a scatter diagram.

(ii)   Given that $n = 9$, $\Sigma x = 266$, $\Sigma y = 248$, $\Sigma x^2 = 8142$, $\Sigma xy = 7460$ find the equation of the regression line of y on x.

(iii)   Plot this regression line on your scatter diagram.

B3   In a class cookery lesson large numbers of chocolate chip cookies are made. A random sample of eight cookies is taken, and the number of chocolate chips is counted:

Exercise 7.1 *continued*

Mass, x grams	23 31 44 45 47 52 55 56
Number of chocolate chips, y	10 17 20 22 21 29 28 33

(i) Given that $n = 8$, $\Sigma x = 353$, $\Sigma y = 180$, $\Sigma x^2 = 16\,525$, $\Sigma xy = 8510$ find the equation of the regression line of y on x.

(ii) Another cookie has a mass of 38 grams. Use your regression line to estimate the number of chocolate chips it contains.

B4 Seven college students take exams in French and German:

Student	A	B	C	D	E	F	G
French score, x	21	41	55	58	61	67	80
German score, y	31	50	57	66	abs	80	87

Student E was absent on the day of the German exam.

(i) Plot the six complete data pairs on a scatter diagram.

(ii) Given that $n = 6$, $\Sigma x = 322$, $\Sigma y = 371$, $\Sigma x^2 = 19\,400$, $\Sigma xy = 21\,984$ find the equation of the regression line of y on x, and plot this regression line on your scatter diagram.

(iii) Use your calculated regression line to estimate the German score which student E might have achieved.

B5 A tyre designer measures the pressure of a tyre when it is cold (12 °C) and at a controlled series of warmer temperatures, as given in the following table:

Couple	A	B	C	D	E	F
Temperature, x °C	12	17	22	27	32	37
Pressure, y bars	2·000	2·041	2·072	2·103	2·135	2·175

(i) Given that $n = 6$, $\Sigma x = 147$, $\Sigma y = 12\cdot526$, $\Sigma x^2 = 4039$, $\Sigma xy = 309\cdot857$ find the equation of the regression line of y on x.

(ii) The tyre designer uses this regression line to estimate the value of the tyre pressure at a temperature of 47 °C. Calculate this estimate, correct to 3 decimal places.

(iii) Explain briefly why it is unwise for the tyre designer to rely on this estimate.

B6 A physics experiment is designed to measure the acceleration, g, due to gravity. Values of x and y are measured, and the gradient of the line of best fit is supposed to be the required value of g. The results are summarised as follows:

$n = 8$, $\Sigma x = 42$, $\Sigma y = 409$, $\Sigma x^2 = 364$, $\Sigma xy = 3566$.

Find the equation of the regression line of y on x. Hence state an estimate for the value of the constant g.

7.2 Product–moment correlation coefficient

Key points

It is not always reasonable to assume that there is a linear relationship between two variables x and y. The **degree of linearity** is measured by a statistic known as the product–moment correlation coefficient.

The **product–moment correlation coefficient** or **pmcc** of a data set is usually denoted by a small Roman letter r. The data set may often be thought of as a sample from a larger population, the population pmcc being denoted by a Greek letter rho, ρ.

The value of a pmcc always lies between -1 and $+1$. A value of $+1$ indicates perfect positive correlation; the points all lie exactly on a straight line with positive gradient. As the pmcc decreases from $+1$ towards 0 the points exhibit more scatter, until $r = 0$ indicates no correlation at all. Negative values of r indicate negative correlation, i.e. the line of best fit has negative gradient.

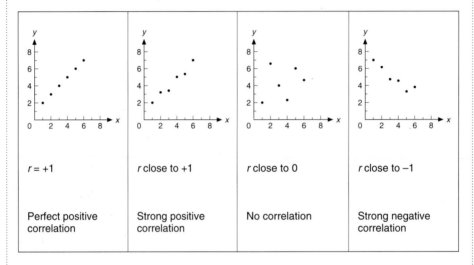

$r = +1$	r close to $+1$	r close to 0	r close to -1
Perfect positive correlation	Strong positive correlation	No correlation	Strong negative correlation

To calculate the value of a product–moment correlation coefficient it is first of all necessary to find these three quantities:

$$s_x^2 = \frac{1}{n}\Sigma x_i^2 - \bar{x}^2 \qquad s_y^2 = \frac{1}{n}\Sigma y_i^2 - \bar{y}^2 \qquad s_{xy} = \frac{1}{n}\Sigma x_i y_i - \bar{x} \cdot \bar{y}$$

Then the product–moment correlation coefficient r is

$$r = \frac{s_{xy}}{s_x \cdot s_y}$$

The pmcc is **independent of the scale of measurement**—if the variables are rescaled in a linear way then the value of the pmcc does not change.

Example 1

The height of a seedling is measured at daily intervals:

Day number, x	1	2	3	4	5	6	7
Height y, mm		5	7	8	11	12	14	13

$n = 7$, $\Sigma x = 28$, $\Sigma y = 70$, $\Sigma x^2 = 140$, $\Sigma y^2 = 768$, $\Sigma xy = 322$.

Calculate the value of the product–moment correlation coefficient.

Solution

$s_x^2 = \frac{1}{7} \times 140 - (\frac{28}{7})^2 = 20 - 16 = 4$

$s_y^2 = \frac{1}{7} \times 768 - (\frac{70}{7})^2 = 109\frac{5}{7} - 100 = 9\frac{5}{7}$

$s_{xy} = \frac{1}{7} \times 322 - (\frac{28}{7}) \times (\frac{70}{7}) = 46 - 40 = 6$

$\therefore r = \dfrac{s_{xy}}{s_x \cdot s_y} = \dfrac{6}{\sqrt{4} \times \sqrt{9\frac{5}{7}}} = 0.9625$ (to 4 decimal places)

To assess the significance of a correlation coefficient we can conduct a hypothesis test. The null hypothesis will always be that there is no correlation, so the population pmcc $\rho = 0$. The alternative hypothesis might be that $\rho > 0$ (one tail), $\rho < 0$ (one tail), or $\rho \neq 0$ (two tail). Critical values may be found from tables. Make sure that you do not accidentally use Spearman tables though, they look very similar!

Example 2

Ten volunteers are asked to perform a simple timed mental task in silence. They are then given a similar problem which is performed under a high level of background noise. The results are as follows:

Volunteer number	1	2	3	4	5	6	7	8	9	10
Time, x (silence)	23	24	26	27	30	35	36	42	45	47
Time, y (noise)	28	23	35	21	27	37	19	32	48	43

$n = 10, \Sigma x = 335, \Sigma y = 313, \Sigma x^2 = 11\,929, \Sigma y^2 = 10\,615, \Sigma xy = 10\,987$.

(i)   Calculate the product–moment correlation coefficient.

(ii) Conduct a hypothesis test to see whether there is any evidence of correlation between the two times. Use a 5% test.

Solution

(i) $s_x^2 = \frac{1}{10} \times 11\,929 - (\frac{335}{10})^2 = 1192.9 - 1122.25 = 70.65$

$s_y^2 = \frac{1}{10} \times 10\,615 - (\frac{313}{10})^2 = 1061.5 - 979.69 = 81.81$

$s_{xy} = \frac{1}{10} \times 10\,987 - (\frac{335}{10}) \times (\frac{313}{10}) = 1098.7 - 1048.55 = 50.15$

$\therefore r = \dfrac{s_{xy}}{s_x \cdot s_y} = \dfrac{50.15}{\sqrt{70.65} \times \sqrt{81.81}} = 0.6596$ (4 decimal places)

(ii) H_0: No correlation $\rho = 0$

H_1: Some correlation $\rho \neq 0$

Two-tail 5% test

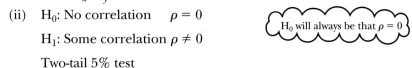

H_0 will always be that $\rho = 0$

From tables, $r_{crit} = \pm0.6319$

Reject H_0. There is evidence of correlation between the two times.

Exercise 7.2

In questions **A1** to **A5** calculate the value of the pmcc for the given data set.

A1

x	1	2	3	4	5	6	7
y	5	7	13	11	14	15	19

A2

x	10	12	19	23	31	45	50	51
y	14	33	51	35	18	40	35	48

A3

x	3	7	8	8	9	14	17	21	22
y	50	47	34	43	16	51	33	22	33

A4

x	1.3	4.9	8.7	10.1
y	55	64	63	70

A5

x	5	10	15	20	25	30	35	40	45	50
y	100	32	68	21	40	54	38	28	45	50

B1 Felicity records the number of hot drinks sold per hour, and the temperature outside, on a random sample of eight occasions at her coffee shop:

Outside temperature, $x\,°C$	15	13	8	11	15	7	9	10
Number of hot drinks sold, y	10	13	26	17	14	23	25	19

$n = 8$, $\Sigma x = 88$, $\Sigma y = 147$, $\Sigma x^2 = 1034$, $\Sigma y^2 = 2945$, $\Sigma xy = 1500$.

(i) Calculate the pmcc for these data.

(ii) Felicity suspects that the temperature and drinks sales exhibit negative linear correlation. Conduct a hypothesis test to see whether the data support her suspicion. Use a 5% significance level.

B2 Eight of the children in Class 3 record the distance they travel to school each day and the time taken for the journey:

Child	A	B	C	D	E	F	G	H
Distance, x km	0.3	1.5	1.9	2.1	2.2	2.3	2.5	3.5
Time, y minutes	6	5	8	10	13	7	10	14

$n = 8$, $\Sigma x = 16.3$, $\Sigma y = 73$, $\Sigma x^2 = 38.99$, $\Sigma y^2 = 739$, $\Sigma xy = 164.2$.

(i) Calculate the pmcc for these data.

(ii) The children decide that Child A's data should be discarded from the data set in order to improve the correlation between distance and time. Suggest one reason why it might be sensible to do this, using values from the table to support your suggestion.

(iii) Calculate the pmcc for the seven children with Child A's data removed.

B3 A garage carries out a survey of new car buyers who also own their own homes. From the responses, a random sample of size 15 is taken. The value of each person's home, £x thousands, and the cost of their new car, £y thousands, are recorded to the nearest thousand pounds, and may be summarised by the following statistics:

$n = 15, \Sigma x = 1312, \Sigma y = 166,$
$\Sigma x^2 = 142\,248, \Sigma y^2 = 2094, \Sigma xy = 14\,679.$

(i) Calculate the pmcc for these data.

(ii) Conduct a hypothesis test, at the 5% significance level, to see whether there is any evidence of a linear correlation between the cost of a home and the cost of a car.

B4 Eight students at a sixth form college take part in a set of tests to evaluate their key skills in the three areas of numeracy, literacy and information technology. Their standardised scores are:

Numeracy score, x	40	48	52	56	58	63	77	90
Literacy score, y	80	36	55	70	35	22	81	70
IT score, z	50	52	47	68	50	88	73	71

(i) Compute the value of a suitable pmcc in order to assess whether there is any correlation between the numeracy scores and the literacy scores.

(ii) Compute the value of a suitable pmcc in order to assess whether there is any correlation between the numeracy scores and the IT scores.

(iii) Conduct hypothesis tests, at the 5% level, on each of the correlation coefficients you have obtained, and summarise your conclusions in plain English.

B5 My local car park has just revised its prices. The new scale is given in the table:

Time of stay, x hours	1	2	3	4	5	6
Cost of stay, y pence		40	70	100	200	250	400

(i) Calculate the value of the pmcc.

(ii) Conduct a hypothesis test to see whether there is any evidence of positive linear correlation between the time of stay and the cost. Use a 5% test.

B6 Nine A-level students compare their predicted UCAS points total with the totals they actually achieve:

Predicted points, x	14	14	16	18	18	18	22	28	30
Actual points, y	10	14	18	22	10	12	24	20	28

$n = 9, \Sigma x = 178, \Sigma y = 158, \Sigma x^2 = 3788,$
$\Sigma y^2 = 3108, \Sigma xy = 3344.$

(i) Calculate the value of the pmcc.

(ii) Conduct a hypothesis test to see whether there is any evidence of positive correlation between the predicted totals and those actually achieved. Use a 5% test.

7.3 The Spearman rank correlation coefficient

Key points

We use **Spearman** when the data are supplied as rank values only, or when we suspect that there is a non-linear correlation between the two variables, x and y. Once the coefficient has been calculated, it can be tested for significance in a similar way to the pmcc. Make sure you use the right tables—the critical values for pmcc and Spearman are usually very close to each other.

The Spearman rank correlation coefficient of a data set is usually denoted by the symbol r_s, the suffix s reminds us that this is Spearman, not pmcc. The corresponding population coefficient is denoted by ρ_s.

To compute a Spearman rank correlation coefficient for a data set, you need to follow these steps:
- **Step 1** Rank the data (if they have not already been ranked)
- **Step 2** List the differences, d, between matching pairs of ranks
- **Step 3** Square these to obtain values of d^2
- **Step 4** Sum them to obtain $\sum d^2$
- **Step 5** Compute the Spearman coefficient

$$r_s = 1 - \frac{6 \times \sum d^2}{n(n^2 - 1)}$$

- **Step 6** Conduct a hypothesis test, if required.

Example 1

Two judges, A and B, rank the competitors in the final of a television cookery competition. They taste the dishes prepared by the eight competitors, and place them in order of merit:

Competitor	A	B	C	D	E	F	G	H
Judge A	1	2	3	4	5	6	7	8
Judge B	3	5	2	8	1	4	7	6

(i) Calculate the Spearman rank correlation coefficient for the data set.

(ii) Conduct a hypothesis test to see whether there is any evidence that the two judges' rank orders are positively correlated. Use a 5% test.

Solution

(i) The data is already ranked, so compute differences:

Competitor	A	B	C	D	E	F	G	H
Judge A	1	2	3	4	5	6	7	8
Judge B	3	5	2	8	1	4	7	6
Difference, d	-2	-3	1	-4	4	2	0	2
d^2	4	9	1	16	16	4	0	4

$\sum d^2 = 54$

Then $r_s = 1 - \dfrac{6 \times 54}{8 \times 63} = 0{\cdot}3571$

(ii) H_0: No correlation, $\rho_s = 0$

H$_1$: Positive correlation, $\rho_s > 0$. One-tail 5% test

From tables $r_{s \, crit} = 0.6429$

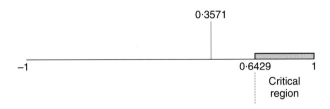

0.3571

−1

0.6429   1

Critical
region

Accept H_0. There is no evidence of correlation between the judges' rankings.

Example 2

A medical student is investigating the possible beneficial effect of regular exercise. From a large database, she selects seven random individuals, and notes the following data about them:

Average number of hours regular exercise per week, x	3	8	4	11	2	3	6
Number of visits to the doctor over the last five years, y	10	4	8	0	3	6	2

(i)   Calculate the Spearman rank correlation coefficient for these data.

(ii)   Conduct a hypothesis test, at the 5% level, to see whether the data provide any evidence that people who do more exercise are less likely to visit the doctor.

Solution

(i)   The data must be ranked first:

> The values which would have taken ranks 2 and 3 have tied in second place, so the total rank available, 5, is shared between them. Questions on tied ranks don't usually come up in exams, but you'll meet them when you work with real data, e.g. projects.

Rank, x	2.5	6	4	7	1	2.5	5
Rank, y	7	4	6	1	3	5	2
Difference, d	−4.5	2	−2	6	2	−2.5	3
d^2	20.25	4	4	36	4	6.25	9

$\sum d^2 = 83.5$

Then $r_s = 1 - \dfrac{6 \times 83.5}{7 \times 48} = -0.4911$

147

(ii) H_0: No correlation, $\rho_s = 0$

H_1: Negative correlation, $\rho_s < 0$. One-tail 5% test

From tables $r_{s\ crit} = -0.7143$

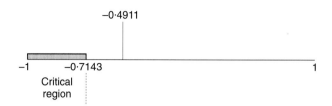

−0.4911

−1   −0.7143   1

Critical
region

Accept H_0. There is no evidence that people who do more exercise are less likely to visit the doctor.

Exercise 7.3

In questions **A1** to **A5** calculate the Spearman coefficient for the given ranks.

A1

x	1	2	3	4	5	6	7
y	3	1	5	4	7	2	6

A2

x	1	2	3	4	5	6	7	8
y	6	1	4	7	5	2	8	3

A3

x	1	2	3	4	5	6	7	8	9
y	9	8	4	6	2	3	7	1	5

A4

x	1	2	3	4
y	4	3	2	1

A5

x	1	2	3	4	5	6	7	8	9	10
y	1	9	5	3	10	7	6	2	8	4

In questions **A6** to **A10** redraw the table to show the ranks of the data, then calculate the Spearman rank correlation coefficient.

A6

x	12	14	17	23	24	28	30
y	21	27	28	40	24	34	31

A7

x	15	18	21	24	27	30	33	36
y	30	28	17	22	19	25	14	25

Watch out for the tied ranks here!

A8

x	1	2	3	4	5	6	7
y	14	17	19	23	22	15	25

A9

x	2.4	3.1	5.8	7.0	7.3	9.5
y	12.1	9.7	5.8	6.1	5.1	7.2

A10

x	7	22	14	25	42	15	35	10	19	31
y	1	10	4	11	16	6	15	2	8	13

B1   I notice that not all the CDs in my collection have the same number of tracks. To investigate this further, I take a random selection of CDs, and note the number of tracks and the length of the longest track:

Number of tracks	6	12	10	13	11	18	17
Longest track, mins:secs	5:54	4:06	6:26	5:00	6:07	5:51	7:10

Exercise 7.3 *continued*

(i) Rank the data.

(ii) Calculate the value of the Spearman rank correlation coefficient.

(iii) Conduct a hypothesis test, at the 5% level of significance, to see whether there is evidence of any correlation between the number of tracks and the length of the longest track.

B2 Martina lives within walking distance of two local Chinese take-aways. She decides to compare their prices by taking a random selection of dishes and noting the price in each restaurant:

Dish	A	B	C	D	E	F	G
Price at 'The Slow Boat', £	0·99	1·99	2·45	2·95	3·40	3·99	4·25
Price at 'The Sizzling Wok', £	0·80	1·95	1·90	2·85	2·40	2·60	3·30

(i) Rank the data.

(ii) Calculate the value of the Spearman rank correlation coefficient. Conduct a hypothesis test, at the 5% level of significance, to see whether the data provide any evidence that those dishes which are more expensive at one restaurant are also more expensive at the other.

(iii) Martina's father says 'It is obvious from your data that "The Sizzling Wok" is better value.' Give one reason why he might be wrong.

B3 In an ice-skating competition the judges have to rank the ten finalists in order of merit for both Technical Quality and Artistic Interpretation. The orders are:

Skater	A	B	C	D	E	F	G	H	I	J
Technical Quality	1	7	3	9	6	2	10	4	8	5
Artistic Interpretation	4	5	1	7	10	6	8	3	9	2

(i) Calculate the value of the Spearman rank correlation coefficient.

(ii) Test the coefficient, at the 10% level of significance, to see whether there is evidence of any correlation between the order of merit for Technical Quality and that for Artistic Interpretation.

B4 Twelve teachers attended a first-aid course. At the end they were given a Theory test and a Practical test. Their scores were:

Teacher	A	B	C	D	E	F	G	H	I	J	K	L
Theory	57	72	91	71	75	77	88	85	59	81	80	63
Practical	52	70	49	56	46	86	59	x	55	81	63	44

(i) Teacher H fainted during the Practical test and was unable to complete it. Rank the data for the remaining 11 teachers, and calculate the value of Spearman's rank correlation coefficient.

(ii) Conduct a hypothesis test, at the 5% level of significance, to see whether there is any evidence that higher scores in the Theory test correspond with higher scores in the Practical.

B5 Eight meteorites are dated by two different processes, and their ages are ranked (1 = oldest, 8 = youngest) as follows:

Meteorite	A	B	C	D	E	F	G	H
Age (Process A)	1	4	3	7	5	2	6	8
Age (Process B)	2	3	6	8	4	1	5	7

(i) Calculate the value of the Spearman rank correlation coefficient.

(ii) Conduct a hypothesis test, at the 5% level of significance, to see whether there is any evidence of positive correlation between the rank orders obtained by the two processes.

Revision questions

C1 The table shows approximate figures for the world's population at 100-year intervals:

Year	1500	1600	1700	1800	1900
Years, x, since 1500	0	100	200	300	400
Population, y millions	425	545	610	900	1625

(i) Plot the points on a scatter diagram.

(ii) Calculate the equation of the least squares regression line of y on x, and draw this line on your scatter diagram.

(iii) Use your regression line to predict approximate values for the world's population in (a) 1650 and (b) 1950.

(iv) In fact, the world's population in 1950 was about 2500 million. Explain briefly why your prediction in (iii) does not agree very well with this figure.

C2 It is said that the ancient Egyptians thought that the length from a person's elbow to their wrist is the same as the length of their foot. Here are the results of measuring a random sample of nine people:

Elbow–wrist length, x cm	21	22	22	24	25	27	27	29	31
Length of foot, y cm	21	21	23	23	24	26	27	28	29

(i) Calculate the pmcc for these data.

(ii) Conduct a hypothesis test to see whether the data provide significant evidence of positive correlation between elbow–wrist length and length of foot. Use a 1% significance level.

(iii) Calculate the equation of the least squares regression line of y on x.

(iv) Use your regression line to predict the length of foot for a person whose elbow–wrist length is 26 cm.

C3 Lois has an old video recorder, and wants to calibrate the counter. She thinks that there should be a linear relationship between the reading on the counter and the time for which the tape has been playing. She notes the following values:

Playing time, x minutes	0	20	40	60	80	100	120
Reading on counter, y	0	500	961	1352	1697	2000	2241

$n = 7$, $\Sigma x = 420$, $\Sigma y = 8751$, $\Sigma x^2 = 36\,400$, $\Sigma y^2 = 14\,903\,000$, $\Sigma xy = 734\,240$.

(i) Calculate the pmcc for these data.

(ii) State suitable null and alternative hypotheses for a hypothesis test to see whether the data provide evidence of positive linear correlation between x and y.

(iii) Conduct the test at the 5% significance level, stating the conclusion clearly.

(iv) Calculate the equation of the least squares regression line of y on x. Explain briefly why Lois should not use this line to predict the counter value at the end of a three-hour video tape.

C4 To test the belief that tall men also tend to be heavy, a researcher collects the following random sample of data:

Height, x cm	155	168	173	178	183	186	188	191
Weight, w kg	70	66	61	86	82	90	87	68

(i) Calculate the Spearman rank correlation coefficient for these data.

(ii) Conduct an appropriate hypothesis test, at the 5% level.

(iii) Explain briefly why a Spearman coefficient is more appropriate than a product–moment correlation coefficient in this case.

Revision questions *continued*

C5 The following results are obtained in an experiment:

x	1	4	5	6	8	9	10	11	12	13
y	1	2	4	3	5	9	8	12	18	17

(i) Plot the data on an (x, y) scatter diagram.

(ii) If you think the trend of the points is approximately linear then calculate the product–moment correlation coefficient; if not, calculate Spearman's rank correlation coefficient.

(iii) Conduct an appropriate hypothesis test on your coefficient, to see whether it provides significant evidence of positive correlation (either linear or rank) between x and y. Use a 5% significance level.

C6 Sean and Debbie are moderating some mathematics coursework tasks. They each look at the same 12 pieces of work, and place them in order of merit:

Piece of work	Order (Sean)	Order (Debbie)
A	1	4
B	8	8
C	5	5
D	6	7
E	2	1
F	12	12
G	9	11
H	3	3
I	10	10
J	7	6
K	11	9
L	4	2

(i) Explain why it would be inappropriate to calculate a product–moment correlation coefficient for these data.

(ii) Calculate the value of Spearman's rank correlation coefficient.

(iii) Conduct a formal hypothesis test to see whether the apparent agreement between their orders of merit is significant at the 1% level. State your conclusion in plain English.

C7 A sample of 30 data points may be summarised as follows:

$n = 30$, $\Sigma x = 1140$, $\Sigma y = 1110$,
$\Sigma x^2 = 1\,299\,600$, $\Sigma y^2 = 1\,232\,100$,
$\Sigma xy = 42\,937$

(i) Calculate the value of the product–moment correlation coefficient.

(ii) Carry out a hypothesis test, at the 5% level, to see whether there is any evidence of correlation between the two variables.

A second sample of 20 data points is summarised as follows:

$n = 20$, $\Sigma x = 810$, $\Sigma y = 790$, $\Sigma x^2 = 872\,450$,
$\Sigma y^2 = 856\,200$, $\Sigma xy = 29\,244$

(iii) Calculate the value of the product–moment correlation coefficient for the combined set of all 50 points.

C8 Explain what is meant by saying that the value of a product–moment correlation coefficient is independent of the scale of measurement.

Peter and Sonia are working together on a chemistry practical task. Peter notes the time taken for a certain reaction to occur at different temperatures:

Temperature, T °C	5	15	25	35	45	55	65	75	85
Time, t minutes			30	29	27	24	20	18	17	18	20

(i) Calculate the value of the product–moment correlation coefficient for Peter's data.

(ii) Conduct a hypothesis test to see whether there is significant evidence (at the 2.5% level) of a negative linear correlation between temperature and reaction time.

Sonia has recorded the same information as Peter, but she has expressed the temperature in °F and the time in seconds.

(iii) Explain, with a reason, whether you would expect the value of the product–moment correlation coefficient for Sonia's data to be greater, smaller or the same as that calculated from Peter's data.

C9 A local council is investigating whether older houses cost more to maintain than newer ones. A random sample of houses is taken, and for each house the age is recorded, along with the amount spent on it by the council within the last two years:

Age of house, T years	3	5	6	6	7	9	12	14	20
Amount spent, £x hundreds	0	4	3	1	12	3	8	5	10

(i) Calculate the value of the Spearman rank correlation coefficient for this data.

(ii) Conduct a hypothesis test to see whether there is significant evidence (at the 5% level) that older houses cost more to maintain.

(iii) Explain briefly why the Spearman coefficient is preferable to the product–moment correlation coefficient in this context.

C10 David and Mike are reading a statistics textbook, and they find the following result:

> When the sample size n is large, the critical value r (two-tail, 5%) for a product–moment correlation coefficient will, to a good approximation, satisfy the equation:
>
> $$r \times \sqrt{\frac{n-2}{1-r^2}} = 1.960$$

(i) Show that $r = 0.2492$ is an approximate solution to this equation when $n = 60$. Show also that this approximate value has a relative error of about 2% when compared with the tabulated value of 0.2542.

(ii) David analyses 90 data points, and calculates a sample value of $r = 0.1832$. Use trial and improvement to deduce an approximate value for r_{crit}, and hence say whether David's test value provides significant evidence of correlation at the 5% level.

(iii) Mike has calculated a Spearman rank correlation coefficient for a sample of size $n = 150$. He intends to conduct a hypothesis test using a critical product–moment correlation coefficient value deduced from the formula given above. Explain briefly whether you think this approach is justified.

Chapter 8

NON-PARAMETRIC TESTS

Key points

A **non-parametric test** is one which makes no assumptions about the shape of the parent distribution. This deceptively simple approach has a wide range of applications in situations where a test based on the Normal distribution might not be appropriate.

The sign test is a test on the median. It makes only one modelling assumption:
- the data points are independent observations from the parent distribution.

The complete test procedure follows this pattern:

- **Step 1** State null and alternative hypotheses

  > Use H_0 and H_1 notation. H_0 is always 'the median = a value'.

- **Step 2** Check the significance level to be used

  > Usually given in the question. If you need to set your own level then tell the examiner you are doing so. 5% is a standard choice.

- **Step 3** Establish the type of tail

  > One tail upper, one tail lower or two tail.

- **Step 4** List the signs of the differences between the data points and the suggested median

  > e.g. $+ - - + - + + + - + +$ $+$

- **Step 5** Count the number of +signs

  > Or count −signs instead.

- **Step 6** Under H_0 the number of such signs is $\sim B(n, \frac{1}{2})$

  > n is the total number of data points.

- **Step 7** Identify the critical region(s)

  > Use cumulative tables of $B(n, \frac{1}{2})$.

- **Step 8** Draw a diagram or write an inequality to compare the test value with the critical region

  > Remember that Binomial models are discrete, so avoid using continuous curves in your diagram.

- **Step 9**   State the conclusion formally

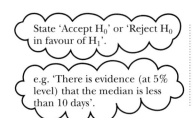

State 'Accept H₀' or 'Reject H₀ in favour of H₁'.

- **Step 10**   Restate it in plain English

e.g. 'There is evidence (at 5% level) that the median is less than 10 days'.

Example I

Last year the average attendance at the Wanderer's home football matches was 27 600. The supporters' club are worried that this season's average might be lower, so they look at a random sample of attendance figures for this season:

15 391   28 442   25 977   38 525   17 425   19 377   21 388

Conduct a sign test to see if there is any evidence that the average is lower this season. Use a 10% significance level.

Solution

H_0: the median $m = 27\ 600$ **(Step 1)**

H_1: the median $m < 27\ 600$

10% significance level, one-tail (lower tail) test.   **(Steps 2 & 3)**

Subtracting 27 600 from each of the data points leaves the following signs: **(Step 4)**

$- + - + - - -$

The observed number of +signs is 2.   **(Step 5)**

Under H_0 the number of +signs is distributed $B(7, \frac{1}{2})$.   **(Step 6)**

Using cumulative tables of $B(7, \frac{1}{2})$,

$P(X \le 1) = 0.0625$

$P(X \le 2) = 0.2266$

As the critical region is a lower tail, start at 0 and count upwards until the cumulative probability is just below 10%.

$\therefore$ Critical region $= \{0, 1\}$ **(Step 7)**
2 does not lie in the critical region.

                                                                                            (Step 8)

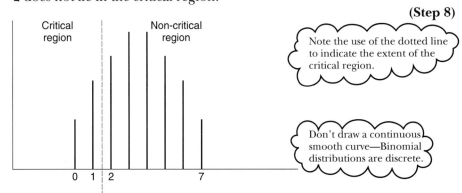

Critical region   Non-critical region

Note the use of the dotted line to indicate the extent of the critical region.

Don't draw a continuous smooth curve—Binomial distributions are discrete.

0 1 2   7

Accept H_0 **(Step 9)**

There is no evidence (at 10% level) that the median attendance is lower this season. **(Step 10)**

Example 2

Sam has been comparing limestone and granite headstones in a number of different graveyards. He has recorded the date of the oldest headstone which is still in good condition for each graveyard, and the results are summarised in the following table.

Graveyard	A	B	C	D	E	F	G	H
Date (limestone)	1921	1908	1943	1927	1933	1899	1921	1903
Date (granite)	1909	1901	1951	1917	1936	1914	1940	1919

Carry out a sign test, at the 10% level, to see whether there is any evidence that the average difference between the dates is zero.

> This is an example of a paired sample test. There are two dates for each graveyard, so you subtract them and test whether the median of the differences is zero.

Solution

H_0: the median of the differences $m = 0$

H_1: the median of the differences $m \neq 0$

10% significance level, two-tail test

Limestone date minus granite date for each graveyard yields the following signs:

$+ + - + - - - -$

The observed number of $+$signs is 3.

Under H_0 the number of $+$signs is distributed $B(8, \frac{1}{2})$.

Using cumulative tables of $B(8, \frac{1}{2})$,

$P(X \leq 1) = 0.0352$

> This is just below 5%, so it forms the upper limit of the left-hand tail.

$P(X \leq 2) = 0.2201$

$P(X \leq 5) = 0.8555$

> This is just above 95% so it forms the upper limit of the central non-critical region.

$P(X \leq 6) = 0.9648$

$\therefore$ Critical region $= \{0, 1, 7, 8\}$.

3 does not lie in the critical region.

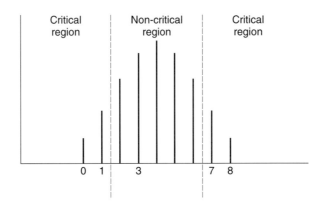

Accept H_0.

There is evidence (at 5% level) that the median of the differences is zero.

Exercise 8.1

In questions **A1** to **A5** you are given a sample size n, the number of $+$signs X and the significance level for a sign test, together with the type of tail. Use tables to find the critical region, and say whether the test statistic X is within the critical region or not.

A1 $n = 14$, $X = 4$, 5% significance level, two-tail test.

A2 $n = 8$, $X = 1$, 10% significance level, one-tail (lower) test.

A3 $n = 16$, $X = 11$, 1% significance level, two-tail test.

A4 $n = 10$, $X = 1$, 5% significance level, one-tail (lower) test.

A5 $n = 20$, $X = 18$, 5% significance level, one-tail (upper) test.

In questions **A6** to **A10** you are given either a single set of data and a suggested median, or a set of matched pairs of data. Carry out an appropriate subtraction, and count the number of $+$signs X. State also the critical region if you were to conduct a 5% two-tail sign test, and say whether your value of X is critical or not.

A6   12   31   28   17   24   38

median = 30

A7   12   11   14   14   12   10   17

median = 13

A8

X	10	55	47	23	36	51
Y	8	70	48	25	35	58

A9   76   99   52   47   51   42   56   66

median = 50

A10

X	12	75	63	44	27	87	28	45
Y	8	66	31	40	29	86	25	33

B1   Richard likes to watch the television 'Two Point Four Children'. The title of this programme is based on the notion that the average number of children in a family in Britain is 2·4.

Richard is not convinced that this figure is correct, so he decides to collect some data and carry out a two-tailed sign test at the 5% significance level. He asks a random sample of his friends the following question: 'How many children are there in your family?' Their replies are: 3, 2, 2, 2, 3, 3, 2, 2, 1, 4.

(i)   State suitable null and alternative hypotheses.

(ii) Carry out the sign test, stating your conclusion clearly.

Richard's friend Marianne reckons that the average number of children per family is more like 2·8 than 2·4.

(iii) Without actually conducting the test explain what the conclusion would be if Marianne were to conduct a two-tailed sign test at the 5% significance level.

(iv) Comment briefly on the usefulness, or otherwise, of the sign test in assessing the value for the average number of children in a family.

B2 A large number of candidates are taking a typing examination. The task is designed to take half an hour, but the candidates are told that they may have up to one hour if they wish. Fifteen candidates are chosen at random, and observed to take the following lengths of time, in minutes, over their typing:

42, 49, 26, 16, 43, 39, 48, 31, 32, 12, 45, 55, 51, 36, 23

(i) State suitable null and alternative hypotheses for a sign test to see whether the candidates are taking half an hour, on average.

(ii) Carry out the test, using a 10% significance level.

B3 Izi is training to be a vet. He is studying the numbers of puppies which different dogs have in their first and second litter, and he thinks that there is a tendency for the second litter to be larger, on average.

Ten dogs are chosen at random from a large database, and the results are as follows:

Dog	A	B	C	D	E	F	G	H	I	J
First litter	5	7	5	4	7	8	5	3	5	12
Second litter	7	8	8	5	6	9	6	6	6	10

Izi decides to conduct a sign test on the median of the differences between the number of puppies in the first and second litters.

(i) State suitable null and alternative hypotheses, explaining carefully why the alternative hypothesis takes this particular form.

(ii) Carry out the sign test at the 2% significance level.

B4 Dorothy has written two novels. She knows that her first novel contained, on average, 200 words per page, but she suspects that her second novel contains fewer words per page. To test this suggestion Dorothy chooses a random sample of 10 pages from her second novel, and counts the following numbers of words: 135, 211, 188, 199, 197, 206, 178, 185, 133, 210.

(i) State suitable null and alternative hypotheses for a sign test.

(ii) Carry out the test at the 2% significance level. Remember to state your conclusion clearly, in plain English.

B5 A steeplechase race consists of an outward section followed by a homeward section. The organisers of the race intend that both sections should be run in the same time, on average, but a reporter suspects that the homeward section is shorter. The reporter logs the times of eight randomly-chosen runners:

Runner	1	2	3	4	5	6	7	8
Outward (seconds)	320	355	331	319	344	325	318	337
Homeward (seconds)	315	371	334	315	331	440	299	317

(i) Carry out a sign test at the 10% level to see whether these data support the reporter's suspicions.

One of the runners suffered an injury on the homeward section.

(ii) Remove the figures for the runner who you think suffered an injury, and repeat the test using the remaining seven data points.

8.2 The Wilcoxon signed rank test

Key points

This powerful technique was developed by Frank Wilcoxon in 1945. It is more sophisticated than the basic sign test, because the sizes of the swings are taken into account. Like the sign test, the Wilcoxon test makes no assumptions about the shape of the parent distribution.

The Wilcoxon signed rank test is a test on the median. It makes only one modelling assumption:
- the data points are independent observations from the parent distribution.

The complete test procedure follows this pattern:
- **Step 1**   State null and alternative hypotheses

    Use H_0 and H_1 notation, H_0 is always 'the median = a value'.

- **Step 2**   Check the significance level to be used

    Usually given in the question. If you need to set your own level then tell the examiner you are doing so. 5% is a standard choice.

- **Step 3**   Establish the type of tail

    One tail upper, one tail lower or two tail.

- **Step 4**   List the (signed) differences between the data points and the suggested median

- **Step 5**   Rank the data, ignoring signs

    The smallest swing has the smallest rank.

- **Step 6**   Re-impose the signs

    Some of the ranks may now carry minus signs, others plus signs.

- **Step 7**   Compute T^+ and T^-. The test statistic T is the lower of T^+ and T^-

    T^+ = sum of the positive ranks
    T^- = sum of the negative ranks
    We often write $T = \min\{T^+, T^-\}$

- **Step 8**   Establish the critical region

    This will always be to the left as T cannot lie above halfway.

- **Step 9**   State the conclusion formally

    State 'Accept H_0' or 'Reject H_0 in favour of H_1'.

- **Step 10**   Restate it in plain English

    e.g. 'There is evidence (at 5% level) that the median is less than 10 days'.

Example 1

A florist supplies carnations for Valentine's day, claiming that the flowers will live on average for 14 days. A member of the public thinks this claim is optimistic, and so he examines a random sample of seven carnations. They turn out to have the following lifetimes in days: 8, 13, 7, 4, 17, 5, 18.

(i) State suitable null and alternative hypotheses for a Wilcoxon signed rank test.

(ii) Conduct the test at the 5% level, stating your conclusion clearly.

Solution

(i) H_0: the median lifetime is 14 days

H_1: the median is less than 14 days. One-tail 5% test

(ii) Signed differences are: $\qquad -6 \quad -1 \quad -7 \quad -10 \quad 3 \quad -9 \quad 4$
(Unsigned) ranks: $\qquad\qquad\quad 4 \quad\; 1 \quad\;\; 5 \quad\;\;\; 7 \quad\;\; 2 \quad\;\; 6 \quad\; 3$
Signed ranks: $\qquad\qquad\;\; -4 \quad -1 \quad -5 \quad -7 \quad +2 \quad -6 \quad +3$

Then $T^+ = 2 + 3 = 5$, and $T^- = 4 + 1 + 5 + 7 + 6 = 23$

The test statistic $T = 5$.

From tables, the critical value T_{crit} is 3.

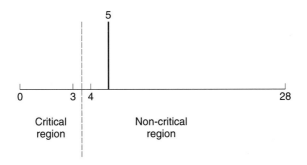

Accept H_0. There is no evidence (at 5% level) that the median is below 14 days.

Example 2

Ten A-level students are given two mathematics papers. Use a Wilcoxon test at the 5% level to see whether the two papers appear to be of equal difficulty.

Student	A	B	C	D	E	F	G	H	I	J
Paper 1 score	55	45	23	76	63	58	77	77	62	38
Paper 2 score	45	39	27	68	53	61	60	63	69	26

This is an example of a paired sample test. There are two scores for each student, so you subtract them and test whether the median of the differences is zero.

Solution

H_0: the median of the differences is zero

H_1: the median of the differences is not zero. Two tail, 5% test

Signed differences:	10	6	−4	8	10	−3	17	14	−7	12
(Unsigned) ranks:	6·5	3	2	5	6·5	1	10	9	4	8
Signed ranks:	+6·5	+3	−2	+5	+6·5	−1	+10	+9	−4	+8

Then $T^+ = 6·5 + 3 + 5 + 6·5 + 10 + 9 + 8 = 48$, and $T^- = 2 + 1 + 4 = 7$.
The test statistic $T = 7$.

Note the tied ranks here. The two 10s should take ranks 6 and 7, so we share them and give 6·5 to each.

From tables, $T_{crit} = 8$

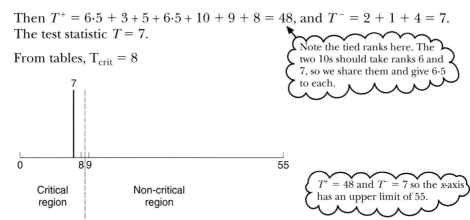

$T^+ = 48$ and $T^- = 7$ so the x-axis has an upper limit of 55.

Reject H_0. There is evidence (at 5% level) that the papers are not of equal difficulty.

Exercise 8.2

In questions **A1** to **A5** you are given a sample size *n*, a test statistic *T* and the significance level for a Wilcoxon test, together with the type of tail. Use tables to find the critical region, and say whether the test statistic *T* is within the critical region or not.

A1 $n = 12$, $T = 12$, 5% significance level, two-tail test.

A2 $n = 6$, $T = 5$, 10% significance level, two-tail test.

A3 $n = 15$, $T = 20$, 1% significance level, one-tail test.

A4 $n = 11$, $T = 9$, 5% significance level, one-tail test.

A5 $n = 20$, $T = 35$, 1% significance level, two-tail test.

In questions **A6** to **A10** you are given either a single set of data and a suggested median, or a set of matched pairs of data. Carry out an appropriate subtraction, and then compute T^+, T^- and the Wilcoxon test statistic *T* in each case.

A6   8   15   9   14   4   18

median = 10

A7   49   32   44   48   33   35   52   39

median = 45

A8

X	41		56	74	35
Y	38		48	62	36

A9   66   58   51   65   68   60   72   53   78

median = 62

A10

X	89		17	48	55	39	61	52
Y	83		22	67	67	54	59	63

B1   Damian is a Mathematics teacher. He writes two end of term tests for the Year 7 pupils in his school, and intends that Paper 2 should be harder than Paper 1. The scores obtained by a random sample of the Year 7 pupils is given in the table:

Pupil	Pete	Mike	Sue	Doris	Pat	Ben	Jo
Paper 1	63	47	71	35	48	58	55
Paper 2	67	39	69	34	37	64	50

(i)   Subtract and rank the data, in preparation for a Wilcoxon signed rank sum test.

(ii)   Carry out the test at the 5% level, and indicate whether you think that the data indicate that Damian succeeded in making Paper 2 harder, on average.

B2   A headteacher has been told that her teachers tend to retire, on average, at age 57. To test this hypothesis she takes a random sample of five recently-retired teachers and notes their ages at retirement as: 55, 60, 58, 52, 51.

(i)   State suitable null and alternative hypotheses for a Wilcoxon signed rank test. Explain carefully why your alternative hypothesis has the form that it does.

(ii)   Conduct the test at the 10% significance level, stating your conclusion clearly.

B3   Sanjay is a dentist. He decides to keep records in a diary of the ages at which his younger patients first show signs of dental decay. His first nine entries are: 16, 10, 5, 23, 16, 22, 9, 12, 18.

Sanjay knows that in a neighbouring district the average age at which tooth decay begins is 21.

(i)   State suitable null and alternative hypotheses for a signed rank test to see whether the average age in Sanjay's district is different from that in the neighbouring district.

(ii)   Carry out this test, at the 5% significance level.

Exercise 8.2 *continued*

(iii) Give two distinct criticisms of the way in which Sanjay has collected his data.

B4 A psychologist is investigating the memory retention of rats. Eight rats are chosen at random from a large population, and have to find their way through to the centre of a maze, where they are rewarded with a piece of cheese. The experiments are repeated six times, and the psychologist is hoping to demonstrate that the rats are able to achieve the task in a progressively shorter time, as they learn their way through the maze.

The rats' times for the first and last runs are recorded in this table.

Rat	A	B	C	D	E	F	G	H
First run (seconds)	82	82	81	61	90	79	76	85
Last run (seconds)	67	90	88	51	89	67	72	83

(i) State suitable null and alternative hypotheses for a Wilcoxon test.

(ii) State the critical region for a one-tail test, at the 10% significance level. Conduct the test, stating your conclusion clearly.

B5 A random number generator on a calculator is supposed to be set so that the average is 0·5. Helen produces eight random numbers on her calculator:

0·337 0·386 0·803 0·02 0·226 0·803
0·254 0·985

(i) Helen wishes to carry out a hypothesis test to see whether these data are consistent with an average value of 0·5. Explain why a Wilcoxon test would be preferable to a test based on the Normal distribution.

(ii) Carry out the Wilcoxon test at the 10% significance level.

Revision questions

C1 Joanna is writing a statistics project. She has been told that a certain novel has words of length 5 letters on average, but she thinks the word lengths tend to be longer than this. She selects eight words at random from the book, and writes them down:

certainly shrubs an of mine a
emotionally brought

(i) Write a suitable null and alternative hypotheses for a Wilcoxon test.

(ii) Carry out the test, using a 5% significance level.

C2 Explain what is meant by a non-parametric test.

Seven darts players reckon that their scores improve after drinking one pint of beer. To test this hypothesis each player throws three darts when sober, and the total is recorded. After drinking a pint of beer the seven players each throw another three darts; once again the total is recorded. The results are shown in this table:

Player	A	B	C	D	E	F	G
Total before drinking	101	85	140	100	100	60	85
Total after one pint of beer	140	81	180	125	101	65	100

(i) Carry out a sign test, at the 5% level, to see whether there is any evidence that the median score has improved after drinking one pint of beer.

(ii) Carry out a Wilcoxon rank sum test, again at the 5% level, to see whether there is any evidence that the median score has improved after drinking one pint of beer.

(iii) Explain which of these two tests is the more sophisticated, giving a reason.

C3 Jenny is studying the ages of men and women when they marry. A random sample of eight entries from the local church records yields the following values:

Couple	A	B	C	D	E	F	G	H
Age of man	28	21	25	56	57	28	40	39
Age of woman	30	19	28	52	52	22	48	27

(i) Carry out a Wilcoxon paired sample test to see whether men tend to be older than the women they marry, on average. Use a 5% significance level.

(ii) Explain clearly any necessary assumptions for the Wilcoxon test to be valid.

(iii) Give one reason why the conclusion to Jenny's test has to be stated carefully.

C4 Twelve drivers were selected at random, and asked how many driving lessons they had before taking their test. Their replies were: 10, 12, 10, 17, 25, 18, 12, 21, 12, 12, 18, 10.

(i) Carry out a sign test to test whether the median number of lessons is 14, against the alternative hypothesis that it is less than 14. Use a 5% test,

(ii) Repeat the test, using a Wilcoxon signed rank test.

(iii) Explain briefly which of the two tests you consider to be better.

C5 Nine friends go on holiday together. On Monday they all play a round of Crazy Golf. The owners of the Crazy Golf course claim that the average score for a round is 90. The actual scores recorded by the players are:

Player	1	2	3	4	5	6	7	8	9
Score	96	83	88	91	87	72	103	89	87

(i) Use a sign test to see whether these scores are consistent with an average score of 90. Use a 10% significance level.

On Wednesday the nine friends play another round of Crazy Golf. There is a strong wind blowing, and they suspect that this will result in a larger higher score, on average. The actual scores recorded on Wednesday were:

Player	1	2	3	4	5	6	7	8	9
Score	103	91	85	94	88	90	98	91	89

(ii) Carry out a suitable sign test to examine the hypothesis that the average score is higher on Wednesday than on Monday. Use a 10% significance level.

C6 A supermarket notices that on Saturday afternoons the average time for which customers queue at the checkouts is 25 minutes. The supermarket introduces a new queuing system, and a random sample of 12 customers yields the following queuing times in minutes: 27, 24, 24, 26, 19, 17, 33, 20, 11, 29, 27, 19.

(i) Carry out a sign test at the 5% significance level, to see whether there is any evidence that the average queuing time has reduced.

The supermarket then decides to open just enough extra checkouts on Saturday afternoons so that the average queuing time will change to 15 minutes. A random sample of ten customers on the first Saturday afternoon under this system gave the following times: 9, 11, 16, 14, 17, 20, 17, 18, 14, 19 minutes.

(ii) State carefully the null and alternative hypotheses which could be used for a Wilcoxon signed rank test on this data.

continued

(iii) Conduct the Wilcoxon test at the 5% level. Hence comment on whether you think the supermarket has succeeded in its aim.

C7 In a school Physics laboratory there are two resistance meters, one digital and the other analogue. A teacher decides to compare them by measuring the resistance of various items as given in the table below:

Item	A	B	C	D	E	F	G
Resistance in ohms (digital meter)	252	523	374	15	2511	855	970
Resistance in ohms (analogue meter)	245	520	370	17	2510	840	960

(i) Carry out a Wilcoxon signed rank test at the 5% level, to test the hypothesis that the two meters are calibrated to give the same value, on average.

(ii) Explain carefully any assumptions you need to make in order that the Wilcoxon test is valid.

C8 A school's sixth form prospectus claims that Mathematics and English are the two most popular A-levels and that, on average, equal numbers of students take each. The Chairman of Governors suspects that Mathematics is actually more popular, so she looks at the numbers of students opting for these subjects in recent years:

Year	Mathematics	English
1989	39	41
1990	39	29
1991	34	31
1992	38	27
1993	38	43
1994	29	21
1995	37	38
1996	39	33
1997	49	36

(i) Carry out a sign test, at the 5% level, to see whether there is any evidence to support the Chairman's suspicions.

(ii) Carry out a similar test using the Wilcoxon signed rank test.

(iii) Comment briefly on the apparent contradiction between these two tests.

C9 A certain make of motor car is supposed to be serviced every 6000 miles. A garage carries out a survey of owners, and from this survey a random sample of eight service intervals are found to be as follows:

6035 5477 5736 5841 6003 6052 5989 5890

A non-parametric test is to be used to test the hypothesis that the median service interval is 6000 miles, against the alternative that it is less than 6000 miles.

(i) Explain what is meant by a non-parametric test.

(ii) Without doing any lengthy calculations, explain why a simple sign test is liable to produce a misleading result with this particular data set.

(iii) Carry out a Wilcoxon signed rank test, using a 5% significance level. State your conclusions clearly.

C10 Karen thinks that words are longer, on average, in French than in English. To test this theory she decides to select 14 words at random, and look at their length (i.e. the number of letters) in both languages. The table shows the 14 words which were selected:

(i) State suitable null and alternative hypotheses for a sign test.

(ii) Carry out the sign test, at the 5% significance level.

(iii) Explain carefully what problem would have arisen if Karen had chosen the word 'blanc' (which means 'white') instead of 'noir'.

French	English
visage	face
voiture	car
moule	mussel
penser	think
croire	believe
chaise	chair
quarante	forty
chien	dog
noir	black
oiseau	bird
encre	ink
poisson	fish
or	gold
neige	snow

ANSWERS

Chapter 1

Exercise 1.1

A1 Mean 7·3, median 6·5, mode 10, midrange 8, range 12, standard deviation 3·49

A2 Mean 6·78, median 7, mode 7, midrange 6·5, range 9, standard deviation 2·74

A3 Mean 115·8, median 118, mode 118, midrange 114, range 22, standard deviation 7·19

A4 Mean 45·4, median 45·5, no mode, midrange 42·5, range 55, standard deviation 16·4.

A5 Mean 5·11, median 6, mode 0, 7 (bimodal), midrange 6, range 12, standard deviation 4·12

A6 Mean 30·4, median 31, mode 31, midrange 29·5, range 3, standard deviation 0·862

A7 Discrete. Mean 1·13, standard deviation 1·03, mode 1

A8 Continuous. Mean 19·1, standard deviation 8·78, modal class 20–30

A9 Discrete. Mean 1·48, standard deviation 1·14, mode 1

A10 Continuous. Mean 33·8, standard deviation 1·72, modal class 34–35

B1 i) Mean 4·6, standard deviation 2·70
ii) mode 8 iii) 0 need not be an error – it represents a baby under 12 months old

B2 ii) Median 8·50 iii) mode 8·99

B3 i) Mean 31 020, standard deviation 19 922
ii)

Upper limit	Cum freq
0	0
12 000	1
16 000	9
20 000	20
25 000	36
40 000	50

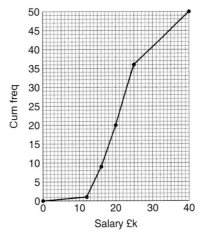

Median is about 22 000, interquartile range about 9000.

B4 i)

Number of fines	Frequency
0	15
1	13
2	7
3	2
4	1
6	1
8	1

ii) Mode 0
iii) Mean 1·275, standard deviation 1·66
iv) Midrange 4. Not useful as it is much higher than most of the data points.

B5 i) Mid points are 5, 15·5, 25·5, 35·5, 45·5, 55·5, 65·5
Mean 35·98, standard deviation 14·9. These are only estimates because the data has been grouped, so the original values have been lost.

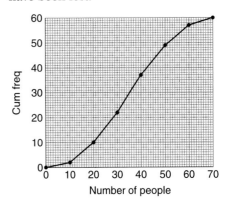

iii) a) Median is about 35 people b) UQ
is about 47, LQ about 24

B6 i) Mean 25 093 grams, standard deviation
107 grams.
ii) Claim is justified – most of the bags
weigh more than 25 kg.

Exercise 1.2

A1 Date is discrete – should use a vertical line
graph.

A2 Medians are missing – should be shown as
vertical dotted lines.

A3 Pseudo-3D pie chart exaggerates
Car. Should use an ordinary 2D pie
chart.

A4 Points should be plotted at upper bounds,
i.e. 3, 5, 7, 9. Median then becomes 5·35
feet.

A5 Empty stems for 50, 60, 70 required.

B1 i)

	Men	Women
20–25	0	1·0
25–30	1·4	2·0
30–35	1·8	2·8
35–40	2·6	1·6
40–50	1·0	0·5
50–60	0·3	0·1
60–80	0·05	0

ii)

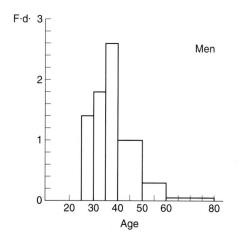

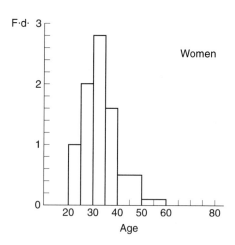

iii) Dispersions are similar but the mean
age for women is lower, as are the median
and mode.

B2 i)

Number of rain-free days	Frequency
0	2
1	5
2	7
3	10
4	9
5	7
6	5
7	1
8	2
9	1
10	1

ii) Median 4, mode 3
iii) Positive skewness.

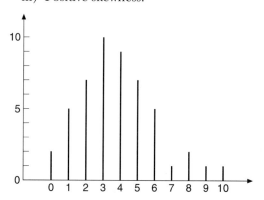

B3

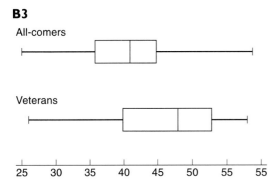

All-comers

Veterans

ii) a) Veterans have a higher average time than all-comers.
b) Both groups have a similar range; the veterans have a higher interquartile range.
c) All-comers' times are reasonably symmetric, veterans are negatively skewed.

B4 i) Mean 4·96, standard deviation 1·34

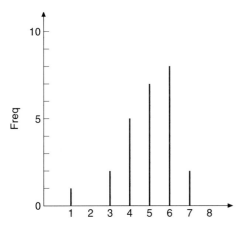

iii) Seven or eight passengers travelling to an airport are likely to have a lot of luggage, so will book a larger vehicle.

B5 i) Shane has twice as many CDs as Olivia, so his pie chart should have twice the area (i.e. about 1·41 times the radius).
ii)

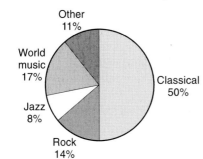

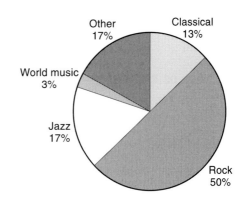

Exercise 1.3
A1 i) 0·06 ii) 0.44
A2 i) 0·125 ii) 0·384 iii) 0·18
A3 i) 0·02 ii) 0·24 iii) 0·28
A4 i) $\frac{1}{9}$ ii) $\frac{5}{6}$ iii) $\frac{1}{2}$

Revision Exercise 1
C1 i) Mean 108·43, standard deviation 14·90
ii) 155·00 lies outside the range 78·63 to 138·23 and thus is an outlier.
iii) a) The mean will increase by £2.00;
b) the standard deviation will not change.

C2 i) Mode 7, median 7, midrange value 7
ii) Range 10, does not convey much information because it is based on only two of the fifty scores.
iii) Mean 7·28, standard deviation 2·46
iv)

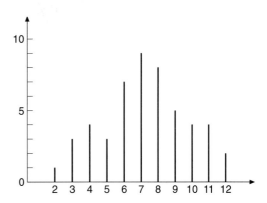

The distribution of the data is approximately symmetrical.

C3 i) Median 23 cm (approx)
ii) Interquartile range 12 cm (approx)
The cumulative frequency curve will be translated by 5 cm to the right.

C4 i)

0	30 60 99
1	20 99
2	25
3	50 50 60 70 80 80 80 80 80 80 90
4	05
5	20

Values such as 0·30, 0·60 and 5·20 lies well away from the main part of the data. They presumably represent unusual dishes.

ii) Mean £3·05, standard deviation £1·30. The value of £0·30 is an outlier.

iii) £0·30 need not be a mistake – it could represent a cheap sundry item, e.g. a portion of mango chutney.

C5 i)

Running time (minutes)	Frequency	Frequency density
10 to 20	1	0·1
20 to 40	5	0·25
40 to 60	9	0·45
60 to 70	8	0·8
70 to 80	11	1·1
80 to 90	10	1·0
90 to 100	16	1·6
100 to 105	9	1·8
105 to 110	11	2·2
110 to 115	13	2·6
115 to 120	12	2·4
120 to 130	13	1·3
130 to 140	6	0·6

ii)

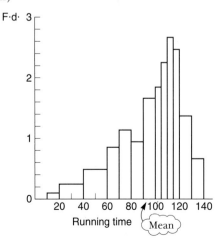

iii) Mean time 94·7 minutes.

iv) The data are negatively skewed.

C6 i)

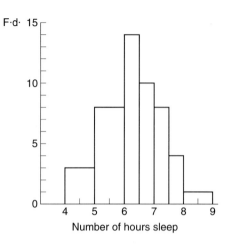

ii) Mean 6·27 hours, standard deviation 0·97 hours. These can only be estimates because the data has been grouped, so the original values have been lost.

iii) The distribution of the data is approximately symmetrical.

iv) The hospital may well have a regular sleeping routine for all patients, so the data cannot be considered to be representative of the population as a whole.

C7 i) a) 0·76; b) 0·12; c) 0·2222

ii) a) 0·7; b) 0·15; c) 0·2857

C8

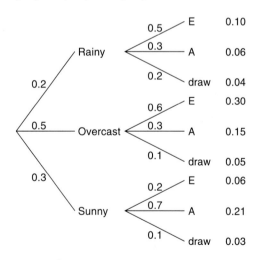

ii) P(England win) = 0·10 + 0·30 + 0·06 = 0·46

iii) P(sunny, given Aus win)

$$= \frac{0·21}{0·06 + 0·15 + 0·21} = 0·5$$

C9 i) $1 - 0.7 \times 0.6 \times 0.9 = 0.622$

ii) $\dfrac{0.3}{0.622} = 0.482$

iii) $350 \times 0.7 \times 0.6 \times 0.9 = 132.3$

C10

	1	3	5	7	9
1	11	13	15	17	19
2	21	23	25	27	29
3	31	33	35	37	39
4	41	43	45	47	49

i) 0.1 ii) 0.4 iii) 0.55 iv) 0.5 v) $\frac{5}{11}$

Chapter 2

Exercise 2.1
A1 Sum of probabilities is greater than 1
A2 One of the probabilities is negative.
A3 i) 2.25 ii) 2.6875 iii) 1.64
A4 i) 2.6 ii) 6.634 iii) 2.58
A5 i) 11.5 ii) 175.25 iii) 13.24
A6 i) 0 ii) 0.286 iii) 0.535
A7 i) 5.5 ii) 39.75 iii) 6.30
A8 i) -1.8 ii) 1.56 iii) 1.25
A9 i) 0.0625 ii) 7.125, 13.98
A10 i) 0.35 ii) 2.8, 3.56

B1 i) 19.25 ii) 1.2875
iii) $20 \times 19.25 = 385 > 365$ so she would expect to earn a commendation, assuming the model for last term is valid for this term's marks also.

B2 i) 24.84 ii) 349.7344, 18.7
iii) $0.2^3 = 0.008 = 0.8\% \approx 1\%$
B3 i) 0.65 ii) 0.91 iii) 0.22
B4 i) 0.9815 ii) 45 pence iii) £82.50
B5 i) Must be non-negative, and sum to 1.
iv) 0.972, 0.986

B6 i) Must sum to 1. $a + b + 0.7 = 1$
ii) $a + 2b + 3.3 = 3.7$ iii) $a = 0.2\ b = 0.1$
iv) 6.31

B7 i) 6.85, 2.4275 ii) 1.56 iii) 0.05 (as size 10 is the only outlier). iv) The model does not cater for half sizes (nor any outside range 4 to 10)

B8 i) $20b = 1$
ii) $10ab + 15ab + 15ab + 14ab = 10.8$ so $a = 4$ iii) 65.76

B9 i) 'more than 4' does not yield a precise value. ii) The category 'more than 4' could be replaced with the value '5'.
iii) 2.35, 1.93 iv) The original model could cater for more than 5 people, but the amended one cannot.

B10 i) 2.2 ii) 1.96 iii) Christmas/Boxing Day might be exceptional, i.e. may not be good examples of the behaviour for randomly chosen nights; also, last year's model need not apply to next Christmas.

Exercise 2.2
A1 Area is not 1.
A2 Suggested pdf is negative between 0 and $\frac{1}{2}$
A3 i) 2.22 ii) 0.667
A4 i) 1.5 ii) 0.259
A5 $\frac{1}{81}$
A6 1
A7 $E(X) = 0.889$
$Var(X) = 0.321$

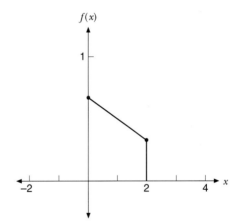

A8 $E(X) = 0.5$
$Var(X) = 0.05$

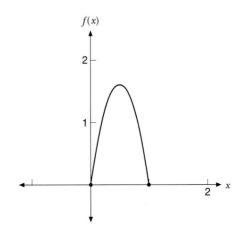

Answers

A9 $E(X) = 1\cdot6099$
$Var(X) = 0\cdot0749$

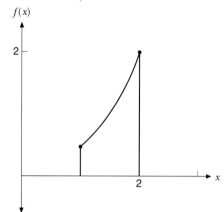

A10 $E(X) = 0\cdot764$
$Var(X) = 0\cdot035$

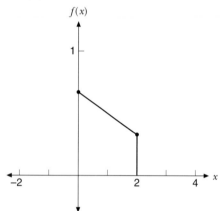

B1 i) $0\cdot21875$ ii) $0\cdot6875$ iii) $0\cdot0523$
B2 ii) $1\cdot75, 0\cdot271$
B3 i) $k = \frac{1}{21}$ iii) $2\cdot929, 0\cdot566$
B4 $E(X) = 0\cdot646$
$Var(X) = 0\cdot0594$

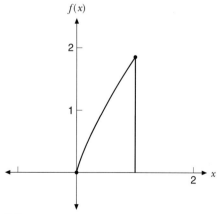

B5 $0\cdot5$
B6 i) $k = \frac{1}{6}$ ii) $1\cdot6778, 0\cdot0601$

Exercise 2.3
A1 $F(x) = \frac{3}{16}x^2 + \frac{1}{8}x$ for $0 \le x \le 2$ ($= 0$ for $x < 0$, $= 1$ for $x > 2$).
A2 $F(x) = -2x^3 + 21x^2 - 72x + 81$ for $3 \le x \le 4$ ($= 0$ for $x < 3$, $= 1$ for $x > 4$).
A3 $F(x) = -\frac{3}{4} + \frac{5}{6}x - \frac{1}{12}x^2$ for $1 \le x \le 3$ ($= 0$ for $x < 1$, $= 1$ for $x > 3$).
A4 $F(x) = \frac{1}{44}x^3 + \frac{3}{88}x^2 + \frac{3}{44}x - \frac{1}{8}$ for $1 \le 3$ ($= 0$ for $x < 1$, $= 1$ for $x > 3$).
A5 $F(x) = \frac{5}{8}x - \frac{1}{64}x^4$ for $0 \le x \le 2$ ($= 0$ for $x < 0$, $= 1$ for $x > 2$).
A6 $F(x) = \frac{16}{27}(2x^3 - x^4)$ for $0 \le x \le 1\frac{1}{2}$ ($= 0$ for $x < 0$, $= 1$ for $x > 1\frac{1}{2}$).
A7 $3\cdot5$
A8 $1\cdot333$
A9 1
A10 $1\cdot8377$

B1 i) $0\cdot2$
ii) $F(x) = -1\cdot4 + 0\cdot8x - 0\cdot05x^2$ for $2 \le x \le 4$ ($= 0$ for $x < 2$, $= 1$ for $x > 4$).

B2 i)

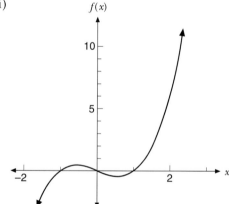

iii) Mode is 2.

B3 i) $f(x) \le 0$ throughout $a \le x \le b$, and
$$\int_a^b f(x)\,dx = 1.$$

ii)

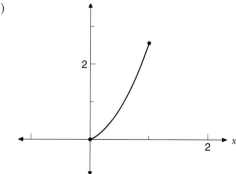

iii) $F(x) = \frac{1}{7}(4x^3 + 3x^2)$ for $0 \le x \le 1$ ($= 0$ for $x < 0$, $= 1$ for $x > 1$).
iv) Mode is 1.

B4 i) $F(x) = \frac{1}{35}(2x^3 - 3x - 10)$ for $2 \le x = 3$ ($= 0$ for $x < 2$, $= 1$ for $x > 3$).
ii) $F(2\cdot6) = 0\cdot496$, $F(2\cdot7) = 0\cdot608$ Median is $2\cdot60$ (2 d.p.)
iii) Mode is 3.

B5 i) $F(x) = \frac{1}{25}(x^3 + 6x^2 - 7)$ for $1 \le x \le 2$ ($= 0$ for $x < 1$, $= 1$ for $x > 2$).
ii) $F(1\cdot6) = 0\cdot49824 \approx 0\cdot5$. Median is a little over $1\cdot6$ as $F(m) = 0\cdot5 > F(1\cdot6)$.
iii) Mode is 2.

B6 ii) $F(x) = \frac{1}{192}(x^4 - 4x^2)$ for $2 \le x \le 4$ ($= 0$ for $x < 2$, $= 1$ for $x > 4$).
iii) Mode is 4.
iv) $3\cdot36$

Exercise 2.4
A1 76, 108
A2 110, 64
A3 90, 40
A4 0, 5
A5 35, 6

B1 40, 25
B2 10, 30
B3 195, 135
B4 0, 289
B5 30 mm, 17 mm (add the variances, not standard deviations)

Revision Exercise 2
C1 i) $0\cdot05$
ii) $12\cdot7$, $1\cdot51$
C2 iii) $0\cdot0025$
iv) $0\cdot99$
C2 i) $0\cdot1$
ii) $4\cdot2$, $2\cdot76$
iii) $0\cdot2$

C3 i) 1, $53\cdot55$. It is fair because the expected prize is equal to the cost of a ticket.
ii) 4, $856\cdot8$. Not fair because the expected prize is less than the cost of a ticket.

C4 i) $0\cdot6$, $0\cdot74$
ii) $8\cdot4$, $145\cdot04$
iii) $0\cdot3$

C5 i) $5\cdot65$, $1\cdot0275$.

ii)

Y	8	10	12	14	16
Prob	0·1	0·4	0·3	0·15	0·05

iii) $11\cdot3$, $4\cdot11$
iv) She only receives an even number of cards.

C6 ii) $F(x) = \frac{1}{96}(x^4 + 2x^2 - 3)$ for $1 \le x \le 3$ ($= 0$ for $x < 1$, $= 1$ for $x > 3$).
iii) $2\cdot378$, $0\cdot235$
iv) 3.

C7 i) $\frac{6}{125}$
ii) $0\cdot352$
iii) $8\cdot07$ and 30 seconds

C8 i) $F(0) = ka$ therefore $a = 0$
ii) $F(1) = 9k + a$ therefore $k = \frac{1}{9}$
iii) $0\cdot472$, $9\cdot528$. $m = 0\cdot472$
iv) 0

C9 i) $f(x)$

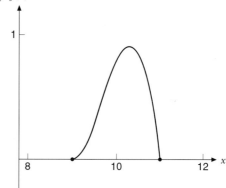

ii) $10\cdot333$
iii) $F(w) = \frac{1}{16}(-3w^4 + 116w^3 - 1674w^2 + 10\,692w - 25\,515)$ for $9 \le w \{\le 11$ ($= 0$ for $w < 9$, 1 for $w > 11$).
iv) $10\cdot2$, $0\cdot16$
v) 102, 16.

C10 i) $f(x)$

ii)
$$F(x) = \begin{cases} 0 & x < 2 \\ 0 \cdot 2(x^2 - 4x + 4) & 2 \le x \le 3 \\ 0 \cdot 05(-x^2 + 14x - 29) & 3 \le x \le 7 \\ 1 & x < 2 \\ & x > 7 \end{cases}$$

iii) 4, 1·1667

iv) 3

v) From the diagram, area from 2 to 3 is less than 0·5. 3·84.

Chapter 3

Exercise 3.1

A1 i) 0·1468 ii) 0·2936 iii) 0·9437

A2 i) 2 ii) $1\frac{2}{3}$ iii) 0·0888 iv) 0·9637

A3 i) 0·3125 ii) 0·2344 iii) 0·6563

A4 i) 3·6 ii) 2·16 iii) 0·2508 iv) 0·7334

A5 i) 0·1318 ii) 0·3560 iii) 0·5339

A6 i) 6 ii) 4 iii) 0·1294
iv) $1 - 0·2311 = 0·7689$

A7 i) 0·3115 ii) 0·0865
iii) $1 - 0·0042 = 0·9958$

A8 i) 2 ii) 1·8 iii) 0·2852 iv) 0·6769

A9 i) 0·6 ii) 0·1115

A10 i) 5 ii) 0·0768

B1 i) 0·2206 ii) 0·1752 iii) 18 iv) not dependent

B2 i) 0·1821 ii) 0·2428 iii) 0·8298
Bionomial might not be valid – a *single street* does not give a *random sample*.

B3 i) *Fixed number* of *independent* trials, with *constant probability* of success.
$n = 10$, $p = 0·1$
ii) a) 0·3874 b) 0·1937
iii) $1 - 0·9298 = 0·0702$

B4 i) $X \sim B(4, 0·15)$ 0·0005 Unlikely.
ii) This seems surprising, but the Binomial model might not be valid – all four tyres are on the same vehicle and so are not chosen randomly.

B5 i) $X \sim B(10, 0·65)$ ii) 0·0689
iii) $1 - 0·9140 = 0·0860$
iv) Not necessarily – e.g. could be an all boys school!

B6 $\frac{20}{250} = 0·08$ Then use B(10, 0·08) to calculate ii) 0·4344 iii) 0·3777
iv) 0·1478.

B7 i) 0·1683 ii) $1 - 0·0581 = 0·9419$
iii) mean 551, standard deviation 5·25
iv) Not a random sample, so trials might not be independent

B8 Using B(3, 0·2) i) 0·096 ii) 0·008
On average, one win per 125 throws. Cost is $125 \times £0·50 = £62·50$ for a £20 prize so he should expect to *lose* in the long run.

B9 Using B(6, 0·2) i) 0·2458 ii) not reasonable – probability of 20% is unlikely to be constant as she improves from novice to instructor

B10 Using B(5, 0·8) i) 0·3277 ii) 0·7373
iii) 0·00032

Exercise 3.2

A1 CR = {0, 1}

A2 CR = {9}

A3 CR = {0, 1, 10, 11, 12, 13, 14}

A4 CR = {0, 1, 2, 3, 4, 5, 6, 7}

A5 CR = {11, 12, 13, 14, 15, 16, 17, 18, 19, 20}

A6 CR = {0, 1, 2, 3, 4, 5, 6, 7, 8, 9, 16}

A7 CR = {0, 1} accept H_0

A8 CR = {7, 8, 9, 10, 11, 12, 13, 14, 15} reject H_0

A9 CR = {0, 1, 2, 3, 4, 5, 13, 14} reject H_0

A10 CR = {0, 1, 2, 3, 4, 5, 6, 7, 17} accept H_0

B1 i) H_0: $p = 0·3$ H_1: $p < 0·3$ ii) CR = {0, 1, 2} $X_{\text{test}} = 4$ Accept H_0.
No evidence that the true figure is lower than 30%

B2 i) $X \sim B(10, p)$ H_0: $p = 0·4$ H_1: $p > 0·4$
ii) CR = {8, 9, 10} $X_{\text{test}} = 6$ Accept H_0.
No evidence that the proportion has increased.
iii) Sample is not random – but is presumably still representative, as shots are independent. Conclusion remains valid.

B3 i) H_0: $p = 0·25$ H_1: $p \ne 0·25$ The engineer is looking for evidence of change.
ii) CR = {0, 7, 8, 9, 10, 11, 12} $X_{\text{test}} = 7$ Reject H_0. There is evidence of a change.

B4 i) H_0: $p = 0·8$ H_1: $p > 0·8$ She wants to *increase* the probability.
ii) CR = {19, 20} $X_{\text{test}} = 19$ Reject H_0.

B5 i) H_0: $p = 0·35$ H_1: $p < 0·35$ The intention is to *reduce* the value of p.
ii) CR = {0, 1} $X_{\text{test}} = 3$ Accept H_0.
iii) Trials are not *independent* – they are consecutive – so conclusion is not valid.

B6 i) H_0: $p = 0·65$ H_1: $p \ne 0·65$ CR = {0, 1, 2, 3, 4, 5, 13, 14} $X_{\text{test}} = 11$ Accept H_0.
ii) Not a *random* sample – so the conclusion is not valid.

B7 i) H_0: $p = 0.5$ H_1: $p \neq 0.5$ as he suspects 'may not be fair'.
ii) CR = {0, 1, 2, 3, 4, 12, 13, 14, 15, 16} $X_{\text{test}} = 5$ Accept H_0.
iii) Trials are still *independent* – so the conclusion is sound.

B8 i) H_0: $p = 0.2$ H_1: $p < 0.2$
ii) CR = {0} $X_{\text{test}} = 1$ Accept H_0.
iii) At 5% level there is no critical region – set is empty.
iv) 'First 12' is not a random sample – poor method of sampling.

B9 i) H_0: $p = 0.3$ H_1: $p < 0.3$
ii) CR = {0} $X_{\text{test}} = 2$ Accept H_0.
iii) Not a sensible question – need to define 'regularly'.

B10 i) H_0: $p = \frac{1}{3}$ H_1: $p > \frac{1}{3}$
ii) CR = {9, 10, 11, 12, 13, 14, 15} $X_{\text{test}} = 7$ Accept H_0.
iii) Conclusion is invalid – questions are not chosen randomly.

Exercise 3.3
A1 i) 0.1353 ii) 0.2707 iii) 0.2707
iv) 0.1804
A2 i) 0.0733 ii) 0.1954 iii) 0.1954
iv) 0.1563
A3 i) 0.0337 ii) 0.1404 iii) 0.1755
iv) 0.1462
A4 i) 0.2231 ii) 0.3347 iii) 0.2510
iv) 0.8088
A5 i) 0.0630 ii) 0.1852 iii) 0.0780
iv) 0.9220
A6 i) 0.1653 ii) 0.2975 iii) 0.2678
iv) 0.8347
A7 i) 0.0821 ii) 0.2052 iii) 0.2565
iv) 0.9858 v) 0.2424
A8 i) 0.0334 ii) 0.1135 iii) 0.1929
iv) 0.9421 v) 0.4416
A9 i) 0.1852 ii) 0.2613 iii) 0.5697
iv) 0.6046

A10 i) Anu is right. ii) Maire is not quite right – the distribution will be bi-modal, with both $\lambda - 1$ and λ as modal values.

B1 i) 0.1888 ii) $T \sim Po(10.5)$
iii) $1 - 0.0071 = 0.9929$
B2 i) $74 \div 50 = 1.48$ ii) 0.3347 iii) 0.34
iv) very good agreement
B3 i) 0.1348 ii) 0.0364 iii) $T \sim Po(11.4)$, 0.1144 iv) 0.4337
B4 i) 0.0498 ii) 0.5768
iii) $(0.2240)^2 = 0.0502$ iv) 0.1339
B5 i) 0.1075 ii) 0.1597 iii) 0.1488

B6 i) 0.1 ii) 0.00000377 iii) Not independent occurrences
B7 i) 0.2565 ii) 0.2226 iii) 0.1678
B8 i) a) 0.2 b) 1.2 ii) 0.0164 iii) 0.0011
iv) 0.3012

B9 i) Each match has two teams, so $24 \times 2 = 48$ data points.
ii) $55 \div 48 = 1.1458$
iii) 0.3166, 0.3641, 0.2094, 0.0803, 0.0231
iv) 15.2, 17.5, 10.1, 3.9, 1.1
v) Reasonably good agreement

B10 i) 240 hours; $240 \div 400 = 0.6$
ii) Discoveries are random, independent and uniform.
iii) a) 0.5488 b) 0.3293 c) 0.0867

Exercise 3.4
A1 0.55
A2 No: p and np are both too large
A3 No: p too large and n too small
A4 4.5
A5 No: p and np are both too large
A6 4.8
A7 No: n is too small
A8 4
A9 No: np is too large
A10 2.5

B1 i) 0.0273 ii) 0.0984 iii) 0.2125
iv) 0.1912
B2 i) 0.0408 ii) 0.1304 iii) 0.2087
iv) 0.3799
B3 i) 0.0111 ii) 0.0500 iii) 0.1125
iv) 0.8264
B4 i) 0.0498 ii) 0.1494 iii) 0.2240
iv) 0.8009
B5 i) Using $B(10, 0.01)$ 0.0914 ii) Using $Po(0.8)$ 0.3595
B6 i) Using $B(40, 0.02)$ 0.1448 ii) Using $Po(1.6)$ 0.7981
iii) Not a random sample, so the calculation is unreliable.

B7 i) $n >$ about 50, $p <$ about 0.1 and $np <$ about 10 are all met.
ii) a) 0.2723 b) 0.2678 good agreement (relative error is less than 2%)

B8 i) Using $Po(3.6)$ 0.2125 ii) Using $B(85, 0.3)$ 0.0418
Cannot use a Poisson as $np = 25.5$ is too large and $p = 0.3$ is too large.

B9 i) Using $B(8, 0.01)$ 0.0746 ii) $B(400, 0.01) \approx Po(4)$ 0.1954

B10 i) Using $B(6, 0.1)$ $1 - 0.9841 = 0.0159$
ii) $B(60, 0.016) \approx Po(0.96)$
prob $= 1 - 0.38289 - 0.36758 -$
$0.17644 - 0.05646 = 0.0166$

Exercise 3.5
A1 $\{0, 1, 2\}$
A2 $\{6, 7, 8, ...\}$
A3 $\{0, 1, 12, 13, 14, ...\}$
A4 $\{0, 8, 9, 10, ...\}$
A5 $\{0, 9, 10, 11, 12, ...\}$
A6 $\{6, 7, 8, ...\}$
A7 $\{0, 1, 12, 13, 14, ...\}$ reject H_0.
A8 $\{6, 7, 8, ...\}$ accept H_0.
A9 $\{0\}$ accept H_0.
A10 $\{0, 1, 2, 15, 16, 17, ...\}$ accept H_0.

B1 i) $H_0: \lambda = 5$ $H_1: \lambda < 5$ ii) CR $= \{0, 1\}$ $X_{test} = 2$ accept H_0.
B2 i) $H_0: \lambda = 1.2$ $H_1: \lambda > 1.2$ ii) CR $= \{4, 5, 6, ...\}$ $X_{test} = 4$ reject H_0.
B3 i) $H_0: \lambda = 8.2$ $H_1: \lambda < 8.2$ ii) CR $= \{0, 1, 2, 3\}$ $X_{test} = 2$ reject H_0.
B4 i) Defects are likely to be random, independent, uniform. $\lambda = 5$
ii) $H_0: \lambda = 5$ $H_1: \lambda \neq 5$ CR $= \{0, 1, 10, 11, 12, ...\}$ $X_{test} = 8$ accept H_0.
B5 i) $P_o(2.5)$ ii) $H_0: \lambda = 2.5$ $H_1: \lambda < 2.5$ CR $= \{0\}$ $X_{test} = 1$ accept H_0.
B6 i) 0.1162 ii) 0.2351
iii) $H_0: \lambda = 6.4$ $H_1: \lambda < 6.4$ CR $= \{0, 1, 2\}$ $X_{test} = 2$ reject H_0

Exercise 3.6
A1 i) 0.144 ii) 0.24 iii) 0.384
A2 i) 1.1111 ii) 0.1235 iii) 0.0009
iv) 0.09
A3 i) 0.3333 ii) 0.2222 iii) 0.5556
A4 i) 3.5 ii) 8.75 iii) 0.1041 iv) 0.0744
A5 i) 0.35 ii) 0.2275 iii) 0.4225
A6 i) 1.6129 ii) 0.9886 iii) 0.0340
iv) 0.0129
A7 i) 0.0358 ii) 0.0916 iii) 0.3906
A8 i) 2.25 ii) 2.8125 iii) 0.2469
iv) 0.6914

B1 0.1029
B2 0.0064
B3 0.0314
B4 i) X counts the number of trials up to and including the first success, so $X \geq 1$.
ii) 0.4 iii) $2.5, 3.75$
B5 0.0783

B6 0.1023
B7 i) 0.1969 ii) 0.0347
B8 $0.1386, 4.1667$

Revision Exercise 3
C1 i) Fixed number of independent trials with a fixed probability of success. $n = 12$, $p = 0.1$
ii) 0.2301 iii) 0.3410 iv) 0.1285
v) 0.2706 vi) 0.3233

C2 i) 0.2097 ii) 0.2775 iii) 0.5614
iv) $H_0: p = 0.15$ $H_1: p > 0.15$ CR $= \{6, 7, 8, ... 17, 18\}$ $X_{test} = 5$ accept H_0.

C3 i) Occurrences are random, uniform, independent. ii) 0.1839
iii) $H_0: \lambda = 1$ $H_1: \lambda > 1$ CR $= \{4, 5, 6, ...\}$ $X_{test} = 3$ accept H_0.

C4 i) 0.3514 ii) 0.1025 iii) $B(52, \frac{1}{3}) \approx Po(4)$
iv) 0.1563
C5 i) 0.4493 ii) 0.0500 iii) 6.61 iv) $Po(2)$, 0.1804

C6 i) a) 0.0523 b) 0.1628 c) 0.2442
d) 0.2352
ii)

0	0.0523
1	0.2151
2	0.4593
3	0.6945

iii) $H_0: p = 0.1$ $H_1: p < 0.1$ CR $= \{0\}$ $X_{test} = 0$ Reject H_0.

C7 0.0041 ii) 0.1558 iii) 0.7983
iv) $H_0: \lambda = 5.5$ $H_1: \lambda < 5.5$ It takes this form because the journalist thinks that the mean is lower.
v) CR $= \{0, 1\}$ $X_{test} = 2$ Accept H_0.

C8 i) 6 ii) Independent trials with a fixed probability of success.
$n = 300\,000$, $p = 0.00002$
iii) n large, p small, np not too large. $\lambda = 6$.
iv) a) 0.1606 b) 0.6063

C9 i) 0.2169 ii) 0.0338 iii) 0.0063
iv) 0.0885
C10 i) 0.1977 ii) 0.2684 iii) 0.7331
iv) 0.0262 v) 0.0641

Chapter 4

Exercise 4.1
A1 1·6, 0·9452
A2 0·6, 0·7258
A3 −2·2, 0·0139
A4 −1·4, 0·9192
A5 0·3, 0·9, 0·1980
A6 −1·2, 0·45, 0·5586
A7 −1·3, −0·3, 0·2853
A8 −0·75, 1·25, 0·6677
A9 −0·15, 0·5596
A10 −0·3, 0·9, 0·5662

B1 0·7475
B2 i) 0·6306 ii) 0·8413 iii) 25%
B3 i) 0·6554 ii) 0·3050 iii) 58%
B4 i) 0·4207 ii) 0·3674 iii) 0·2119
  iv) 0·4087
B5 i) 0·8413 ii) 0·9522 iii) 0·7936 4·8%
B6 i) 0·3085 ii) 0·3829 iii) $T \sim N(5, 0·8)$
  iv) 0·2398

B7 i) 'weights of sausages are $N(55, 25)$ so
  weights of the packs must be $N(440, 1600)$'
  ii) Independence. iii) 0·4937

B8 i) 0·7977 ii) 0·7977 $N(14·5, 1·8)$, 08682
B9 i) 0·2743 ii) 0·3220 iii) $D \sim N(−3, 61)$,
  independence. iv) 0·3505
B10 i) 0·3413 ii) 0·1915 iii) $T \sim N(1, 5)$
  iv) 0·6726

Exercise 4.2
A1 78, 14
A2 67, 70
A3 19·2, 8·9
A4 137, 60
A5 23·2, 8·3
A6 7·2, 3·1
A7 36, 26
A8 19, 6
A9 −2·2, 11·2
A10 115, 18·4

B1 i) $\sigma = 3·89$ ii) Estimate because it is
  based on a sample of 40 observations.
  iii) 33%
B2 ii) $\dfrac{60 - \mu}{\sigma} = 0·6745$ iii) 8·77, 54·1

B3 i) $\dfrac{3·8 - \mu}{\sigma} = −0·2533$,

  $\dfrac{5·35 - \mu}{\sigma} = 0·6745$ ii) 1·671, 4·22

B4 i) $\dfrac{450 - \mu}{\sigma} = −0·3853$,

  $\dfrac{550 - \mu}{\sigma} = 0·9542$ ii) 479, 74·7 iii) 39%

B5 i) 6·43 ii) 5·71

Exercise 4.3
A1 Using $N(28, 16·8)$, 0·4462
A2 Not appropriate – n too small.
A3 Using $N(21, 13·65)$, 0·2744
A4 Using $N(10, 8)$, 0·5137
A5 Not appropriate – p too small.
A6 Using $N(40, 30)$, 0·4022
A7 Using $N(84, 25·2)$, 0·1366
A8 Not appropriate – p too large.
A9 Not appropriate – n too small.
A10 Using $N(200, 66\frac{2}{3})$, 0·2006

B1 $B(100, 0·25) \approx N(25, 18·75)$ 0·5087

B2 i) $B(10, \frac{1}{3})$ ii) 0·2276 iii) $B(528, \frac{1}{3}) \approx N(176, 117\frac{1}{3})$
  iv) 0·2420. Assumed to be a random sample.

B3 i) Using $B(6, 0·35)$, 0·3529 ii) Using
  $N(70, 45·5)$, 0·9402

B4 i) $N(26·6, 17·29)$ valid as n is large and p is
  fairly central.
  ii) 0·7820 iii) January is a winter month,
  when more slips are likely to occur.

B5 i) Agree – for X the value of p is too small.
  ii) Binomial: 0·18451 Normal: 0·18924
  Error 0·0257 ≈ 2·6%
  iii) Binomial: 0·0576 Normal: 0·0583 Error
  1·2%
  iv) As expected, the approximation for Y is
  more accurate.

Exercise 4.4
A1 0·4386
A2 Not appropriate – λ is too small.
A3 0·6735
A4 Not appropriate – λ is too small.
A5 0·2255
A6 0·6612
A7 0·9464
A8 Not appropriate – λ is too small.
A9 i) 0·2915 ii) 0·3011 iii) Good
  agreement (3·3%)
A10 i) 0·0909 ii) 0·0937 iii) Good
  agreement (3·1%)

B1 i) 25 ÷ 2 = 12·5

ii) Using N(12·5, 12·5)   0·1288
iii) The average of one stile every 2 kilometres might not apply to a high-level mountain walk.

B2 i) Occurrences are random, uniform and independent. Using Po(2) 0·1353
ii) Po(12) 0·2351

B3 i) Using Po(1) a) 0·3679 b) 0·0803
ii) Using N(20, 20) 0·3592

B4 i) $\lambda = 6·7$ ii) 16·08 iii) Using N(16·08, 16·08) 0·8648

B5 i) 0·3374 ii) $n = 7$ (so $\lambda = 8·4$ giving 99·98%) iii) Po(16·8) $\approx$ N(16·8, 16·8) 0·7792

Revision Exercise 4

C1 i) $30 - \mu = 0·2793\sigma$, $40 - \mu = 1·555\sigma$
ii) $\mu = 27·8$ and $\sigma = 7·84 \approx 8$.
Mean = 0820 + 28 = 0848.
iii) Using N(28, 8^2)   0·00298; 2·38

C2 i) Using B(10, 0·3)
probability = $0·3828 \approx 0·38$
ii) B(100, 0·38) $\approx$ N(38, 23·56)   0·3175

C3 i) • Continuity correction missing;

• Lower probability

$$\varphi\left(\frac{-0·5 - 6}{\sqrt{6}}\right) \text{ missing}$$

• Not a good idea to use a Normal approximation anyway, as λ is too small.
ii) • X ~ B(120, 0·05) may be approximated by X ~ Po(6)
Then using cumulative tables of Po(6)
$P(X < 5) = 0·2851$

C4 i) 0·6915 ii) 0·9773 iii) D ~ N(3, 5)   0·0899

C5 i) $\sigma = 1·5$ ii) $0·2525 \approx 0·253$ iii) B(100, 0·253) ~ N(25·3, 18·899) 0·9089

C6 i) 0·3385 ii) $\sigma = 74$ hours iii) Using B(100, 0·75) ~ N(75, 18·75) 0·8980

C7 i) Marks are discrete but Normal distribution is continuous.
ii) 0·3773 iii) 5·9% iv) 31

C8 i) Po(0·6) 0·5488 ii) Po(24)~N(24, 24) 0·9985

C9 i) $23 - \mu = -0·5244\sigma$, $32 - \mu = 1·036\sigma$
ii) $\mu = 26·0$ and $\sigma = 5·77$
iii) B(60, 0·3) ~ N(18, 12·6) 0·9827

C10 iii) Po(40) ~ N(40, 40) 0·6052

Chapter 5

Exercise 5.1

A1 3, 20, 1·5, 1·225
A2 2·828, 30, 0·5, 0·707
A3 2·236, 20, 0·5, 0·707
A4 36, 166, 4, 2
A5 3·742, 75, 2, 1·414
A6 150, 100, 25, 4
A7 0·6563
A8 0·8849
A9 i) $\bar{X}$ is approximately Normal
ii) Mean is 44, variance is $12 \div 64 = 0·1875$, so $\bar{X} \sim$ N(44, 0·1875)

A10 i) Mean is 100, variance 1·5
ii) 0·1559
iii) Parent is not Normal – so the Central Limit Theorem is necessary to claim that $\bar{X}$ is approximately Normal.

B1 i) 0·7258 ii) $\bar{X} \sim$ N(6, 6·25) iii) 0·9918
B2 i) $\bar{X}$ is approximately Normal, with mean 52 and variance 0·5 ii) 0·9190
B3 i) $Y \sim$ N(80, 9) and $Z \sim$ N(80, 2·25)
ii) 0·4522 iii) 0·4996
B4 i) 32 kg ii) $\bar{X} \sim$ N(31·4, 0·207)
iii) 0·9063
B5 i) 3·5 ii) 0·9652 iii) 3·5 iv) 0·9336

Exercise 5.2

A1 i) 13·75 ii) 2·4375 iii) 2·786
A2 i) 3·55 ii) 3·1475 iii) 3·313
A3 i) 0·5425 ii) 0·0279 iii) 0·0335
A4 38·48 ii) 1·3016 iii) 1·627
A5 i) 0·4225 ii) 0·0798 iii) 0·0886
A6 i) 42·1 ii) 0·79 iii) 0·8316
A7 i) 77·97 ii) 11·0880 iii) 11·2301
A8 i) 6·24 ii) 5·3064 iii) 6·633
A9 i) 14·2 ii) 65·2933 iii) 66·4
A10 i) 67·2 ii) 27·4267 iii) 28·3724

B1 i) Mean 1·74, variance 0·0455
ii) $1·598 \leqslant \mu \leqslant 1·882$
iii) Normal distribution must be assumed because the sample is too small for the Central Limit Theorem to apply.

B2 i) 43·8 ii) $42·25 \leqslant \mu \leqslant 45·35$
B3 i) Mean 62·727, variance 129·8347
ii) $59·6881 \leqslant \mu \leqslant 65·7664$
B4 i) Mean 24·3727, variance 1·1656
ii) $23·612 \leqslant \mu \leqslant 25·133$
B5 i) Mean 14·277, variance 3·8002
ii) $13·870 \leqslant \mu \leqslant 14·684$

iii) If heights were not Normal you could still construct a confidence interval, as the sample is large enough for the Central Limit Theorem to apply.

B6 i) Mean 144·2375, variance 12·2148
ii) $14·11 \leq \mu \leq 147·36$

B7 i) Mean 123·6 ii) $116·53 \leq \mu \leq 130·67$

B8 i) Mean 48·083, variance 157·2431
ii) Mean 48·083, variance 171·5379
iii) $(48·083 - 11) \div \sqrt{171·5379} = 2·83$ which is approximately 3 standard deviations.
iv) They do not appear to come from a Normal distribution – data does not look symmetric, and a value 3 standard deviations away from the mean is not likely to occur in a sample of 12 values.
v) Unwise to use Central Limit Theorem – the sample is too small.

B9 i) Not necessary to assume a Normal parent as the sample is large enough for the Central Limit Theorem to apply.
ii) $\hat{\mu} = 26·0286$, $\hat{\sigma}^2 = 55·4774$
iii) $24·564 \leq \mu \leq 27·493$

B10 i) Mean 5238, variance 2 345 316
ii) Mean 15 238, variance 2 345 316
iii) $14 971 \leq \mu \leq 15 505$

Exercise 5.3
A1 $\pm 2·576$
A2 $1·645$
A3 $-1·282$
A4 $\pm 2·262$
A5 $2·998$
A6 $\pm 1·960$, reject H_0
A7 $2·326$, accept H_0
A8 $-1·282$, accept H_0
A9 $\pm 2·179$, accept H_0
A10 $-2·306$, accept H_0

B1 i) $H_0: \mu = 10$ $H_1: \mu \neq 10$
ii) $z_{test} = -2·771$, $z_{crit} = \pm 1·960$, reject H_0.
iii) It is not necessary to assume a Normal parent – the sample is large enough for the Central Limit Theorem to be used.

B2 i) Normality must be assumed because the sample is too small to use the Central Limit Theorem.
ii) Assume that the population standard deviation remains at 9·6. Assume that the sample is random. $H_0: \mu = 70$, $H_1: \mu > 70$, $z_{test} = 1·398$, $z_{crit} = 2·054$, accept H_0. No evidence of an increase.

B3 i) Mean 50·29, variance 1·0469
ii) $H_0: \mu = 50$ $H_1: \mu \neq 50$
iii) $t_{test} = -0·938$, $t_{crit} = \pm 2·821$, accept H_0.

B4 i) $H_0: \mu = 2$ $H_1: \mu < 2$
ii) $z_{test} = -2·835$, $z_{crit} = -2·054$, reject H_0.

B5 i) $H_0: \mu = 20$ $H_1: \mu > 20$
ii) $t_{test} = 7·566$, $t_{crit} = 2·718$, reject H_0.

B6 i) $H_0: \mu = 40$ $H_1: \mu > 40$
ii) $z_{test} = 1·437$, $z_{crit} = 1·645$, accept H_0.
iii) $\hat{\sigma}^2 = 5·276$ which agrees well with the assumed value of 5·5.

B7 i) $\hat{\sigma}^2 = 0·4$
ii) $t_{test} = 1·342$, $t_{crit} = 1·895$, no evidence that the mean is longer than 5 minutes.

B8 i) $H_0: \mu = 32$ $H_1: \mu < 32$
ii) $z_{test} = -3·394$, $z_{crit} = 2·326$, reject H_0.
iii) Normal tables used – the population variance is known.

B9 i) $H_0: \mu = 105$ $H_1: \mu \neq 105$
ii) $z_{test} = -0·8889$, $z_{crit} = \pm 2·242$, accept H_0.
iii) No need to assume Normality as sample is large enough to use Central Limit Theorem.

B10 i) $x - 240$ has mean 2, variance 110. x has mean 242, variance 110.
ii) Data must be *random* observations from a *Normal* distribution.
iii) $t_{test} = 0·6030$, $t_{crit} = \pm 2·228$. Data is consistent with a mean of 4 minutes.

Exercise 5.4
A1 $0·074 \leq P \leq 0·192$
A2 $0·647 \leq P \leq 0·753$
A3 $0·142 \leq P \leq 0·220$
A4 $0·089 \leq P \leq 0·143$

A5 i) $0·296 \leq P \leq 0·454$ ii) 'Population' refers to the set of those university students from whom the sample has been drawn.

A6 $0·278 \leq P \leq 0·478$
A7 i) $0·72$ ii) $0·668 \leq P \leq 0·772$
A8 i) $0·0611 \leq P \leq 0·2055$ ii) It is assumed he had chosen a *random* sample.

B1 i) $H_0: P = 0·1$ $H_1: P \neq 0·1$
ii) $z_{test} = -1·265$, $z_{crit} = \pm 2·576$, accept H_0.

B2 i) $H_0: P = 0·15$ $H_1: P < 0·15$
ii) $z_{test} = -1·829$, $z_{crit} = -2·054$, accept H_0.

B3 i) $H_0: P = 0·12$ $H_1: P \neq 0·12$
ii) $z_{test} = -1·152$, $z_{crit} = \pm 1·960$, accept H_0.

B4 i) $H_0: P = 0·5$ $H_1: P > 0·5$
ii) $z_{test} = 3·926$, $z_{crit} = 1·645$, reject H_0.

B5 i) $0.218 \leq P \leq 0.382$
ii) $H_0: P = 0.1$ $H_1: P \neq 0.1$
iii) $z_{test} = -1.118$, $z_{crit} = \pm 1.960$, accept H_0.

Exercise 5.5
A1 4.4764
A2 -3.091
A3 1.750
A4 1.434
A5 -0.894
A6 10.7
A7 82.17
A8 86.10
A9 17.13
A10 73.51

B1 i) $H_0: \mu_N - \mu_S = 0$ $H_1: \mu_N - \mu_S < 0$
ii) $z_{test} = -4.969$, $z_{crit} = -1.960$, reject H_0.
B2 i) $z_{test} = -3.462$, $z_{crit} = -2.326$, there is evidence that toffees have a lower mean mass.

B3 i) $H_0: \mu_R - \mu_Y = 0$ $H_1: \mu_R - \mu_Y \neq 0$
ii) Measurements must be independent observations from two Normal distributions with a common variance.
iii) $\hat{\sigma} = 0.531$ $t_{test} = -2.127$, $t_{crit} = \pm 2.457$, accept H_0.

B4 i) $z_{test} = 2.240$.
ii) Normal tables, as σ is assumed to be 2.
iii) $z_{crit} = 1.645$, reject H_0.

B5 i) mean 11.68, standard deviation 0.773
ii) mean 10.43, standard deviation 0.523
iii) 0.5002
iv) $H_0: \mu_m - \mu_f = 0$ $H_1: \mu_m - \mu_f > 0$
v) $t_{test} = 3.189$, $t_{crit} = 1.796$, reject H_0.

B6 i) A common standard deviation is assumed.
ii) $H_0: \mu_P - \mu_S = 0$ $H_1: \mu_P - \mu_S \neq 0$
iii) $\hat{\sigma}^2 = 7.566$ $t_{test} = -1.138$, $t_{crit} = \pm 2.042$, accept H_0.

B7 i) Independent Normal distributions with a common variance.
ii) $\bar{x} = 25.5$, $s_x^2 = 4.25$, $\bar{y} = 26.17$, $s_y^2 = 6.22$, $\hat{\sigma}^2 = 5.858$
iii) $H_0: \mu_A - \mu_B = 0$ $H_1: \mu_A - \mu_B \neq 0$
$t_{test} = -0.643$, $t_{crit} = \pm 2.086$, accept H_0.

B8 i) He might have simply taken the mean of 1.95 and 2.05.
ii) 2.098
iii) $t_{test} = -2.459$, $t_{crit} = \pm 2.086$, reject H_0.

Revision Exercise 5
C1 For a sample of n observations of a random variable X the sample mean $\bar{X}$ will be approximately Normal, provided n is reasonably large.
i) 165, 1.793 Approximately Normal.
ii) 170
iii) 0.9974. No need to assume Normality because the sample is large enough to invoke the Central Limit Theorem.
iv) Probably unwise: although the figure of 65 passengers is well below 70, weightlifters are likely to be much heavier than randomly-chosen passengers.

C2 i) $\hat{\sigma} = \sqrt{\dfrac{50}{49}} \times 16 = 16.162$

ii) $91.5 \leq \mu \leq 100.5$
iii) Central Limit Theorem is used because sample is large and the parent distribution is not known to be Normal.

C3 $40.45 \leq \mu \leq 43.95$, $0.067 \leq P \leq 0.173$

C4 i) $z_{test} = -3.415$, $z_{crit} = \pm 1.960$ the machine seems to be set wrongly.
ii) $z_{test} = -1.075$, $z_{crit} = \pm 1.960$. The machine seems to be set correctly.

C5 i) 9.55, 0.797
ii) $H_0: \mu = 10$ $H_1: \mu \neq 10$
iii) $t_{test} = -1.494$, $t_{crit} = \pm 2.365$, accept H_0.

C6 i) $0.185 \leq P \leq 0.315$
ii) 359

iii) $1.96 \sqrt{\dfrac{0.5 \times 0.5}{1068}} = 0.03$ so poll is accurate to within 3% (at 95% confidence)

C7 $z_{test} = -2.165$, $z_{crit} = \pm 1.960$, reject H_0.
C8 $H_0: \mu = 225$ $H_1: \mu < 225$
ii) $t_{test} = -3.087$, $t_{crit} = -1.796$, reject H_0.
C9 i) $H_0: \mu_{12} - \mu_{14} = 0$ $H_1: \mu_{12} - \mu_{14} > 0$
ii) $z_{test} = 1.947$, $z_{crit} = 1.645$, reject H_0.

C10 i) Observations come from two independent Normal distributions with a common variance.
ii) $\hat{\sigma}^2 = 35.0455$
iii) $t_{test} = -2.679$, $t_{crit} = \pm 2.430$, reject H_0.

Chapter 6

Exercise 6.1
A1 2.95
A2 1.467

A3 3·5
A4 7·717
A5 2·242
A6 3·647, 5·991
A7 0·93, 9·488
A8 7·438, 6·251
A9 6·3, 11·34
A10 13·867, 12·59

B1 i) H_0: distribution is uniform, H_1: distribution is not uniform
ii)

O	24	17	26	21
E	22	22	22	22

iii) $X^2 = 2·091$, $\chi^2_{crit} = 6·251$ Accept H_0.

B2 i) H_0: distribution is uniform, H_1: distribution is not uniform
ii) $X^2 = 11·75$, $\chi^2_{crit} = 11·07$ Reject H_0.
iii) Sample is not random, as calls are consecutive.

B3 i) H_0: Ratio is 5:3:4, H_1: Ratio is not 5:3:4
ii) Under H_0 expected frequencies are 25:10:15 so all Es $\geq$ 5.
iii) $X^2 = 0·81$, $\chi^2_{crit} = 7·378$ Accept H_0.

B4 i) H_0: Ratio is 1:2:3:4, H_1: Ratio is not 1:2:3:4
ii) $X^2 = 0·383$, $\chi^2_{crit} = 7·815$ Accept H_0.
iii) Not likely to affect the conclusion.

B5 i) H_0: Ratio is 1:5:3:1, H_1: Ratio is not 1:5:3:1
ii)

O	11	25	15	14
E	6·5	32·5	19·5	6·5

iii) $X^2 = 14·538$, $\chi^2_{crit} = 7·815$ Reject H_0.

B6 i) 120
ii) Using $B(4, 0·25)$ we obtain $120 \times 0·421875 = 50·625 \approx 50·6$
iii) 38·0, 50·6, 25·3, 5·6, 0·5
iv) $X^2 = 25·285$, $\chi^2_{crit} = 7·815$ Reject H_0.

B7 i) $33·614 \approx 33·6$
ii) 33·6, 72·0, 61·7, 26·5, 5·7, 0·5
iii) $X^2 = 60·871$, $\chi^2_{crit} = 9·488$ Reject H_0.

B8 i) 10·5, 12·7, 7·6, 3·0, 0·9, 0·3
ii) H_0: data may be modelled by $P_o(1·2)$
H_1: data may not be so modelled
iii) Es are too low. Regroup data so that X is 0, 1, or 2 or more.
$X^2 = 1·705$, $\chi^2_{crit} = 5·991$ Accept H_0.

iv) 'The last 35 matches' is not a random sample – could cast doubt on the conclusion.

B9 i) $149 \div 100 = 1·49 \approx 1·5$
ii) 1·43 As mean $\approx$ variance this lends further support to the Poisson model.
iii) 22·3, 33·5, 25·1, 12·6, 4·7, 1·8
iv) To ensure that all Es are at least 5, must compress to 5 cells. $v = 5 - 1 = 4$
$X^2 = 0·452$, $\chi^2_{crit} = 9·488$ Accept H_0.

B10 i) Geometric distribution. Mean 6.
ii) $55 \div 6 = 9·17 \approx 9·2$ 7·6, 6·4, 5·3, 4·4
iii) Grouped so that all Es are at least 5.
iv) 9·2, 7·6, 6·4, 5·3, 8·1, 5·6, 5·4, 7·4
v) $X^2 = 8·621$, $\chi^2_{crit} = 14·07$ Accept H_0.

Exercise 6.2

A1

	A	B	C	
P	30	54	48	132
Q	40	72	64	176
R	35	63	56	154
	105	189	168	

A2

	A	B	
P	32	28	60
Q	40	35	75
R	64	56	120
	136	119	

A3

	A	B	C	D	
P	36	45	33	36	150
Q	48	60	44	48	200
	84	105	77	84	

A4

	A	B	C	
P	13·4	19·5	22·1	55
Q	12·6	18·5	20·9	52
	26	38	43	

A5

	A	B	C	
P	5	8	7	20
Q	20	32	28	80
R	15	24	21	60
	40	64	56	

$v=4$

A6

	A	B	C	D		$\nu=6$
P	11·1	20·9	40·0	34·1	106	
Q	9·7	18·1	34·7	29·6	92	
R	11·2	21·0	40·3	34·4	107	
	32	60	115	98		

B1 i) H_0: type of food/onset of migraine are independent
H_1: type of food/onset of migraine are not independent
ii) $X^2 = 2·276$, $\chi^2_{crit} = 5·991$ Accept H_0.

B2 i) H_0 age/type of drink are independent
H_1: age/type of drink are not independent
ii) $X^2 = 21·473$, $\chi^2_{crit} = 9·488$ Accept H_0.
iii) December is not representative of the whole year (e.g. people who buy Christmas spirits might not do so at other times of year)

B3 i) H_0: efficiency of service/season are independent
H_1: efficiency of service/season are not independent
ii) As a 2 by 2 table has only one degree of freedom, Yates is desirable.
iii) $X^2 = 1·872$, $\chi^2_{crit} = 3·841$ Accept H_0.

B4 i) H_0: choice of food is independent of residential area.
H_1: choice of food is not independent of residential area.
ii)

40	20	16	4	80	
30	15	12	3	60	
50	25	20	5	100	
120	60	48	12	240	

iii) Some Es are <5. Combining columns C and D ensures that all Es are ≥15.
iv) $X^2 = 16·695$, $\chi^2_{crit} = 9·488$ Reject H_0.

B5 H_0: year/grade are independent
H_1: year/grade are not independent
ii)

10·9	6·5	8·3	12·3	80	
9·7	5·8	7·4	11·0	60	
9·4	5·7	7·2	10·7	100	
120	60	48	12	240	

iii) All Es are ≥5.
iv) $X^2 = 9·111$, $\chi^2_{crit} = 12·59$ Accept H_0.

Exercise 6.3
A1 Mean 1·7, $\mu = 1·7$
A2 Mean 2, $\mu = 2$
A3 Mean 0·75, $p = 0·25$
A4 Mean 1·5, $p = \frac{2}{3}$
A5 Mean 1·1, $\mu = 1·1$
A6 Mean 1·38, $\mu = 0·725$
A7 Mean 2, $p = \frac{1}{2}$

B1 i) 1·75
ii) H_0: the data may be modelled by a Poisson distribution Po(1·75)
H_1: the data may not be so modelled
iii) Combining last two cells of '5 or more'
$X^2 = 0·668$, $\chi^2_{crit} = 9·488$ Accept H_0.

B2 i) 0·9
ii) Testing for a Poisson fit with an estimated parameter of 0·9 and merging so the classes are 0, 1, 2 and 3 or more,
$X^2 = 1·592$, $\chi^2_{crit} = 5·991$ Accept H_0.

B3 i) Mean is 1·89, estimated value of p is 0·4725
ii) H_0: the data may be modelled by a Binomial distribution B(4, 0·4725)
H_1: the data may not be so modelled
iii) $X^2 = 15·084$, $\chi^2_{crit} = 7·815$ Reject H_0.

B4 i) 0·9
ii) H_0: the data may be modelled by a Poisson distribution Po(0·9)
H_1: the data may not be so modelled
iii) Merging so the classes are 0, 1, 2 and 3 or more, $X^2 = 2·029$,
$\chi^2_{crit} = 5·991$ Accept H_0.

B5 7·3, 87·9, 264·0, 200·7, 40·1
iii) $v = 5 - 2 - 1 = 2$ (two estimated parameters)
iv) $X^2 = 2·582$, $\chi^2_{crit} = 9·210$ Accept H_0.

B6 i) 3; $\frac{1}{3}$
ii) 75·7, 50·4, 33·6, 22·4, 14·9, 10·0, 20·0
iii) $X^2 = 73·747$, $\chi^2_{crit} = 11·07$ Reject H_0.

B7 i) Mean is 1·8, estimated value of p is 0·3
ii) H_0: the data may be modelled by a Binomial distribution B(6, 0·3)
H_1: the data may not be so modelled
iii) $X^2 = 3·829$, $\chi^2_{crit} = 7·815$ Accept H_0.

Revision Exercise 6
C1 i) H_0: the data may be modelled by a uniform distribution
H_1: the data may not be so modelled
ii) $X^2 = 6·4$, $\chi^2_{crit} = 16·92$ Accept H_0.

C2 i)

X	0	1	2	3	4	5	6
Frequency	7·5	29·9	49·8	44·2	22·1	5·9	0·7

ii) Last two cells must be combined as the expected frequencies must be at least 5.
iii) $X^2 = 7·922$, $\chi^2_{crit} = 11·07$ Accept H_0.

C3 i) The occurrences are random, uniform and independent. $\lambda = 3$.

ii) $200 \times e^{-3} \times \dfrac{3^3}{3!} = 44·81 \approx 44·8$
iii)

No of errors X	0	1	2	3	4	5+
Frequency	10·0	29·9	44·8	44·8	33·6	36·9

$X^2 = 11·435$, $\chi^2_{crit} = 12·83$ Accept H_0.

C4 i) H_0: nationality/reason for visit are independent
   H_1 nationality/reason for visit are not independent
ii) $X^2 = 1·664$, $\chi^2_{crit} = 12·59$ Accept H_0.
iii) Leaving forms in rooms does not necessarily ensure a random sample, so the conclusion may not be reliable.

C5 $X^2 = 1·701$ (or 2·222 without Yates), $\chi^2_{crit} = 3·841$ (5% level)   Accept H_0.

C6 i) 1·2
ii) Using 0, 1, 2 and 3+ with Es of 18·1, 21·7, 13·0 and 7·2, $X^2 = 0·422$, $\chi^2_{crit} = 5·991$ Accept H_0.

C7 i) 1·5
ii) Using 0, 1, 2 and 3+ with Es of 28·8, 24·7 and 13·1, $X^2 = 2·869$, $\chi^2_{crit} = 5·991$ Accept H_0.

C8 i)

	Type of music			
	Classical	Rock	Jazz	Other
Age 16–25	30	48	18	12
Age 26–35	20	32	12	8
Age over 35	5	8	3	2

ii) Merging the two columns will ensure that all Es are at least 5
iii) $X^2 = 9·804$, $\chi^2_{crit} = 9·488$ Reject H_0.

C9 ii) 5, 10, 15, 20, 25, 30, 25, 20, 15, 10, 5
iii) H_0: the data may be modelled by a (triangular) distribution on fair dice
   H_1: the data may not be so modelled
   $X^2 = 2·943$, $\chi^2_{crit} = 18·31$ Accept H_0.

C10 i) The raw data has been lost so mid-points of intervals must be used – the result will only be an estimate. Also the first and last intervals are open-ended – the mid-point method is unreliable here.
ii) Standardising the boundaries between the intervals produces $-1·5625$, $-0·9375$, $-0·3125$, $0·3125$, $0·9375$, $1·5625$. Expected frequencies are 11·8, 23·0, 40·6, 49·1, 40·6, 23·0, 11·8. Test statistic $X^2 = 3·709$, $\chi^2_{crit} = 9·488$; the Normal model is a good one. There are $7 - 1 - 2 = 4$ degrees of freedom as two parameters have been estimated.

Chapter 7

Exercise 7.1
A1 $y = 5·07 + 4·74x$
A2 $y = 107·0 - 0·879x$
A3 $y = 26·6 - 0·257x$
A4 $y = 1·40 + 0·116x$
A5 $y = 6·4 + 1·01x$
A6 random on random $y = 48·3 - 0·468x$
A7 random on random $y = 4·32 + 0·597x$
A8 random on non-random $y = 44·2 - 0·364x$
A9 random on non-random $y = 100·42 - 4·04x$
A10 random on random $y = 0·729 + 0·917x$

B1 i) $y = 0·25 + 0·184t$ ii) Thickness 6 mm (rounded from 5·77)
B2 $y = 13·82 + 0·465x$
B3 i) $y = -3·89 + 0·598x$ ii) 19 choc chips (rounded from 18·8)
B4 ii) $y = 9·32 + 0·978x$ iii) Estimated German score is 69.
B5 ii) $y = 1·921 + 0·00679x$ iii) Estimated pressure is 2·240 bars.
iii) It has been extrapolated well beyond the range of the data.
B6 $y = -0·780 + 9·887x$. Estimated value of g is 9·887.

Exercise 7.2
A1 0·9491
A2 0·2390
A3 $-0·4306$
A4 0·8893
A5 $-0·3966$

B1 i) $-0·9222$
ii) $r_{crit} = -0·6215$ Evidence of negative linear correlation.

B2 i) 0·7535
ii) Time is high compared with distance. Maybe this child walks to school and the others do not.
iii) 0·7722

B3 i) 0·0600
ii) $r_{crit} = \pm0.5140$ No evidence of correlation.

B4 i) 0·1940, ii) 0·6075
iii) In each case, there is no evidence of correlation.

B5 i) 0·9629
ii) $r_{crit} = 0.7293$ There is evidence of positive linear correlation.

B6 i) 0·7327
ii) $r_{crit} = 0.5822$ There is evidence of positive linear correlation.

Exercise 7.3
A1 0·4643
A2 0·0714
A3 -0.5667
A4 -1
A5 0·0667
A6

x	1	2	3	4	5	6	7	0·5714
y	1	3	4	7	2	6	5	

A7

x	1	2	3	4	5	6	7	8	-0.4464
y	8	7	2	4	3	5·5	1	5·5	

A8

x	1	2	3	4	5	6	7	0·6071
y	1	3	4	6	5	2	7	

A9

x	1	2	3	4	5	6	-0.6
y	6	5	2	3	1	4	

A10

x	1	6	3	7	10	4	9	2	5	8	1
y	1	6	3	7	10	4	9	2	5	8	

B1 ii) -0.1429
iii) Critical values ±0.7857 Accept H_0.
B2 ii) 0·8571 Critical value 0·7143 Reject H_0.
iii) Dishes may be of differing size or quality.
B3 ii) 0·5879
iii) Critical values ±0.5636 Reject H_0.
B4 i) 0·3273
ii) Critical value 0·5364 Accept H_0.
B5 i) 0·8095
ii) Critical value 0·6429 Reject H_0.

Revision Exercise 7
C1 i)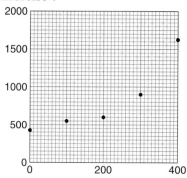

ii) $y = 270 + 2.755x$
iii) a) 683 million b) 1510 million
iv) Graph suggests that the linear model does not apply towards the upper end of the range, and extrapolation is likely to be unreliable anyway.

C2 i) 0·9739
ii) Critical value 0·7498 is significant
iii) $y = 3.376 + 0.840x$
iv) 25 cm

C3 i) 0·9928
ii) $H_0: \rho = 0$ $H_1: \rho > 0$
iii) $r_{crit} = 0.6694$ Reject H_0
iv) $y = 129 + 18.7x$
v) Should not extrapolate beyond the range of the data, especially as there is evidence of non-linearity towards the end of the range.

C4 i) 0·4524
ii) Critical value 0·6429   Accept H_0
iii) He is only testing whether taller men are also heavier, not whether there is a linear relationship, so Spearman is more appropriate.

C5 ii) $r = 0.9171$ (or $r_s = 0.9636$)
iii) $r_{crit} = 0.5494$ (or $r_{scrit} = 0.5636$)
Significant evidence of positive correlation

C6 i) Should not use as pmcc because the given figures are ranks, not scores.
ii) 0·9161
iii) Critical value 0·6783; the agreement is significant

C7 i) 0·0006
ii) Critical value 0·3610 No evidence of correlation
iii) -0.0009

C8 The value of a pmcc is not affected by a

(linear) change of scale of either of the variables involved.
i) -0.8944
ii) Critical value -0.6664
iii) As the pmcc is independent of the scale of measurement then Sonia's value should be the same.

C9 i) 0.6792
ii) Critical value 0.6000 Significant evidence
iii) The council is not investigating whether there is a linear relationship, merely whether older houses cost more to maintain, so a rank coefficient is preferred.

C10 ii) 0.2045, not significant
iii) Yes – critical values of Spearman and pmcc and virtually indistinguishable for large sample sizes such as 150.

Chapter 8

Exercise 8.1
A1 $\{0, 1, 2, 12, 13, 14\}$ 4 is not critical
A2 $\{0, 1\}$ 1 is critical
A3 $\{0, 1, 2, 14, 15, 16\}$ 11 is not critical
A4 $\{0, 1\}$ 1 is critical
A5 $\{15, 16, 17, 18, 19, 20\}$ 18 is critical
A6 $X = 2$ CR is $\{0, 6\}$ not critical
A7 $X = 3$ CR is $\{0, 7\}$ not critical
A8 $X = 2$ CR is $\{0, 6\}$ not critical
A9 $X = 6$ CR is $\{0, 8\}$ not critical
A10 $X = 7$ CR is $\{0, 8\}$ not critical

B1 i) H_0: median $= 2.4$ H_1: median $\neq 2.4$
ii) $X = 4$ CR $= \{0, 1, 9, 10\}$ Accept H_0.
iii) The conclusion would be the same
iv) It is not a useful test – it cannot discriminate between say median $= 2.1$ and median $= 2.9$.

B2 i) H_0: median $= 30$ H_1: median $\neq 30$
ii) $X = 11$ CR $= \{0, 1, 2, 3, 12, 13, 14, 15\}$ Accept H_0.

B3 i) H_0: median of differences $= 0$ H_1: median of differences < 0
ii) $X = 2$ CR $= \{0, 1\}$ Accept H_0.

B4 i) H_0: median $= 200$ H_1: median < 200
ii) $X = 3$ CR $= \{0, 1\}$ Accept H_0. No evidence of a decrease in the median number of words.

B5 i) $X = 5$ CR $= \{7, 8\}$ Accept H_0. No evidence to support the reporter's suspicions.
ii) Removing 325, 440 $X = 5$ CR $= \{6, 7\}$ Again, accept H_0.

Exercise 8.2
A1 CR $= \{0, 1, \ldots 13\}$ critical
A2 CR $= \{0, 1, 2\}$ not critical
A3 CR $= \{0, 1, \ldots 19\}$ not critical
A4 CR $= \{0, 1, \ldots 13\}$ critical
A5 CR $= \{0, 1, \ldots 37\}$ critical
A6 $T^- = 8$ $T^+ = 13$ $T = 8$
A7 $T^- = 26$ $T^+ = 10$ $T = 10$
A8 $T^- = 1$ $T^+ = 9$ $T = 1$
A9 $T^- = 1$ $8.5\ T^+ = 26.5$ $T = 18.5$
A10 $T^- = 24\ T^+ = 4\ T = 4$

B1 i) $-3, 6, 2, 1, 7, -5, 4$
ii) $T = 8$ CR $= \{0, 1, 2, 3\}$ Paper 2 does not appear to be harder.

B2 i) H_0: median $= 57$; H_1: median $\neq 57$. He is simply testing whether the average is 57 or not.
ii) $T = 4$ CR $= \{0\}$ Accept H_0.

B3 i) H_0: median $= 21$; H_1: median $\neq 21$.
ii) $T = 3$ CR $= \{0, 1, 2, 3, 4, 5\}$ Reject H_0.
iii) a) The first nine patients do not constitute a random sample.
b) The sample is biased as he is selecting from his younger patients only.

B4 i) H_0: median of differences $= 0$ H_1 median of differences > 0.
ii) $T = 9$ CR $= \{0, 1, 2, 3, 4, 5\}$ Accept H_0.

B5 i) The distribution is not likely to be Normal, and the sample is too small to invoke the Central Limit Theorem, so he cannot use a test based on the Normal distribution. The Wilcoxon test makes no assumptions about the shape of the distribution and so is preferable.
ii) $T = 17$ CR $= \{0, 1, 2, 3, 4, 5\}$ Accept H_0.

Revision Exercise 8
C1 i) H_0: median $= 5$ H_1: median > 5
ii) $T = 17$ CR $= \{0, 1, 2, 3, 4, 5\}$ Accept H_0.

C2 A non-parametric test makes no assumptions about the shape of the distribution.

i) $X = 1$ CR $= \{0\}$ Accept H_0.
ii) $T = 2$ CR $= \{0, 1, 2, 3\}$ Reject H_0.
iii) Wilcoxon is more sophisticated, since it takes the size of the swings into account.

C3 i) $T = 11 \cdot 5$ CR $= \{0, 1, \ldots, 5\}$ Accept H_0.
ii) Data are independent observations on matched pairs.
iii) Her conclusion only applies to church weddings in her locality.

C4 i) $X = 5$ CR $= \{0, 1, 2\}$ Accept H_0.
ii) $X = 34$ CR $= \{0, 1, \ldots, 17\}$ Accept H_0.
iii) Wilcoxon is better since it takes the size of the swings into account.

C5 i) $X = 3$ CR $= \{0, 1, 8, 9\}$ Accept H_0 – scores are consistent with an average of 90.
ii) $T = 2$ CR $= \{0, 1, 2\}$ Reject H_0 – scores on Wednesday appear to be higher.

C6 i) $X = 5$ CR $= \{0, 1, 2\}$ Accept H_0 – no evidence that queuing time has reduced.
ii) H_0: median $= 15$ H_1: median $\neq 15$
iii) $T = 21 \cdot 5$ CR $= \{0, 1, \ldots, 8\}$ Accept H_0 – supermarket does appear to have succeeded.

C7 i) $T = 2$ CR $= \{0, 1, 2\}$ Reject H_0.
ii) Independent observations on matched pairs of data.

C8 i) $X = 6$ CR $= \{8, 9\}$ Accept H_0 – no evidence that Mathematics is more popular.
ii) $T = 7$ CR $= \{0, 1, \ldots, 8\}$ Reject H_0 – there is evidence that Maths is more popular.
iii) Wilcoxon takes the size of swings into account, so conclusion ii) is preferred.

C9 i) A non-parametric test makes no assumptions about the shape of the distribution.
ii) The positive swings tend to be very small while the negative swings are large, so a simple sign test is likely to mislead.
iii) $T = 8$ CR $= \{0, 1, \ldots, 5\}$ Accept H_0. There is no evidence that the median is below 6000.

C10 i) H_0: median of differences $= 0$ H_1: median of differences > 0
ii) $X = 10$ CR $= \{11, 12, 13, 14\}$ Accept H_0.
iii) $5 - 5 = 0$ which is neither a positive nor a negative sign.

INDEX